Ted Jones is a writer and journalist who specialises in travel and the arts. He is the author of *The French Riviera: A Literary Guide for Travellers* (Tauris Parke Paperbacks, 2007).

❧

'I'm fascinated to learn that Milton visited Galileo, that Freud could be "bowled over", and that Emerson described the Duomo as "like an archangel's tent". Bravo, Ted Jones, for gathering a trove of writers' responses to Tuscany and for writing such an engaging context for their travels. Knowing of those who traveled before us deepens our own responses to a place. This book enriches my own journeys in this fabled land.'

Frances Mayes,
author of *Every Day in Tuscany: Seasons of an Italian Life*

Praise for *The French Riviera*

'The ultimate travel book for anyone who likes sun and literature. I found it irresistible.'
Peter Mayle

'There are two views of the French Riviera. One says it is an overdeveloped blot on the landscape; the other that it is the epitome of style. If you veer towards the latter, and enjoy literary history, this book is for you. Drawing on the stories of more than 150 writers, Jones does a great job of buffing up the legend.'
Anthony Sattin, *Sunday Times*, Books of the Week

'Thoughtful, entertaining and vivid, Jones's *The French Riviera* sweeps us along the coast . . . Cap Ferrat comes to life. Jones's book is sad only because it reminds us of how much of the Riviera's tranquil beauty has been sacrificed. The list of literary lovers of the Riviera almost beggars belief. It is delightful to have their eloquent, acerbic, lyrical responses collected here, in a book that deserves to become a favourite with all travellers.'
Miranda Seymour, *Sunday Times*

'There is much to relish. The author is assiduous in recording who wrote what where and when, in seeking out memorial plaques and mourning lost landmarks.'
E.S. Turner, *Times Literary Supplement*

'A vivid guide to the Côte d'Azur in the eyes of some of the greatest writers of their time.'
Jane Mays, *Daily Mail*

'Certainly among the best of recent books on the area. Jones has done a lot of research and presents his results in a clear and lively style. The book will appeal obviously to those with literary interests but it's also designed to please those who enjoy Sunday paper-style gossip (broadsheet, of course).'
Patrick Middleton, *The Riviera Reporter*

'unsurpassed in literary name-dropping'
David Armstrong, *San Francisco Chronicle*

❧

Florence and Tuscany

A LITERARY GUIDE FOR TRAVELLERS

❧

Ted Jones

I.B. TAURIS

LONDON · NEW YORK

Published in 2013 by I.B.Tauris & Co Ltd
6 Salem Road, London W2 4BU
175 Fifth Avenue, New York NY 10010
www.ibtauris.com

Distributed in the United States and Canada
Exclusively by Palgrave Macmillan
175 Fifth Avenue, New York NY 10010

ISBN: 978 1 84885 836 7

A full CIP record for this book is available from the British Library
A full CIP record is available from the Library of Congress

Library of Congress Catalog Card Number: available

Typeset by JCS Publishing Services Ltd, www.jcs-publishing.co.uk

Printed and bound in Great Britain by TJ International Ltd, Padstow, Cornwall

CONTENTS

❧

ILLUSTRATIONS

Photos 16, 22, 23: David Mundstock; all others: Ted Jones

PREFACE

On the evening of 15 October 1764, the English historian Edward Gibbon was in Rome, 'musing amongst the ruins of the Capitol, while the barefoot friars were singing vespers in the temple of Jupiter', and he knew with absolute certainty that he must write *The History of the Decline and Fall of the Roman Empire*. I had no such inspirational moment: I was aware only that for some years I had wanted to write a book about the writers of Tuscany. The only deterrent was that *Decline and Fall* took Gibbon 23 years to write. I wasn't sure if I had that long.

In Florence a year later, in 1765, the Scottish author Tobias George Smollett wrote in his *Travels through France and Italy* that he did not intend to write about 'every thing which is commonly visited in this metropolis'. 'All these objects', he wrote, 'have been described by twenty different authors. I shall not trouble you with a repetition of trite observations.' His words were written more than two centuries ago but they are even more appropriate today, when an internet search of 'books about Tuscany' elicits ten thousand responses, and minute historical details are accessible in seconds. Smollett wrote about *his* Tuscany. I shall write about Tuscany as it was seen by other writers.

These writers' collective impressions are a total experience of Tuscany: its scenery, its sky and the people under it as much as its history, art and literature. This homogeneity has been expressed by writers in many different ways: Percy Bysshe Shelley, who lived and died there, eulogised its 'mountains, seas, and vineyards, and the towers of cities they encircle!'

So many writers have been attracted to Tuscany that my problem soon became not which to write about, but which to exclude.

Because this edition is in English, I have tended to give preference to Anglo-Saxon authors, and to omit those who, even if famous in their own languages, are less known internationally. Missing also – or almost – are those writers who scurried through Tuscany on their way to somewhere else. Goethe stayed no longer than three hours; J. G. Ballard's autobiography allotted Tuscany only a paragraph; H. G. Wells's Tuscan trysts were commemorated in one single place name; and the seriously ill Sir Walter Scott was so anxious to reach his native Scotland before he died that he hurried by, leaving no record of it at all (he made it back home with only two months to spare).

I applied similar criteria to places: thus Prato, a city with a population of nearly 200,000 – but seemingly authorless – is omitted, while little Certaldo (population 16,000) is included. How could I exclude Boccaccio's home town?

A work of this type may have one author but it is the effort of many: writers who have gone before have collaborated with contemporary ones. I am indebted to all the writers of Tuscany (much of whose original research was achieved without the benefit of search engines) and am contrite if, despite my efforts, I have inadvertently infringed any of their copyrights. I would also like especially to thank my wife for her boundless ideas, unfailing help and forbearance; Graziella Amerio for Italian translations; Roberta Boboli of APT, Florence and Claudia Bolognesi of the Consorzio Turistico di Volterra; Jessica Cuthbert-Smith for assiduous and positive editing; Professor Ceri Davies of Swansea University for Latin translation; Mary Hawkins, who introduced me to Tuscany; the Open University, which introduced me to Mary Hawkins; Julia Bolton Holloway, custodian of the English Cemetery of Florence and La Misericordia di Livorno, trustees of that of Livorno; David Mundstock of Intrepid Explorer for photography; Michael Pearcy of Words and Pictures for his generous help and advice with illustrations; and the staffs of the London Library and the English-American Library and the Bibliotèque Municipale of Nice.

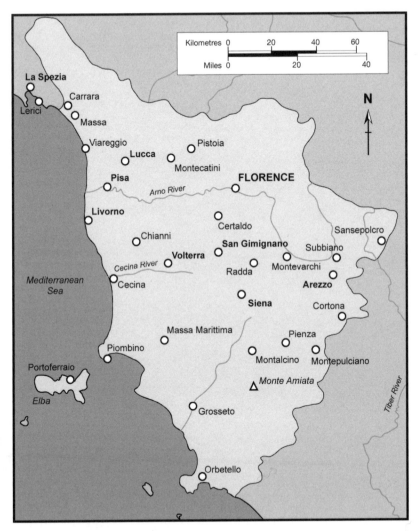

Tuscany

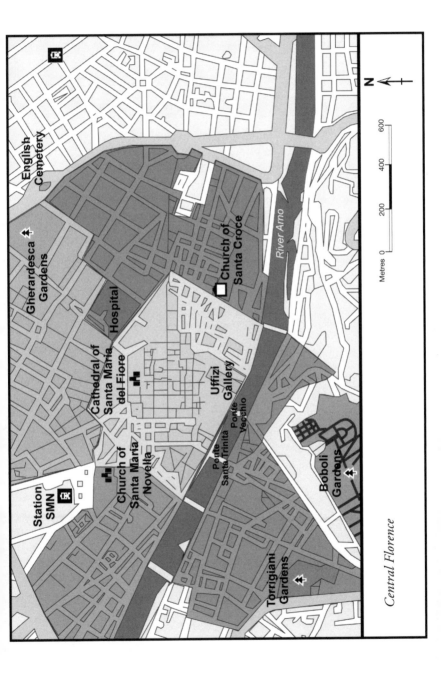

Central Florence

English Cemetery

Gherardesca Gardens

Cathedral of Santa Maria del Fiore

Hospital

Church of Santa Croce

Church of Santa Maria Novella

Station SMN

Uffizi Gallery

Ponte Santa Trinita

Ponte Vecchio

River Arno

Boboli Gardens

Torrigiani Gardens

N

Metres 0   200   400   600

∽

FOR JOAN

∽

❧ 1 ❧

INTRODUCTION

*You cannot conceive what a divine country this is just now; the vines
with their young leaves hang as if they were of beaten gold.*

(John Ruskin, 1845)

With its historical villages and towns and verdant, undulating
countryside, its treasury of medieval and Renaissance works of art
and, above all, its ancient tradition of authorship, Tuscany is the
obvious setting for a literary guide. Writers from northern Europe
have been coming to Tuscany for six centuries.

The early exchanges between Britain and Tuscany were anything
but cultural: from pre-Christian times, traffic along the coastal
Via Aurelia, the road linking ancient Rome with France and
eventually Britain, had consisted mainly of Roman conquerors
and their trudging slaves. Later, in the Middle Ages, the inland
Via Francigena – by then preferred over the Via Aurelia because
it was less vulnerable to pirate attacks from the sea – put central
Tuscany, and cities such as Florence and Siena, on the Holy Road to
Rome, and for centuries it was traversed by itinerant monks taking
Christianity to the heathen north, and pilgrims travelling in the
opposite direction, seeking salvation. Later, trade routes, responding
to demands for English wool and textiles and Tuscan oil, wines and
finery, brought commercial traffic between the two countries.

Inevitably, the writers followed, but it is significant that the first
English poet to visit Tuscany, Geoffrey Chaucer in 1373, came, not
as a writer, but as part of a trade mission, charged by his employer,
King Edward III, with negotiating landing rights at English ports.
Chaucer's negotiations in Genoa were successful, but in the long

term it was the literary outcome of his journey that was of greater importance. Chaucer extended his trip, not only to see Florence for the first time, but also in the hope of meeting the Florentine poets who were his contemporaries.

The three greatest writers in Italian history, Dante Alighieri (1265–1321), Francesco Petrarca (1304–74) – Petrarch – and Giovanni Boccaccio (1313–75), were all Tuscans. Chaucer, an admirer of all three, had already paid them the compliment of borrowing their rhyme and metre patterns – and sometimes even their story lines – thus becoming the first author to demonstrate the need for copyright laws. By some coincidence of location and culture, Tuscany had been providing the world of letters with inspiration and settings through the works of the Florentine poet Dante and his successors since long before Chaucer's arrival. Poetry has remained the most important element of Italian literature – described by the twentieth-century Italian writer Italo Calvino as 'poor in novelists but rich in poets'. We will see that poets have also featured disproportionately among Tuscany's expatriate literati.

Just as Chaucer has been called the father of English literature, so Dante can be called the father of the Italian language. After his banishment in 1302, Dante's writings while in exile included *De vulgari eloquentia* (*On the Eloquence of the Vernacular*), in which he advocated the use of the dialect that was understood by the ordinary people of Tuscany. Because Dante persisted in writing in the Tuscan language – at the time only one of a babel of dialects to be found in the Italian peninsula – rather than ecclesiastical or academic Latin, his language came to be adopted by later writers and was readily available when printing presses and cheap paper arrived in Italy. By the time of the nineteenth-century Risorgimento, when Italy became a sovereign state, the language of Dante continued to be adopted by later writers, and so became the language of the united Italy.

Within decades of the death of Dante, Tuscany was struck by the worst plague in history: an outbreak so virulent that it ravaged the whole continent, and came to be known as the Black Death.

The infection was brought by rats arriving in southern Italy in the 1340s, in ships carrying spices from the Far East. Over the next half-century, the plague would have a profound effect on the demography of Tuscany, killing more than two-thirds of its population.

Chaucer may have been the first English writer to visit Tuscany, but he could hardly claim to have been a trailblazer; the literary exodus from the north was still a long way off. The French essayist and philosopher Michel Eyquem de Montaigne called in briefly in 1581, looking for a cure for his kidney stones, but it would be another three centuries before the next recorded sighting of a British author.

Then, like buses, two arrived almost at once: John Milton in 1634, followed four years later by John Evelyn. A mere hundred years later, in the mid-eighteenth century, another couple arrived, this time together: Horace Walpole, son of British Prime Minister Sir Robert Walpole, and his 23-year-old travelling companion and old Etonian schoolmate, the poet Thomas Gray. They were the vanguard of the trickle of eighteenth-century Anglo-Saxon writers that included, later in the century, James Boswell and Tobias Smollett. The trickle broadened to a stream with the Grand Tour, that eighteenth- and nineteenth-century aristocratic gap year, in which noble British families sent their young male heirs to continental Europe to round off their classical studies with exposure to its cultural treasures – and at times to a variety of socially transmittable diseases.

With the growth of the Victorian middle class, the discovery of travel as a leisure activity, (encouraged by a devout Thomas Cook), and the advent of affordable travel, the stream became a torrent, and, despite Lord Byron's optimistic promise that 'in two or three years the first rush will be over', it shows no sign of abatement. Tuscany became a magnet for foreign writers and has remained an irresistible attraction for centuries.

The writers came from many countries: from France, Alexandre Dumas and Stendhal; from Germany, Johann von Goethe and Rainer Maria Rilke; Denmark's Hans Christian Andersen; from

Russia, Dostoevsky and Chekhov; and, from the middle of the nineteenth century, the Americans – Mark Twain, Henry James, Edith Wharton and Sinclair Lewis. They were all far outnumbered by the British: the Shelleys, the Brownings, Lord Byron, Charles Dickens, Thomas Hardy, David Herbert Lawrence, Aldous Huxley, E. M. Forster, Muriel Spark, Dylan Thomas – and many more. Such was the preponderance of Britons among the early migrants that resident continentals, having as yet no word for 'tourist' used its nearest equivalent: 'English'. Alexandre Dumas, in his *Une Année à Florence* (*A Year in Florence*), claimed that *all* foreigners, 'regardless of hair colour, age or gender', came from London. When he was staying at the Hôtel d'York in Nice (then the Italian Nizza) in the 1840s, he saw a coach pull up at the front door. When he asked where the guests were from, the manager answered, 'They're definitely English, but whether they are French or German I don't know.'

Fiction writers have found in the Tuscan people and landscape an inexhaustible source of characters and settings. Few expatriate authors returned to their home countries without the green shoots of their 'Italian novel' in their luggage: Harriet Beecher Stowe with her Renaissance saga, *Agnes of Sorrento*; George Eliot with hers, *Romola*; D. H. Lawrence with *Aaron's Rod*; Nathaniel Hawthorne and his *The Marble Faun* (published in England as *Transformation*); or Sinclair Lewis and *World So Wide*, to name a few. E. M. Forster's novelistic green shoots took some time to blossom, but in the years following his stays in Tuscany he published two: *A Room with a View* and *Where Angels Fear to Tread*. If Tuscany was fertile soil for novelists, non-fiction writers needed to look little farther than the nearest castello, palazzo or landscape.

What was it that brought, and continues to bring, these many poets, novelists, biographers, playwrights and historians to Tuscany? It is certainly a place of calm; a haven from the pressures and distractions of life in northern cities; its climate, unlike their native one, is consistently pleasant. Another attraction was good health: it was generally believed – and endorsed by the likes of Tobias

Smollett, D. H. Lawrence and the poet Elizabeth Barrett Browning – that the Mediterranean climate offered relief from respiratory ailments. London artist Seymour Kirkup came there in his late twenties for medical reasons and survived into his nineties. Modern medical historians claim that, in the longer term, the plague had a beneficial effect in that descendants of its survivors enjoy greater immunity to viral infections such as influenza and HIV than non-Europeans do.

Many impecunious writers, such as Nathaniel Hawthorne, became economic migrants, finding that they could make their pounds or dollars go further in Italy. Others came seeking freedom from the constraints of English society: D. H. Lawrence (whose capacious beachside villa cost him £25 a year) wrote, '[Italy] leaves the soul so free. Over these [northern] countries, Germany and England, like the grey skies, lies the gloom of dark moral judgment and condemnation. Italy does not judge.' (*Lady Chatterley's Lover* was published in Florence in 1919 – 41 years before the English edition.) Other constraints were parental (Elizabeth Barrett Browning), religious (James Boswell) and – particularly following the Oscar Wilde trial in 1895 – sexual. The American author David Leavitt described the homosexuality laws as 'a blackmailer's charter': Oscar Wilde's friend and biographer, the Irish-American author Frank Harris, described the situation somewhat imaginatively in his biography of Wilde: 'Every train to Dover was crowded; every steamer to Calais thronged with members of the aristocratic and leisured classes.' Percy Shelley wrote to his cousin, Thomas Medwin, 'Italy is the place for you – the very place – the Paradise of exiles – the retreat of Pariahs.'

Writers were attracted by a greater variety of settings, for not only were Italy's cities different from northern cities, but they were different from each other. The American historian N. M. Maugham wrote, 'the differences between Italian towns are as striking as those between Athens, Corinth, or Sparta must have been. This is more than a geographical contrast; the fierce antagonisms of the Middle Ages resulted in extreme individualism.'

Above all, what continue to attract and inspire writers and artists of all genres are the wealth of Tuscany's artistic, architectural and historical treasures, the warmth and love of life of its people and the variety of its highly cultivated countryside. 'The intensive culture of vine and olive and wheat', wrote D. H. Lawrence, 'by the ceaseless industry of naked human hands and winter-shod feet, and slow-stepping soft-eyed oxen does not devastate a country . . . it is a work of many centuries. It is the gentle sensitive sculpture of all the landscape.' 'Nothing is new in Tuscany,' the pioneering travel writer H. V. Morton declared, 'we were merely the latest of those who had laughed and joked upon that hilltop under the same blue sky.'

1 Tuscan landscape near Siena

✌ 2 ✌

FLORENCE
The Renaissance City

*An inexplicable miracle, an enchanted land of geniuses whose
achievements evoke admiration and astonishment.*
(John Najemy, *History of Florence, 1200–1575*)

I first arrived in Florence on a sunny but chilly February day many
years ago, as a student. It was my final year at university, and I
intended to devote the time exclusively to one subject: Italian art
of the fourteenth century – what Italians call the *trecento* – on the
optimistic assumption that I would thus have time in which to
appreciate the city's other attractions.

I soon realised that if I were to complete the course in one year,
I must not be tempted to look at anything outside the *trecento*. I
would have to find a way to resist the siren calls of the Renaissance
treasures, the paintings and palaces, sculptures and cathedrals that
confronted and tantalised at every turn. I had to pretend that the
Renaissance – those two or three centuries, beginning around
1400, during which art and science were 'reborn' in Florence and
spread throughout northern Europe – never happened. As a reward
for this sacrifice, I promised myself that I would return to Florence
after my studies and enjoy all those churches and palazzos, the
Michelangelos, Botticellis and da Vincis that I had to ignore then.

I did learn to love the *trecento*, and was soon enraptured by all
those medieval castles, the Franciscan and Dominican monasteries,
the sacred altarpieces and the frescoed Madonnas; but returning to
the Florence of the Renaissance took rather longer than I expected;

I had to earn a living. Now, retired and living just a few hours' train journey from the city, I have been back many times, and have never tired of Florence and its treasures, regardless of period: Etruscan, Roman, medieval or Renaissance.

The American writer Sinclair Lewis, in his last novel, *World So Wide*, called Florence 'a city of ancient reticences and modern energy'. Florence is not one, but a number of cities: the first a vibrant commercial and financial centre, the birthplace of banking; the city whose very name became, in 1252, the first international unit of currency – the *fleurin* or florin – seven and a half centuries before the Euro. There is also the Florence, appropriately for the city in which Dante's *Divine Comedy* was born, that is a modern depiction of chaos: too many cars crowd into streets that were not built to hold them, their speed frenzied and their smell and noise demonic. Cars in Italy make a noise inversely proportional to their size, as if to assert their rights to the inadequate space: small cars make more noise than big cars, and scooters are noisier than both.

As Charles Dickens put it, there is 'another and a different city of rich forms and fancies, always lying at our feet'. In the vortex of this whirlpool is yet another: Florence the museum, birthplace of the Renaissance. It is easy to understand why early travellers, lucky enough never to have had to cope with traffic any more anarchic than the occasional horse-drawn carriage or sedan chair, were enchanted by its harmony and beauty.

It should not be assumed that the Piazza del Duomo, although a traffic-free zone, is a haven of tranquillity. How could one expect to enjoy such treasures alone, especially in midsummer, when the city is besieged by tourists? As early as 1845, the English author and critic John Ruskin was complaining in a letter to his father, 'The square is full of listless, chattering, smoking vagabonds, who are always moving every way at once.' Today, day trippers, arriving by the busload from Turin, Milan and Rome and from cruise liners in Livorno and Civitavecchia, follow guides carrying garish banners, to be herded into an international phalanx of gawpers and photographers: note-taking Japanese hanging on their guides' every word, clinging close together lest they become detached from their group, while American high-schoolers chatter as their guides expound unheard. The city powers, in an attempt to stem the flow, have restricted the number of coaches parked at any one time to 150. They might as well try to staunch Niagara Falls. The camera-clicking hordes photographing the pigeon-sullied statue of David outside the Palazzo Vecchio don't care that he is only a copy – a mere century-old *arriviste*, while the *real* David – the one sculpted by Michelangelo in 1504 – stands pristine and pigeon-free in a museum only half a mile away. But, as the travel writer Jan Morris says, 'tourism encourages unreality'.

Real or unreal, who can deprive the tourists of their right to be there? Ever since the Grand Tour, visitors have resented other visitors doing exactly what they themselves are doing: two hundred years ago, a curmudgeonly Lord Byron complained that the Mediterranean was 'pestilent with English – a man is a fool who travels now in France and Italy till this tribe of wretches is swept home again'.

In fact, the 'pestilence' of English tourists had begun long before Byron's day and, contrary to his predictions, has continued long after him. In 1860, the English author George Eliot (Mary Ann Evans) wrote, 'We are at the quietest hotel in Florence, having sought it out for the sake of getting clear of the stream of English and Americans.' The American writer Dan Fellows Platt, in his *Through Italy with Car and Camera*, wrote, 'People have made of this paradise a hell, in particular a motorists' hell' – and he was writing in 1907. The *residential* Anglicisation of Florence, however, which began in the late eighteenth century and reached its peak in the nineteenth, is now in decline. It is difficult to estimate, in these days of open European frontiers, the number of permanent British residents, but it would probably be a mere fraction of the 35,000 estimated by the British consul in 1910. The British government finally closed its consulate in Florence at the end of 2011, after five hundred years, and replaced it with an Honorary Consul – to the great disappointment of the mayor, Signor Renzi. The falling Briton count is being more than compensated by Americans, including those 'reverse patriots' decried by Sinclair Lewis: the descendants of Italian Americans.

Having visited Florence many times in recent years, I have concluded that, not only is a year not enough to enjoy its abundance, but a lifetime will not be enough. More learned writers and art historians than I have recognised this problem, which the English historian John Julius Norwich described in *The Italian World* as 'cultural indigestion'. Disillusioned, he found Florence, 'frankly, a disappointment', and blamed his own excessive anticipation:

Perhaps I had expected too much, which would not have been surprising; perhaps, too, the weather had something to do with it, for the radiant summer was gone and I saw the city through a grey drizzle. Sadly, and despite frequent return visits, that first impression has never entirely left me. I have tried, again and again, to love Florence. The fault is entirely mine; mine, too, is the loss.

The German historian Bernd Roeck, in *Florence 1900,* found that: 'There comes a moment when one is awash with regular enjoyment and thinks that this is how it must be; when the churches, Madonnas, and Lamentations of Christ become a matter of total indifference and one longs for something else, without really knowing what.' The Italians even have a name for this disorienting condition: *hyperkulturia*, introduced by the Italian psychiatrist Graziella Magherini in her 1979 book, *Stendhal's Syndrome*. Her title is based on the French writer's gushing reaction to Florentine art: 'I was in a state of ecstasy with the heavenly sensations brought on by great art; . . . my heart beat so strongly that I was afraid I might fall.'

Visitors who hope to 'do' Florence on one brief visit tend to suffer the same artistic overload – even writers. The Irish-American writer, Mary McCarthy, in *The Stones of Florence*, casts a cold, if ironic, eye: 'For the contemporary [1959] taste, there is too much Renaissance in Florence: too much David, too much rusticated stone, too much glazed terracotta, too many Madonnas with Bambinos.' A travel-worn Mark Twain, on his first trip outside the United States, damned the city with faint praise:

> Florence pleased us for a while. I think we appreciated the great figure of David in the grand square, and the sculptured group they call the Rape of the Sabines. We wandered through the endless collections of paintings and statues of the Pitti and Uffizi galleries, of course. I make that statement in self-defence; there let it stop. I could not rest under the imputation that I visited Florence and did not traverse its weary miles of picture galleries.

To the world-weary English novelist Aldous Huxley, Florence was 'a third-rate provincial town colonized by English sodomites and middle-aged lesbians'.

Ernest Hemingway's only recorded visit to Florence was in the spring of 1927, when he travelled with his journalist friend, Guy Hickok of the *Brooklyn Daily Eagle*, in a battered old Ford. The trip purported to be a topical study of Mussolini's Fascist Italy. The resultant article, 'Italy, 1927', appeared in the *New Republic* magazine in August of that year. In it, Hemingway claims to have crossed northern Italy from coast to coast in both directions, visiting Ventimiglia, La Spezia, Pisa, Florence, Rimini, Forlì, Imola, Bologna, Parma, Piacenza, Genoa and back to Ventimiglia – a distance of some 2,000 kilometres (1,200 miles), all in just 10 days. Apart from that article – described by his biographer, Kenneth Lynn, as 'semi-factual, semi-fictional' – the only written product of the journey was a picture postcard from Rimini, leading one to wonder if the article's final sentence: 'Naturally, in such a short trip, we had no opportunity to see how things were with the country or the people', was an editorial apology.

Florence's appeal is to the more leisured visitor. The English author and journalist Leigh Hunt, who spent almost three years there, said on returning to England, 'I loved Florence, and saw nothing in it but cheerfulness and elegance. I loved the name, I loved the fine arts and old palaces . . . I loved the good-natured, intelligent inhabitants'. Travel writer Jan Morris wrote, 'The truth is that to me Florence is more than just a city: It is the idea of a city. No place on earth offers me an image more concentrated and more exact – the look of it, its history, its style and reputation all bundled into one intoxicating fancy.'

Tobias Smollett, the eighteenth-century Scottish surgeon-turned-author, was among the early British visitors to Florence. As a novelist, Smollett was an inspiration to contemporary writers, and many who came after him have acknowledged his influence – none more forcefully than Charles Dickens. Smollett, asthmatic, consumptive and jaundiced, hoped that the Mediterranean climate would ease his respiratory problems. He arrived in Nice in 1763 at the age of 42 and used it as a base for his journeys to Provence, Rome and Tuscany, which he recorded in his *Travels through France and Italy*, published in 1766. In his book, he described Florence as 'a noble city, that still retains all the marks of a majestic capital, such as piazzas, palaces, fountains, bridges, statues and arcades'.

Unlike the travellers of today, most of whom arrive in Florence by air or rail, the early arrivals had time to appreciate the panoramic first view of the city from the surrounding hills. James Fenimore Cooper, the author of Western novels, the most famous of which is *The Last of the Mohicans*, was one of the first American writers to visit Tuscany. He recalled his first view of the city in 1828: 'the city of Florence appeared, seated on a plain, at the foot of the hills, with the dome of its cathedral starting out of the field of roofs like a balloon about to ascend.' The first impression of the American novelist Nathaniel Hawthorne evoked the triumphant journey of Christian in *The Pilgrim's Progress*:

> by and by, we had a distant glimpse of Florence, showing its great dome and some of its towers out of a sidelong valley, as if we were between two great waves of the tumultuous sea of hills; while, far beyond, rose in the distance the blue peaks of three or four of the

Apennines, just on the remote horizon. There being a haziness in the atmosphere, however, Florence was little more distinct to us than the Celestial City was to Christian and Hopeful, when they spied it from the Delectable Mountains.

Charles Dickens decided, in 1845, in view of the failure of *Martin Chuzzlewit*, that he and his family could live less expensively in Italy, and obtained contracts for articles and a travel book to be called *Pictures from Italy*. He was enchanted by the city:

> I need not tell you that the churches here are magnificent. But how much beauty of another kind is here, when on a fair, clear morning, we look from the summit of a hill, on Florence! See where it lies before us in a sun-lighted valley, bright with the winding Arno, and shut in by swelling hills; its domes, and towers, and palaces, rising from the rich country in a glittering heap, shining in the sun like gold!

No one has yet been able to explain fully the amazing fusion of artistic, intellectual and scientific talents that converged in one city, initiating the era of cultural change that we now know as the Renaissance, or how, over a period of 200 years, one small city state roughly the size of today's Portsmouth could nurture such artists as Giotto, Leonardo da Vinci, Michelangelo, Raphael, Donatello and Botticelli, writers of the calibre of Dante, Petrarch and Boccaccio, and scientists such as Galileo. (Portsmouth-born geniuses do not come so readily to mind.) It was fortuitous that the Renaissance should coincide with the political dominance of the Medici, whom Dickens called 'the Good and Bad Angels of Florence' – an enlightened dynasty with the wealth and power for their city to flourish – and historians such as Dante, Machiavelli and Vasari to record it. It was, as the American historian John Najemy wrote in his *History of Florence 1200–1575*, 'an enchanted land of geniuses whose achievements evoke admiration and astonishment'. 'What city,' asked Gene Brucker, not merely in Italy, but in all the world, is more securely placed within its circle of walls, more proud in its palazzi, more bedecked with churches, more imposing in its gates, richer in piazzas, happier in its wide streets, greater in its people, more glorious in its citizenry, more inexhaustible in wealth, more fertile in its fields?

A long-term resident of Florence, the English poet Walter Savage Landor, marvelled, in his *Imaginary Conversations* that 'A town so little that the voice of a cabbage-girl in the midst of it may be heard at the extremities, reared within three centuries a greater number of citizens illustrious for their genius than all the remainder of the continent'.

Florence began life as a Roman military encampment in the first century BC. Over the next 13 centuries it grew and prospered, at least twice overflowing its city walls, until at the beginning of the fourteenth century its population was 120,000, or about three times that of London, making it one of the largest cities in the world. According to the sixteenth-century sculptor Benvenuto Cellini, 'Caesar decided to call the city Florence [Fiorenza], as it was a very beautiful name and very apposite, and it seemed, with its suggestion of flowers, to make a good omen.' The legend is supported by the prominence of the *giglio*, or lily, in the city's flag, and the dedication of its cathedral to Santa Maria del Fiore.

Because the plague arrived in southern Italy from the east, Florence was the first city in Europe to suffer its devastation. No protective measures existed at the time, and the plague and its successive outbreaks killed almost three-quarters of the city's population. Despite this, by the time the first English writer, Geoffrey Chaucer, arrived in 1373, the city's population was still 50 per cent larger than that of London.

The city's next crisis was politico-religious: thirteenth- and fourteenth-century Florence was dominated by the rivalries between the Ghibellines, supporters of the Holy Roman Emperor, and the Guelphs, supporters of the Pope. The conflict had repercussions in the local politics of the city states, particularly those of Florence and Siena, in their struggles for political supremacy. The fortunes of the two factions fluctuated according to the relative powers of emperors and popes: thus staunchly Guelph cities such as Florence and Siena were frequently in conflict, not only with pro-Ghibelline cities like Pisa and Arezzo, but with each other. These complex relationships had inevitable influences in the world of art: works were commissioned as much on social, political or economic grounds as on artistic ones. This led to greater mobility of artists and writers according to the changing fortunes of their political leaders.

As you enter the Duomo, the cathedral of Florence, almost the first thing you notice on the left-hand wall is a painted monument of an equestrian figure by the highly regarded Paolo Uccello, the plinth of which bears the name 'JOANNES ACUTUS'. Some say it was a corruption of the subject's nickname '*L'Acuto*' – the crafty one – but it could be that 'Joannes Acutus' was as near as a fourteenth-century Italian painter could get to the horseman's real name: John Hawkwood. Hawkwood was born in Essex, the son of a tanner. Having proved his bravery and military skills in the army of Edward III, he was knighted on the field of battle. After the war, he gathered together a private army that he called the White Company and set himself up in Italy as a *condottiero*, or mercenary soldier, with the intention of exploiting the rival allegiances of pre-united Italy, turning out, like a modern footballer, for the highest bidder: variously, for Pisa against Florence, Florence against Pisa, and for and against the papal forces – not necessarily at the same time. From modest roots, he rose to become the best-known mercenary of his day, achieving fame on the battlefields of northern and central Italy, where he served for more than thirty years. 'He managed his affairs so well', wrote his biographer, William Caferro, 'that there was little peace in Italy in his times.'

Hawkwood was so successful that in 1378 Edward III sent Geoffrey Chaucer to Florence to try to entice him back into the service of the English King. Whether or not the transfer fee offered was insufficient is not known, but Chaucer failed in his mission. Hawkwood turned down his King's offer and decided to stay in Tuscany, where he married an Italian woman and spent the remaining 34 years of his life, becoming a respected figure in Florentine society – one worthy of a memorial in the Duomo. Tuscany has one other souvenir of him: the crumbling tower near Cortona that is all that remains of the thirteenth-century crenellated castle presented to him by a grateful Florence.

It was not through charity that Hawkwood merited such a saintly memorial. He was a professional fighter with little respect for religion. A fourteenth-century Italian storyteller, Franco Sacchetti, told a story of Hawkwood encountering two priests on the road: 'May God grant you peace,' said the priests. The angry Hawkwood explained that, since he made his living through war, he had no need for their God's peace. 'Keep your peace,' he said. 'The peace you wish me would make me die of hunger.'

Hawkwood's notoriety extended far beyond his own lifetime. His adventures are recalled not only by Alexandre Dumas, but in the works of the Renaissance humanist Niccolò Machiavelli and by Edward Gibbon.

As already mentioned, Chaucer's attempt to recruit Hawkwood was not his first visit to Florence: that was in 1373, following an earlier diplomatic mission to Genoa in the service of the King. The son of a prosperous vintner, Chaucer was reasonably well educated, with an understanding of both Latin and French – the languages of Church and court – and as the husband of one of the Queen's staff, he had become a trusted member of the royal household. Chaucer had been captured by the French at the siege of Rheims while serving in the invasion of Brittany, and his ransom was paid in part by the King. Having visited northern Italy while still in his twenties, Chaucer also probably had a good understanding of Lombardian Italian, which was probably the reason for his selection for the trade mission.

The first English literary migrant to arrive in Florence after Chaucer was John Milton. Born in London in 1608, he was originally destined for the Church, and was writing in Latin and Italian before he wrote his first English verse, so it is not surprising that he was eager to visit Italy. Milton was the pioneer 'Grand Tourist' before the term was invented, sailing from Marseilles along the French and north Italian coasts to Nice, Genoa and Livorno. After a brief stop in Pisa, he reached Florence in July 1638, 'which', he said, 'I have always admired above all others because of the elegance, not just of its tongue, but also of its wit, [where] I lingered for about two months'. His candour and erudition, and his familiarity with neo-Latin poetry, made him many friends among Florentine intellectuals, and after spending four months in Rome, he returned to Florence for a further two months, during which time he lectured to academies in Lucca and Florence.

While in Florence, Milton visited the 74-year-old Galileo, who was by then almost blind, in his villa in the southern suburb of Arcetri. Galileo had been exiled by the Jesuits for the offence of declaring that the sun, rather than the earth, was the centre of the universe, and he was living under the protection and patronage of the Grand Duke of Tuscany, Ferdinando II de' Medici. In June 2010, the four-hundredth anniversary of *Sidereus Nuncius* – 'the Starry Messenger' – Galileo's revelation of his sensational observations, Galileo received much-delayed recognition: the restored Institute and Museum of the History of Science reopened under its new name of Museo Galileo.

The meeting between Milton and Galileo, with its rare contiguity of art and science, would later be depicted by a number of artists and writers. Three years after his return to England, Milton married, and, despite worsening eyesight, continued to write. He became totally blind within 10 years, after which he wrote by dictating to his wife. In his most important work, *Paradise Lost*, Milton recalled his meeting with the Florentine astronomer:

> . . . like the moon, whose orb
> Through optic glass the Tuscan artist views
> At evening, from the top of Fesole,

Or in Valdarno, to descry new lands,
Rivers, or mountains, in her spotty globe.

Later, Sigmund Freud, the creator of psychoanalysis, who stayed in Florence a number of times between 1895 and 1898, visited the Torre del Gallo, Galileo's last home in Florence, and was entranced:

We had read about the Torre del Gallo, a belvedere in the hills from where Galilei, who stayed there for a long time, observed the skies. When we arrived it was already dark. The caretaker turned on the lights and showed us Galilei's room, various portraits, his telescope and so on. We were completely bowled over by the solemnity and tranquillity of the place, the view and the garden.

Freud was so excited that he asked the owner, Count Galletti, if he took in lodgers. 'In short, the following day we moved in on a full board basis.'

John Evelyn, the English writer, agronomist and pioneer environmentalist – he was the author of *The Inconvenience of Air and Smoke of London Dissipated* – followed Milton, visiting Florence for the first time in 1644. He was a contemporary and later close friend of the diarist Samuel Pepys, who described Evelyn as 'In fine, a most excellent person', and 'a man so much above others'.

Like Pepys, Evelyn was a prolific diarist, whose diaries covering the years 1641–1706 were discovered in an old clothes-basket a century after his death and published in 1818. He began his travels in Europe in 1640, because, as a loyal supporter of King Charles I, he wanted to escape the attention of Cromwell during the Civil Wars. While at the home of the British ambassador in Paris – a regular meeting-place of English Royalist exiles – Evelyn met the ambassador's daughter Mary Browne, whom he later married. He initially returned to England but resumed his journeys in 1642, travelling across France to the Mediterranean and along the coast of Provence by felucca – a sail-assisted rowing boat – arriving at the port of Livorno in 1644. The port had been built earlier in the century by another Englishman, Robert Dudley, Earl of Warwick, and financed by Grand Duke Ferdinando II, whose larger-than-life statue stands on top of the monument at the port entrance.

From Livorno, Evelyn travelled to Pisa and Florence, where he stayed for five days before going on to Rome. Unimpressed by what he called the 'heath'nish pomp' of Rome, he returned to Florence. Following the fall of Oliver Cromwell's Protectorate and the Restoration of the monarchy in 1660, Evelyn held a number of important government posts under Charles II and wrote books on a wide range of topics, including gardening, ecology and arboriculture, but he is best remembered for his *Diaries*, which, like those of Pepys, give valuable information on cultural and domestic issues of the day.

2 Central Florence from the Piazza Michelangelo, Florence

Central Florence

The city of Florence is a complete picture book, if you only turn the
leaves.   (Hans Christian Andersen)

Getting around the heart of old Florence is easier if you imagine a central triangle linking its three most important piazzas: the Piazza della Signoria, the Piazza del Duomo and the Piazza della Repubblica. The Piazza della Signoria (also known as the Piazza dei Signori – piazzas in Florence manifest their importance by having at least two names) is the political heart of Florence. Its religious heart is the Piazza del Duomo (also known as the Piazza San Giovanni), which contains the Duomo (Cathedral), the Baptistery and the Campanile (bell tower). The Piazza della Repubblica, despite its relatively modern appearance, is the city's historical heart, for this was the original Roman Florence, where stood the forum, temples, theatres and, of course, baths.

The Duomo

Similar to thee I will not, better than thee I cannot.
                      (Michelangelo, quoted by Richard Lassels, 1670)

The Duomo is more correctly known as the Church of Santa Maria del Fiore, to whom it is dedicated. Construction began in 1296, on the site of an earlier church. The objective of the commune in building it was to create 'the most beautiful and honourable church in Tuscany'. Construction, delayed by the plague and diversion of funds to other projects, was not completed until 1436; thus, when Chaucer visited Florence, the interior crossing of the transepts and nave of the cathedral had lain exposed to the weather for two centuries. It would be another hundred years before the complex engineering problems of building the largest brick-built dome ever constructed were finally solved, by a 40-year-

old Florentine goldsmith named Filippo Brunelleschi. The story
of the construction is told by the Canadian author Ross King
in his *Brunelleschi's Dome: How a Renaissance Genius Reinvented
Architecture.* The competition for the contract to build the dome

3 Brunelleschi's Dome, the Duomo, Florence

was announced in 1418, but it was not until 30 August 1436 that the Bishop of Fiesole climbed to the very peak to lay the final stone and bless the dome, to the accompaniment of trumpets and fifes and the peals of every church bell in the city. Brunelleschi's construction plans included the provision of kitchens, a lounge area and sleeping accommodation between the double walls, so that his workmen would not find it necessary to waste time going down and up.

However many times you visit the Piazza del Duomo, and from whichever direction, the edifice comes as a surprise on turning the last corner. It is a rediscovery, like revisiting an old painting that you thought you remembered and finding it even more beautiful than you expected. Alexandre Dumas remarked on this phenomenon: 'We followed the crowd, which led us to the Duomo, which it seemed I saw for the first time, so much had its proportions grown. The Campanile seemed especially gigantic, its illuminated peak seeming to mingle with the stars.' Unlike in Pisa, where the cathedral is in a vast open square and visible from afar, in Florence one's awareness of the architectural detail is a gradual process. Within the Piazza del Duomo, it is difficult to find a spot from which to view the whole complex, and photography of the whole is almost impossible without special equipment – or a helicopter. The most exciting way to take in the whole complex has been described by the American author Henry James: 'Coming out of the Annunziata you look down a street vista of enchanting picturesqueness. The street is narrow and dusky and filled with misty shadows, and at its opposite end rises the vast bright-coloured side of the Cathedral.' The eighteenth-century English novelist William Beckford wrote: 'Nothing in art [is] more ornamented than the exterior, and few churches so simple within.' Awe-inspiring outside, but – except for its size – relatively unspectacular inside, the Duomo has cenotaphs to the memory of Michelangelo, Galileo and Machiavelli. The city had voted to mount an equestrian statue of Sir John Hawkwood, and asked the Florentine sculptor Donatello to design one, but, either because the connotation of equestrian statues with royalty was anathema to a republican state, or to save money, Donatello's bronze statue ended up instead in Padua, outside the Pontifical Basilica of St Anthony of Padua, where it commemorates an Italian mercenary, Gattamelata. Sir John Hawkwood is commemorated by only the painting by Uccello mentioned earlier.

Like Pisa's Leaning Tower, the Duomo is the first monument that the visitor wants to see in Florence: 'I ran out to feast my eyes with its wonders,' wrote James Fenimore Cooper in 1828. His fellow American and contemporary, the poet Ralph Waldo Emerson, also made straight for it on his first visit to Florence in 1833: 'How like an archangel's tent is this great Cathedral of many-coloured marble set down in the midst of the city.' 'The soaring pinnacles above the doors', wrote George Eliot, 'are exquisite; so are the forms of the windows in the great semi-circle of the apsis; and on the side, where especially the white marble has taken on so rich and deep a yellow, that the black bands cease to be felt as a fault.'

When D. H. Lawrence met his wife Frieda off the train at four o'clock on a December morning in 1919, she insisted on seeing the Duomo, and recorded her experience: 'I saw the pale crouching Duomo and in the thick moon-mist the Giotto tower disappearing at the top into the sky.' The couple also visited the quarter in June, brightly lit to celebrate the festival of its patron saint, San Giovanni. Lawrence was enchanted: 'with the light above illuminating the pale and coloured marbles ghostly, and the red tiles of the dome in the night sky, and the abrupt end of the [Campanile's] lily-stem without a flower, and the old hard lines of the Baptistery's top, there is a lovely ethereal quality to the great cathedral group.' It is little wonder that, 30 kilometres to the north-west in Pistoia, there is a street named Via dell'Apparenza – the Street of the Appearance. It is the spot at which Brunelleschi's dome first comes into the traveller's view.

Not all writers were as moved as the Lawrences. The German author Goethe strode by in 1786: 'I made no more than a three-hours' stop in Florence. I hurried through the place post-haste – the cathedral, the baptistery and all that,' while the egalitarian Mark

Twain expressed his customary disapproval of ecclesiastical excess; the Duomo was:

> a vast pile that has been sapping the purses of her citizens for five hundred years and is not nearly finished yet. Like other men, I fell down and worshipped it, but when the filthy beggars swarmed around me the contrast was too striking . . . Why don't you rob your church? Three hundred happy, comfortable priests are employed in that cathedral.

The beggars, the priests and Twain are long dead, but the Duomo and its treasures are still there for all to appreciate.

The Baptistery

The central building of Etrurian Christianity
(John Ruskin, *Mornings in Florence*)

Eve Borsook, a Canadian writer who came to Florence in the 1950s as a Fulbright Scholar and has remained there ever since, in her *The Companion Guide to Florence*, calls the Piazza del Duomo and its buildings 'adventures in science and technology'. Ghiberti's bronze Baptistery doors (of which the Russian novelist Dostoevsky wanted to print life-size photographs so that he could study them when he got home) were 'unprecedented technical as well as artistic achievements'. No one had ever built a dome on such a scale before Brunelleschi's, and Ghiberti's doors – with an avuncular Ghiberti looking benignly down at them as if through a porthole – have come to be called the 'Gates of Paradise'. Mary Shelley, wife of Percy Bysshe Shelley and author of *Frankenstein*, wrote of them, 'Let us turn to the gates of the *Battistero*, worthy of Paradise. Here we view all that man can achieve of beautiful in sculpture, when his conceptions rise to the height of grace, majesty, and simplicity. Look at these, and a certain feeling of exalted delight will enter at your eyes and penetrate your heart.' The main competitors for the commission to build the doors, Ghiberti and Brunelleschi, were the same as those who later applied to build the dome, bringing a certain artistic justice in the fact that, years later, when the two former goldsmiths competed for the construction of the dome, Brunelleschi was given his chance.

The Campanile

That glory of Giotto and Florence together.
(Robert Browning, *Old Pictures in Florence*)

The Campanile has inspired more praise from visiting writers than any other monument in Florence. It was designed by Giotto, one of the first great painters of the Renaissance; construction began in 1334 with Giotto in charge, but he was already 67 and near the end of his career. He did not live to see its completion, and it was left to Andrea Pisano to complete Giotto's designs. John Ruskin said of it in his *Mornings in Florence*, published in 1901, 'of living Christian work, none [is] so perfect as the Tower of Giotto. He was appointed to build the Campanile because he was then the best master of sculpture, painting, and architecture in Florence, and supposed in such business to be without superior in the world.' On his death in 1337, Giotto was buried in the Duomo.

Hippolyte Taine, the French philosopher and historian, wrote, 'Medieval man certainly likes to build upwards. He aims towards the sky, erecting lofty towers that taper into pointed peaks.' The 85-metre-high bell tower, with its layers of white, pink, green and black marble, is the enduring proof of this aspiration. Ralph Waldo Emerson thought it 'a sort of poem in architecture. One might dream of such a thing, but it seems strange that it should have been executed in lasting stone.'

The American poet, Henry Wadsworth Longfellow, author of *The Song of Hiawatha*, wrote:

In the old Tuscan town stands Giotto's tower,
The lily of Florence blossoming in stone
A vision of delight, and a desire.

Having myself trudged up its 414 steps, I would agree with George Eliot, who preceded me in 1860 – 'a very sublime getting-upstairs indeed – our muscles are much astonished'.

4 *The Giotto Tower, the Duomo, Florence*

Henry James, seldom guilty of excessive brevity, wrote,

> Perhaps the best image . . . of the positive presence of what I have called temperate joy, in the Florentine impression and genius, is the bell-tower of Giotto, which rises beside the cathedral. No beholder of it will have forgotten how straight and slender it stands there, how strangely rich in the common street, plated with coloured marble patterns, and yet so far from simple or severe in design that we easily wonder how its author, the painter of exclusively and portentously grave little pictures, should have fashioned a building which in the way of elaborate elegance, of the true play of taste, leaves a jealous modern criticism nothing to miss.

Piazza della Signoria

Here, on these very stones, Florence had risen a score of times in the name of liberty. (Stendhal, *Rome, Naples and Florence*)

The vast open space that is the Piazza della Signoria comes as a relief after its claustrophobic approach, and gives one a real sense of being at the centre of things, dominated as it is by the monumental municipal Palazzo Vecchio, or Palazzo dei Priori. It is the political and administrative centre of Florence and the meeting place of the city's rulers – the priori – since 1299. Its height, its stone facings and crenellated tower give a powerful impression of permanence and invincibility.

The French novelist Marie-Henri Beyle, who adopted the pen name 'Stendhal', visited Florence fresh from post-Revolution France, and saw the Piazza della Signoria as a symbol of revolution: a romanticised Bastille. 'This evening', he wrote in his *Une Dépêche sur la Toscane* (*Dispatch on Tuscany*),

> I was sitting in a cane chair in front of a café in the middle of a large square facing the Palazzo Vecchio. The crowd and the chilly

air; the one heedless of the other; did not prevent me from musing on all that had occurred in that square. This was the very place where on twenty occasions Florence attempted to gain its freedom and here flowed blood for an impossible constitution.

True to national stereotype, the gouty Stendhal was compelled to comment on Florentine drinking habits. 'It is customary here to put snow into the wine glasses. I put only a little in, not being too well in body, having pain in the sides many times, and all the time ejecting an incredible amount of gravel'. He explained later, 'I had drunk a great quantity of Trebbiano [wine], when heated by travelling and by the season.'

Charles Dickens wrote of the piazza in his *Pictures from Italy*: 'In the midst of the city – in the Piazza of the Grand Duke, adorned with beautiful statues and the Fountain of Neptune – rises the Palazzo Vecchio, with its enormous overhanging battlements, and the Great Tower that watches over the whole town.' It was the only architectural feature in Florence that was mentioned by the Victorian novelist Henry Rider Haggard – if imprecisely – in his *Winter Pilgrimage*: 'The palace of the Signoria is surmounted by a famous and beautiful tower of wondrous architecture that soars I forget how many hundred feet into the air.'

The tower also caught the awestruck eye of the Bohemian poet Rainer Maria Rilke in 1898. His *Das Florentinische Tagebuch* (*Florentine Diary*) reports that 'the Palazzo Vecchio rises before me, oppressive in its abrupt compact bulk, and I can feel upon me its heavy grey shadow. From the building's crenellated shoulders soars the bell tower; stretching out its muscular neck into the nightfall. It is so high that I am seized by dizziness as I lift my eyes towards its helmeted head.'

D. H. Lawrence's eponymous hero in *Aaron's Rod*, had a similar impression:

In another minute he was passing between massive buildings, out into the Piazza della Signoria. There he stood still and looked round him in real surprise and real joy. The flat, empty square with its stone paving was all wet. The great buildings rose dark. The dark sheer front of the Palazzo Vecchio went up like a cliff to the battlements, and the slim tower soared dark and hawk-like, crested, high above.

As if to reinforce this image of strength and defiance, a massive white marble David stands guard at the entrance to the Palazzo, sling over one shoulder. He may be only a copy of Michelangelo's original David, but the message to potential enemies is clear: you may be a giant, but you cannot win over guile and ingenuity. Faults in David's proportions – sometimes blamed on imperfections in the marble from which he was sculpted – have drawn critical comment in the past. The multi-talented American novelist and paediatrician William Carlos Williams, in his *A Voyage to Pagany*, thought David ugly, with 'too big hands' and 'over-anxious Jewish eyes', and the English essayist and critic William Hazlitt thought David's head 'too big for the body', with 'a helpless expression of distress'.

It was in this piazza that Savonarola, Florence's fanatical spiritual leader and preacher, used to preach his fire-and-brimstone sermons that kept its people enthralled for a decade, and held his infamous Bonfire of the Vanities. Items considered 'vanities' by Savonarola included ornaments and frivolities of any kind. In her novel *Romola*, George Eliot gives some examples: 'music-books, and musical instruments in all the pretty varieties of lute, drum, cymbal and trumpet; there were masks and masquerading-dresses . . . implements of feminine vanity – rouge-pots, false hair, mirrors, perfumes, powders, and transparent veils intended to provoke inquisitive glance – all were put to flame'. It was in this same piazza, on a spring day in 1498, that the passionate preacher was tried, declared a heretic and hanged – before himself becoming a victim of the bonfire. It was here, too, on a moonlit summer evening in 1800, that Stendhal watched as 'the rising moon, by imperceptible degrees, began to print the massive shadow of the

Palazzo Vecchio upon the scoured flagstones of the Piazza'; and it was here also that Lucy Honeychurch, heroine of the English novelist E. M. Forster's *A Room with a View*, sauntered: 'She fixed her eyes wistfully on the tower of the palace, which rose out of the lower darkness like a pillar of roughened gold. It seemed no longer a tower, no longer supported by earth, but some unobtainable treasure throbbing in the tranquil sky.' As she muses, Lucy is suddenly traumatised by seeing two stereotypical Italians in mortal combat over a debt of 5 lire, and faints into the eager arms of George Emerson.

The assorted statues in the Piazza della Signoria and in the Florentine Loggia dei Lanzi, in front of the Palazzo Vecchio, combine, despite their varied types and provenance, to create a single harmonious whole, as seen by the novelist Mary McCarthy:

> More than any other piazza in Italy, the Piazza della Signoria evokes the antique world, not only in the colossal deified statues, the David, the Neptune . . ., the hideous Hercules and Cacus, but in the sober Loggia dei Lanzi, with its three lovely full arches and its serried statuary groups in bronze and marble. Some are antique Greek and Roman; some are Renaissance; some belong to the Mannerist epoch; one to the nineteenth century. Yet there is no disharmony among them.

It was on the steps of the Loggia dei Lanzi in the Piazza della Signoria that the English novelist Thomas Hardy sat for a long time 'on a soft green misty evening following rain' in the summer of 1887 after he had returned from a trip to Rome:

> It is three in the afternoon, and the faces of the buildings are steeped in afternoon stagnation. The figure of Neptune is looking an intense white against the brown-grey houses behind, and the bronze forms round the basin [of the fountain] are starred with rays on their noses, elbows, knees, bosoms and shoulders. The shade from the Loggia dei Lanzi falls half across the Piazza.

The piazza's most admired statue is not David, but the magnificent bronze Perseus of Benvenuto Cellini – another former goldsmith. Elizabeth Barrett Browning would often go for a walk after tea, 'to sit in the Loggia and look at the Perseus', and D. H. Lawrence, speaking through his leading character in *Aaron's Rod*, thought Perseus 'looked female, with his plump hips and his waist, female and rather insignificant'. Perseus even found his way into an American novel: in 1851, describing Captain Ahab in *Moby Dick*, Herman Melville wrote: 'His whole high, broad form seemed made of solid bronze, and shaped in an inalterable mould, like Cellini's cast Perseus.'

A more recent view, from the American poet Robert Lowell, whose four chaotic years in Florence in the 1950s were punctuated by illness and mental breakdowns, is a whimsical one. His poem 'Florence' was dedicated to the Seattle-born Mary McCarthy:

> Oh Florence, Florence, patroness of the lovely tyrannicides!
> Where the tower of the Old Palace pierces the sky
> like a hypodermic needle.

These days the piazza is a favourite setting for wedding photographs, and on weekend afternoons is much frequented by rapturous nuptial couples in horse-drawn carriages, pursued by photographers, both professional and impromptu.

La Casa di Dante

As a tower, firmly set, shakes not its top for any blast that blows.
(Dante Alighieri, *Divine Comedy: Inferno*)

In the centre of Florence, within the triangle formed by the three main piazzas, is the little Via Santa Margherita, where one of Italy's – and the world's – greatest literary figures, Dante Alighieri, was born in 1265. He was betrothed at the age of 12 and the marriage, while not a love match, produced four children; but his affection was devoted exclusively to Beatrice Portinari, whom he never married, and who became the Beatrice of the *Divina Commedia* (*Divine Comedy*) and other works. One of Dante's earlier works, *La Vita Nuova* (*New Life*), was written after the death of Beatrice, as her memorial.

5 *The house of Dante, Florence*

Boccaccio, in his *Life of Dante*, told how the two met:

This girl then, such as I describe her, and perhaps even more beautiful, appeared at the *festa* – not I suppose for the first time, but for the first time in power to create love – before the eyes of Dante, who, though still a child, received her image into his heart with so much affection that from that day henceforward, as long as he lived, it never again departed from him.

La Vita Nuova, a collection of sonnets and songs, tells of Dante's love for Beatrice, his premonition of her death in a dream, her actual death, and his ultimate resolve to write a work that would be a worthy monument to her memory.

Dante's house, tall and towered, is hidden at the end of a narrow street and is not easy to find. It is now the Museo Casa di Dante, exhibiting memorabilia of the writer and his work, and charts that depict his life as a soldier and a writer, and explain the iconography of his *Divine Comedy*.

Dante spent much of his life in exile; his mother died when he was young, and his father was a successful lawyer and fervent Guelph sympathiser. The conflict between Guelphs and Ghibellines was especially bitter in Florence, where Dante, like his father, supported the Guelphs. A shield bearing the red lily of Florence on a white background, stands in his house. Towards the end of the century, Dante fell victim to this complex rivalry. He had fought in the early battles that defeated the Ghibellines of Arezzo, but later the Florentine Guelphs themselves split into separate factions, known as 'Blacks' and 'Whites'. In 1300, as one of the municipal priori, (councillors) Dante was sent to Rome to negotiate with the pope, but in his absence the Blacks seized power in Florence, and in 1302, Dante, a White, was ordered to pay a large fine. On refusing – or being unable – to do so, he was exiled from Florence under the threat of being burned alive, should he return. Wisely, he chose exile, and travelled in French Provence and in other provinces of Italy – all independent states at the time.

He wrote as he travelled – to Lucca (1313) and Verona (1316), where he finished his *Divine Comedy*, then to Ravenna, on Italy's Adriatic coast. He does not seem to have made any serious attempts to return to live among the Florentines, whom he had described variously as 'stingy, jealous and haughty', 'malign', 'ungrateful', 'discord-ridden', 'mongrelised', 'corrupt', 'vainglorious' and 'never satisfied'. If this was how the most famous of Florentines viewed the fellow citizens who exiled him in 1302, it is no surprise that there was so little enthusiasm for the return of the living Dante. What is more surprising is that for seven centuries the city has campaigned strenuously for the repatriation of the dead one from Ravenna.

His best-known work is *The Divine Comedy*; Dante himself called it only *La Commedia*: the '*Divina*' was added by ardent followers after his death. It is an allegorical and semi-autobiographical account on the lines of *The Pilgrim's Progress*, of a pilgrim's journey, told in three parts: the *Inferno*, a description of Hell, *Purgatorio*, described as a mountain, at the peak of which stands the third part, *Paradiso*, the paradise in which Dante finds his beloved Beatrice. Many of Dante's experiences as an exile found their way into *The Divine Comedy*. Like *The Pilgrim's Progress*, it is a work of moral enlightenment, full of topical references and philosophical allusions. Dante wrote it over a period of about 15 years, sometime between the age of 42 and his death. The work contains his image of Hell, its gates inscribed with his much-quoted words: 'All hope abandon, ye who enter in.' The work was not a favourite of a British Grand Tourist in 1740, Horace Walpole, who thought it 'absurd and disgusting', but it was widely appreciated in Europe in Dante's lifetime, and was loved throughout the world, its admirers including poets such as Chaucer, Milton, Byron, Shelley, Carlyle, William Blake and the Americans Emerson, Ezra Pound and Longfellow. T. S. Eliot praised Dante's ability to 'make the spiritual visible'. Dante spent his last years of exile in Ravenna, and is buried there, but was on a visit to Venice when he contracted malaria and died in September 1321, at the age of 56.

Il Sasso di Dante

The laurelled Dante's favourite seat.
(William Wordsworth, *Memorials of a Tour in Italy*, 1837)

On the south side of the Piazza del Duomo stands an alleged memento of Dante: Il Sasso di Dante (Dante's Seat). It is the marble plinth on which he is rumoured to have sat while contemplating the cathedral. The seat has since supported a number of poetic posteriors, including – uncomfortably – my own. Robert Browning honoured it, as, in 1845, did Dickens – commemorating the experience in *Little Dorrit*, describing Dante as an eccentric gentleman who 'used to put leaves round his head, and sit on a stool for some unaccountable purpose, outside the cathedral at Florence'. Two years later, the seat was occupied by the Cumbrian poet William Wordsworth, who wandered lonely in Italy for five months in the summer of 1837, spending five weeks in Florence. He wrote a sonnet to commemorate his enthronement:

> I stood and gazed upon a marble stone.
> The laurelled Dante's favourite seat. A throne . . .

6 *Dante's Seat, Florence*

Wordsworth wrote many more poems about Florence, including two sonnets on Michelangelo and another inspired by Raphael's painting of St John the Baptist in the Pitti Palace. Wordsworth was a regular celebrant at the Church of Santa Croce, and later regretted that he did not visit Florence until he was in his late sixties, because he believed it would have inspired more of his earlier work.

A new marble *sasso* has recently appeared in the piazza, but locals claim that it is a public relations event to promote the sales of an adjacent bar, the name of which is 'Il Sasso di Dante'. To avoid confusion, Dante's original granite seat is now labelled 'The *true* seat of Dante'.

Church of Santa Croce

The most interesting and perfect little gothic chapel in all Italy.
(John Ruskin, *Mornings in Florence*)

After the Duomo, the Church of Santa Croce is the most important in the city. It contains, as the French writer Madame de Staël noted, 'possibly the most brilliant assembly of corpses in the whole of Italy', including the tombs of the sculptors Michelangelo and Lorenzo Ghiberti, the poet Alfieri, the scientist Galileo and the writer Machiavelli. Dante is represented only by a larger-than-life statue outside the main entrance and a monument inside; as mentioned earlier, his remains are entombed in Ravenna, where he died in exile – a fact lamented by both Lord Byron, in *Childe Harold's Pilgrimage*: 'Ungrateful Florence! Dante sleeps afar'; and Mark Twain, in *The Innocents Abroad*: 'We saw Danté's tomb in that church, also, but we were glad to know that his body was not in it; that the ungrateful city that had exiled him and persecuted him would give much to have it there, but need not hope to ever secure that high honour to herself.'

In 1519 the Florentines petitioned Pope Leo X (Lorenzo the Magnificent's son, Giovanni de' Medici) to instruct Ravenna to let them have Dante's body. Among the petitioners was one Michelangelo, who added a note offering to build Dante's memorial himself, but despite the fact that Leo was not only a Florentine but also a Medici, the petition was refused. In June 2008, seven centuries after Dante's banishment, the city council of Florence passed a motion rescinding his sentence – one further ploy aimed at the repatriation of his remains, but it was no more successful than the previous attempts, and Dante's remains still lie in a modest tomb beside the fifth-century Church of San Francesco in Ravenna.

The Santa Croce was begun in 1294 – about the same time as the Duomo – as a Franciscan church, and was intended to be one of the Christian world's largest, which was probably not an aim that the ascetic mendicant St Francis would have supported, but he was dead by then and the Franciscans, having become purveyors of absolution and eternal life, were rich and no longer mendicant. The church was not completed until 1863, when it received the neo-Gothic western façade that was described by E. M. Forster in *A Room with a View* as 'a black-and-white façade of passing ugliness'. In the church, Forster's hapless heroine, Lucy, tries to rescue a toddler being doused in holy water – but the 'dripping but hallowed' child 'stumbled over one of the sepulchral slabs so much admired by Mr Ruskin, and entangled his feet in the features of a recumbent bishop'.

Ruskin's school-masterly advice to visitors wishing to look at art in Florence was: 'Know your first volume of Vasari . . . look about you, and don't talk, nor listen to talking.' About the Church of Santa Croce he is more specific: 'Wait then for an entirely bright morning; rise with the sun, and go to Santa Croce, with a good opera-glass in your pocket. Walk straight to the chapel on the right of the choir. Wait patiently till you get used to the gloom.' The visitor who can withstand the Ruskin hauteur will find a treasure-house of Giotto frescoes painted between 1296 and 1304, most of them in the chapels of the Bardi and the Peruzzi families, and representing scenes from the lives of St Francis and St John the Evangelist. They were later mysteriously whitewashed over, and not uncovered until 1853. In his *Purgatory*, Dante describes the relationship between the painter Giotto and Cimabue, his mentor, whose *Crucifixion* is also in the church:

> In painting Cimabue thought that he
> Should hold the field, now Giotto has the cry,
> So that the other's fame is growing dim.

In 1840, Alexandre Dumas, in his *Une Année à Florence*, patronised the Santa Croce as 'Florence's Panthéon', probably because he found a Bonaparte there. Charlotte, daughter of Napoleon's older brother Joseph, had been buried there only the previous year. Dumas found the church 'mediocre, and like most Florentine churches, unfinished, and even more crude than the others', but, once across the threshold, it was 'une autre chose' ('something else'). There is, in fact, another tomb there marked, simply, 'Bonaparte', but its tenant is not identified.

Mark Twain, on his cruise in the *Quaker City* in 1867, also visited the church. He tells in *The Innocents Abroad* that he and his travelling companion 'went to the Church of Santa Croce from time to time, to weep over the tombs of Michael Angelo, Raphael and Machiavelli, (I suppose they are buried there, but it may be that they reside elsewhere and rent their tombs to other parties – such being the fashion in Italy).' Raphael's tomb is in fact in Rome, but the Twain of those days was never one to let accuracy spoil a good story.

Eleven years later, Twain returned to Florence, and again in 1892 and 1893 with his wife and children, when they stayed in the Villa Viviani in Settignano, overlooking the city: it was a 28-room mansion from which their view was:

> the fairest picture on the planet, the most enchanting to look upon, the most satisfying to the eye and the spirit. To see the sun sink down, drowned in his pink and purple and golden floods, and overwhelm Florence with tides of colour that make all the sharp lines dim and faint and turn the solid city into a city of dreams, is a

sight to stir the coldest nature and make a sympathetic one drunk with ecstasy.

Twain was equally ecstatic about the villa itself: 'The flowery terrace on which it stood looked down upon sloping olive groves and vineyards . . . in the distant plain lay Florence, pink and gray and brown.' It was in the Villa Viviani that Twain wrote his novel *Pudd'nhead Wilson*. Ten years later, in November 1903, the family returned to Florence, and rented the Villa di Quarto in the southern outskirts of the city, where he wrote *Tom Sawyer Abroad*. After the idyllic Villa Viviani, the Villa di Quarto was a bitter disappointment: Twain called it 'this ducal barrack'. It was a sixteenth-century house that had once been a Medici manor, and later, in the mid-nineteenth century, the home of Jérôme Bonaparte, Napoleon's youngest brother and the former King of Westphalia. There Jérôme would often welcome his friend and countryman, Alexandre Dumas. Dumas recalled that, when out sailing one day with Jérôme's sons, they pointed out to him the island of Monte Cristo, which struck him as a good title for a book. When, fifty years after the departure of Jérôme, the Twain family arrived by train from Genoa to rent the Villa di Quarto, it was owned by the Contessa Massiglia.

We had to wait until 2010 to find the reasons for Twain's disenchantment with the Villa di Quarto, and his feud with the Contessa. They were not revealed until his *Autobiography*, the publication of which he had forbidden until 100 years after his own death. Because of his wife's failing health, Twain had made a number of attempts to have a telephone installed in the Villa di Quarto so that he could call a doctor in the event of an emergency. The bureaucratic formalities with the telephone company were soon resolved, but the problem was the Contessa, who used every devious device possible to prevent the telephone from being installed, including cutting the telephone wires and threatening to sue the telephone company if they should erect a telephone post on her land without her written permission – which she had no intention of giving. 'I was not yet able to realize', wrote Twain, 'that I was not dealing with a human being but with a reptile: I was losing my belief in hell until I got acquainted with the Countess Massiglia.' La Contessa, until her marriage to an Italian count two years earlier, had been Mrs Frances Paxton, a coal-dealer's daughter, of Cherry Street, Philadelphia. To Twain she would always be 'the American bitch who owns this Villa', and his vilification of her became increasingly creative in later years. In his *Autobiography* she is 'malicious, malignant, vengeful, unforgiving, selfish, stingy, avaricious, coarse, vulgar, profane, obscene, a furious blusterer on the outside and at heart a coward'.

In order to escape 'the fangs of this titled animal', Twain decided to purchase a residence in nearby Fiesole, but his hopes were dashed the following year, 1904, when, the day before the purchase was to be completed, his wife Olivia – his beloved Livvy – died. It was the end of Mark Twain's plans to settle permanently in Florence.

A near neighbour to the tombs of Michelangelo and Machiavelli in the Santa Croce is the ostentatious memorial to the Italian poet and dramatist Vittorio Alfieri. It was completed in 1810 by Canova – later sculptor to Napoleon and his family – and was paid for by Alfieri's wealthy mistress, who herself posed for the figure of the grieving 'Italy' that dominates the monument. Although it is today considered one of Canova's best pieces, it did not impress Sophia, the wife of Nathaniel Hawthorne: 'It is not good for anything to me,' she wrote. The journal of Alfieri – later Count Alfieri – recalls his summer spent in Florence as a young man of 28 in 1777: 'I met there a beautiful and friendly woman. A distinguished foreigner, it was impossible not to notice her, and, once having noticed, to appreciate her infinite charm. I would see her at the theatre, and, once seen, she would remain in my thoughts and in my heart.' She was 25-year-old Luisa Stolberg, Countess of Albany and wife of the Young Pretender to the English throne, Charles Edward Stuart. He was the 'Bonnie Prince Charlie' who had left Scotland in 1746 after his defeat at the Battle of Culloden had put an end to his attempts to gain the crown. After numerous affairs, he had married Luisa in Rome in 1772, when she was 19 and he 52, and they moved to Florence two years later to live in the Palazzo San Clemente on the Via Gino Capponi.

The marriage was far from blissful. Luisa officially separated from Charles Edward Stuart after 12 years, having unofficially left him at least four years earlier to live with Alfieri, with whom she remained for the last 20 years of his life. After his wife left him, Charles Edward churlishly bestowed her title, Countess of Albany, on his illegitimate daughter Charlotte, who came to live with him in Florence and later Rome for his last years. Charles Edward had by then become almost totally alcohol dependent and, although he still attended the opera regularly, he had to have his sofa specially adapted so that he could watch the stage from a recumbent position. When the performance was over he would be discreetly awakened and sent home to the Palazzo San Clemente. He died in Rome in 1788 at the age of 68 and his remains were laid to rest in the crypt of St Peter's Basilica in the Vatican, next to those of his brother and his father, beneath an epitaph naming him, as he had always claimed: 'Charles Edward, son of James III, King of England'.

On Alfieri's death in 1803, the Countess, to quote the English novelist E. V. Lucas, 'selected the French artist Fabre to fill the aching void in her fifty-years-old heart; and Fabre not only filled it until her death in 1824, but became heir to all that had been bequeathed to her by both Stuart and Count Alfieri'. On the Countess's death in 1824 from dropsy, Fabre presented Alfieri's works to Michelangelo's magnificent Laurentian Library, and on his own death in 1837, charitably bequeathed all his possessions, including those inherited from Alfieri and the Stuarts, to his natal city, Montpelier, in France. Although Montpelier may have inherited most of Fabre's work, Florence may have had the last laugh, for not only did Luisa fail to become England's Catholic queen, but Fabre's picture of her, with Alfieri gazing at her adoringly, now hangs in the Uffizi Gallery.

Luisa's capricious love life was further maligned by Henry James in his novel *A Little Tour in France*, in which, in one of his more laconic moments, he applauded her ability to 'associate sentimentally with diverse figures: a disqualified sovereign, an Italian dramatist and a bad French painter'.

Santa Maria Novella

You will begin to wonder that human daring ever achieved anything so magnificent.   (John Ruskin, *Mornings in Florence*)

Arriving by train at Florence's main station – known as Florence Santa Maria Novella or SMN – the first ancient church you see, across the Piazza della Stazione and behind the market stalls is, not surprisingly, the Church of Santa Maria Novella, with its striking Gothic and Renaissance façade in green and white marble.

7 *The Church of Santa Maria Novella, Florence*

Compared with the Franciscan Santa Croce, whose original church was begun in 1294, the Santa Maria Novella, whose Dominican construction began in 1246, is, despite its name, the older. The Santa Maria Novella was also the first of the two to complete its façade in the fifteenth century: the finishing touches to the marble façade of the Santa Croce were not added until 1863, the gift of an English resident, Sir Francis Sloane.

Like most mendicant orders, for economic reasons the Dominicans built their church outside the city walls. It was originally known as the Santa Maria tra le Vigne, or 'in the vineyards', and it acquired its modern name when the city extended its walls.

Internally, the Santa Maria Novella is as well endowed with artistic masterpieces as the Duomo is scant; from the Giotto crucifix hanging high above the nave to works by Masaccio and Lippi, and Brunelleschi's wooden crucifix – of which the author Leigh Hunt asked, 'Is not this the best in Europe?' Its chapter room is also known as the Spanish Chapel, for it was used by the court of Eleanor of Toledo, the Spanish wife of Cosimo I de' Medici and Grand Duchess of Tuscany.

There used to be a Madonna and Child in the church, which was mistakenly declared by the parochial Vasari to be the work of the Florentine Cimabue, but the painting was later attributed to the Sienese painter Duccio di Buoninsegna, and relegated to the Uffizi. Ruskin wrote, 'I find Vasari's mistakes usually of this *brightly* blundering kind.'

The Santa Maria Novella's earliest literary association is that it was in its frescoed cloisters that Boccaccio set the opening chapter of his greatest work, the *Decameron*, which begins:

In the year 1348 after the fruitful incarnation of the Son of God, that most beautiful of Italian cities, noble Florence was attacked by deadly plague. It started in the East, either through the influence of the heavenly bodies or because God's just anger with our wicked deeds sent it as punishment to mortal men, and in a few years killed an innumerable quantity of people.

In the Santa Maria Novella, after Mass one day in 1348, a group of seven young ladies got together and decided to leave the city and find a country retreat where they could wait in safety until the plague had passed. They were joined by three young nobles and the 10 friends – the *Decamerone* – are said to have chosen as their fictional refuge Boccaccio's actual Florence home, the Villa Palmieri, in the village of San Domenico on the hillside of Fiesole. More than four centuries later, in 1775, the house was acquired by the newly ennobled Earl Cowper, and in 1840 it was the home of a French novelist. As Alexandre Dumas describes it in his book *La Villa Palmieri*: 'It was in this house that Boccaccio wrote his *Decameron*. I thought its name would bring me happiness, and set up my office in the same room in which, four hundred and ninety-three years earlier, Boccaccio had established his.'

Half a century later, in both 1889 and 1893, the residents of the Villa Palmieri were the widowed Queen Victoria and her abundant retinue. Not long after Victoria's stay, the villa was the home of the novelist on whom she had conferred a knighthood: Sir Henry Rider Haggard. Best known as a writer of adventure stories with African settings such as *King Solomon's Mines* and *She*, Haggard spent the winter of 1900–1 in Florence, as part of a tour that included Palestine and Cyprus, which he describes in his *Winter Pilgrimage*. He and his family later lived in the former Convent of Annalena, a fifteenth-century Medici palace on the Via Romagna. It had been founded as a convent by Sister Annalena, and after her death served variously as a Catholic girls' school, a residence for Napoleon's sister Caroline and – at different times – a brothel and a wartime shelter for Jewish women, before becoming the Pensione Annalena, which it is today. Haggard became fascinated with the history of Savonarola and retraced the priest's footsteps – at the Church of San Marco and the Palazzo Vecchio – with a view to basing a novel on his life, but the novel was never written. Like Tobias Smollett in his *Travels through France and Italy*, Haggard, writing a century later in *Winter Pilgrimage*, made no pretence of having artistic expertise. He began his chapter on Florence with: 'For generations past, visitors to Italy have written about Florence. I propose to leave that noble army unrecruited. Here the reader will find no account of the architecture of its cathedrals, no list of the best pictures.' He almost kept his word: the exception being Donatello's *Annunciation* in the Church of Santa Croce – but otherwise he confined his attention to such earthy matters as nocturnal funerals, priestly attire and the agonised death of Savonarola.

Queen Victoria, writing in 1883 to her future granddaughter-in-law, Princess Mary of Teck, later to become queen as the wife of King George V, and grandmother of Queen Elizabeth II, said: 'it was with much regret that I heard you were gone to Florence, for living in a town full of attractions and temptations to expense made me very anxious.' By the time that Victoria began her own visits to Florence, six years later, she had evidently overcome her anxiety about its attractions and temptations to expense, for she travelled complete with royal train, carriage and horses, a donkey and cart, and an entourage that included private secretaries, a French chef, four sous-chefs, scullions, coachmen, outriders, a dozen grooms and stablemen, a troop of Indian servants, a teacher of Hindustani and a kilted Highland gillie – 80 people in all, not including family members.

Florence was Queen Victoria's alternative retreat during her 17-year love affair with southern France, her first stay in the city in 1889 being sandwiched between holidays in Biarritz and Grasse, and her second, in 1893, between her holidays in Hyères and Nice. As had been her custom on the Riviera, each afternoon in Florence she would go out in her donkey cart to a different place of interest, and the evenings would be reserved for matters of state: dinner with the King and Queen of Italy or other visiting royalty or political VIPs. During these first two visits to Florence, Earl Cowper lent her Boccaccio's Villa Palmieri, and on the Queen's next and final visit in 1894, she stayed in the Villa Fabbricotti in Montughi. The Villa Palmieri is still a private mansion, but the Villa Fabbricotti is now a youth hostel.

In the Piazza Santa Maria Novella, in front and to the left of the church is the building in which the 20-year-old poet Longfellow lodged in 1928, now the Hotel Minerva. 'In front of my parlour windows', he wrote, 'was the venerable Gothic Church of Santa Maria Novella, in whose gloomy aisles Boccaccio has placed the opening scenes of his *Decamarone*'. Longfellow was there to research the life of Dante for his projected translation of *The Divine Comedy*, which, following a number of further visits to Florence, was eventually published in America forty years later. Longfellow also studied the works of other Florentine writers, and wrote his *Tales of a Wayside Inn* as a tribute to Boccaccio.

It was at that same Hotel Minerva, 10 years later, that another American stayed: the writer and lecturer Ralph Waldo Emerson lodged here, hoping to spend the spring months improving his Italian and researching material for his lecture tours. He does not appear to have seen any irony in the fact that his address to Harvard University the previous year had advocated American 'intellectual independence: we have listened for too long to the courtly muses of Europe'. The courtly muses called him again six years later to study Michelangelo and Plutarch for more lecture material, and he returned yet again at the age of 70 for a longer stay.

The Uffizi Gallery

Adorned with the selected chefs d'œuvres of the best artists.
(Mary Shelley, *Rambles in Germany and Italy*)

Stretching from the Piazza della Signoria to the river Arno is Florence's most important art gallery, the vast Galleria degli Uffizi. Designed by Giorgio Vasari, it was built in the late sixteenth century to house the art collections of the Medici family, and the *uffizi*, (literally, offices) of the city's major guilds. The collections were left to the city by the last survivor of the Medici family, the widowed Anna Maria Luisa, when she died in 1743. They include Greek and Roman sculptures and Florentine art from Gothic to Renaissance periods and later. For the German writer, Bernd Roeck, the Uffizi was altogether too much: he 'could summon up no further ecstasy'.

Tobias Smollett was more precise: 'If I resided in Florence,' he said in his *Travels through France and Italy* in 1766, 'I would give something extraordinary for permission to walk every day in the gallery. Among the great number of pictures in this Tribuna, I was most charmed with the Venus by Titian, which has a sweetness of expression and tenderness of colouring, not to be described.' Herman Melville was another of Venus's admirers, and Hans Christian Andersen called her 'mortal beauty in all its fullness'.

Titian's Venus d'Urbino was not universally appreciated: a century later, she was described less enthusiastically by Mark Twain, who wrote in *The Innocents Abroad*:

> You enter the Uffizi and proceed to that most-visited little gallery that exists in the world – the Tribune – and there, against the wall, without obstructing rag or leaf, you may look your fill upon the foulest, the vilest, the obscenest picture that world possesses – Titian's painting of the Venus d'Urbino. It isn't that she is naked and stretched out on a bed; no, it is the attitude of one of her arms and hand.

Such an outraged reaction from America's pioneer of the ironic form to a masterpiece of the Italian Renaissance came as such a surprise to me that I have had to assume, either that a piece of Twain irony has flown over my head, or that the author was having a Puritanical day. The American censors went further, and banned even Twain's *description* of the painting. Twain may have reconsidered this comment, because later in the book he writes, 'How the fatigues and annoyances of travel fill one with bitter prejudices sometimes! I might enter Florence under happier auspices a month hence and find it all beautiful, all attractive.'

The young John Ruskin was even less enthusiastic about the collections, and wrote that, impressive as the galleries might be, 'I had as soon be in the British Museum, as far as enjoyment goes, except for the Raphaels.' But he was only 21 years old at the time: within five years he was writing to *The Times*, insisting that the

National Gallery buy no more Rubens until it had acquired some older Italian works.

The Uffizi, like the Florentine weather, left Herman Melville cold. The work that he thought was its greatest artistic treasure was the one that had so appalled Mark Twain: Titian's Venus. Melville arrived in Florence in the spring of 1857, and although the weather was anything but spring-like, the hardy man of the sea was generous enough to admit that 'Florence is a lovely city, even on a cold rainy day.' Like many of his countrymen, he stayed at the Hôtel du Nord and took breakfast at Doney's. His first artistic excursion was to the Pitti Palace, where he was captivated by Michelangelo's Three Fates, but his comment on a painting of Lucrezia Borgia, as quoted by Alice Leccese Powers in her *Italy in Mind*, was 'Good looking dame. Rather fleshy.' A keen agronomist, Melville visited – presumably suitably rain-proofed – a number of Florentine gardens. The fact that he called in at Liverpool on his way home to see his fellow New Englander, Nathaniel Hawthorne, the American consul there, suggests that Hawthorne's visit to Florence the following summer might have been prompted by Melville.

The most viewed artist in the Uffizi is Sandro Botticelli. From having been an early star of the Renaissance period, his works fell out of fashion until the late nineteenth century, when, thanks largely to Florence-based American art dealers such as Bernard Berenson and the colourful prose of American writers, Botticelli more than recovered his position, and the Uffizi now honours him by dedicating a room to his works. An assessment of Botticelli from Henry James read: 'He was rarity and distinction incarnate, and of all the multitudinous masters of his group incomparably the most interesting.' We shall see later how the temporary absence of one of Botticelli's works made international headlines during the Second World War.

Unlike Titian's controversial Venus painting, the *statue* known as the Medici Venus, which Ralph Waldo Emerson called 'the statue that enchants the world', has enjoyed almost universal acclaim. It is of third-century BC Greek origin, and was 'liberated' by Napoleon's troops from the villa of the Emperor Hadrian in Rome. Tobias Smollett preferred 'the back parts', which 'are executed so happily as to excite the admiration of the most indifferent spectator', to the face, 'there is no beauty in the features'. Leigh Hunt was no less excited: he thought her body 'perfection', but found 'neither the gesture of the figure modest, nor the face worthy even of the gesture'. Nathaniel Hawthorne's wife Sophia described her as 'a being that lives to gladden the world, incapable of decay or death; as young and fair as she was three thousand years ago'; Hans Christian Andersen claimed she was 'heavenly beauty! I have been sitting in front of her for more than an hour'; while Mary Shelley said: 'the matchless statue of the Queen of Beauty reigns over the whole.' She was echoed half a century later by Fyodor Mikhailovich Dostoevsky, who considered the statue 'a work of genius', but another Russian, the dramatist Anton Chekhov, did not: after visiting the Uffizi at the age of 31, he wrote to his family in St Petersburg, 'it's my opinion that if she were dressed in modern clothes she'd look quite hideous, especially around the waist.'

The English Cemetery

Blue Tuscan sky endomes our English words of prayer.
  (Elizabeth Barrett Browning, 'A Child's Grave at Florence')

The sparseness of Florence's English Cemetery comes as a contrast after the more ornate and densely packed Mediterranean cemeteries, but it shares with its Catholic equivalents the sense of calm amid chaos; of being in the midst of a maelstrom of traffic and strangely at peace. The Cimetière Père Lachaise in Paris is another such haven. The so-called 'English' Cemetery – in fact it is non-Catholic rather than English, as a glance at the headstones reveals – is an appropriately mandorla-shaped traffic island in the Piazzale Donatello, north-east of the city, and because of racing traffic and the absence of traffic lights, pedestrian access is hazardous. Since few of its incumbents arrive on foot – and none ever leave – there are no pedestrian crossings, so a visit can be a life-threatening experience, which is also apt.

Before 1827, non-Catholics who died in Florence had to be buried in Livorno. The cemetery acquired the name 'English' because Protestants, most of whom were English, had to be buried outside the medieval city walls.

Another similarity to the Père Lachaise is that the Florence English cemetery has an illustrious, if smaller, literary cast. Its most famous figure is Elizabeth Barrett Browning, who died in 1861, leaving behind her husband Robert and son Pen. Her near neighbours in a miniature Anglo-Saxon writers' corner include the novelist Frances 'Fanny' Eleanor Trollope, mother of the novelists Anthony and Thomas Adolphus Trollope. Frances Trollope started to write in her fifties from financial necessity, but continued through addiction, setting up a cottage industry of fiction, to which she contributed 115 books. Her productivity came at the expense of attending to her own children, in particular the novelist Anthony Trollope, author of *The Chronicles of Barsetshire*, whom she carelessly left behind in England as a child while she moved to Florence with her older and more favoured son, Thomas Adolphus, who also became a prolific author. In all, the industrious Trollope ménage produced a total of 306 novels, as calculated by Olive Hamilton, author of *The Divine Country: The British in Tuscany*. Thomas's wife, the musician and writer Theodosia Trollope, whom Elizabeth Browning described as 'more intense than intensity itself', now lies buried alongside her mother-in-law. The more successful son, Anthony Trollope, 15 years younger than Thomas, made only cursory visits with his wife to the Villino Trollope, Frances's home in the Piazza dell'Indipendenzia, preferring to live in England, where he was equally dedicated to his other careers, of senior executive in the Royal Mail (he was responsible for installing Britain's red cylindrical letterboxes) and Member of Parliament. He did not set any of his novels in Florence, but began his novel *Doctor Thorne* there, and contributed a number of satirical articles on Florence to the *Pall Mall Gazette*.

After Frances's arrival at the Villino, it became a sort of mini-Bloomsbury for itinerant writers. Thomas wrote in his memoir, *What I Remember*: 'within weeks, my mother's home became, as usual, a centre of attraction and pleasant intercourse and her weekly receptions were always crowded.' Frances's invitation list looked like the programme for a nineteenth-century literary festival, and included the Americans Nathaniel Hawthorne, James Russell Lowell and Harriett Beecher Stowe, and Britons George Eliot, the Brownings, Charles Dickens and of course Thomas Adolphus. Thomas even became a contributor to Dickens's magazine, *Household Words*. A tetchy – or envious – Elizabeth Browning wrote to England, 'Mrs Trollope has recommended her "public" mornings which we shrink away from. She "receives" every Saturday morning in the most heterogeneous way possible. It must be amusing to anybody not overwhelmed by it, and people say that she snatches up "characters" for her "so many volumes a year" out of the diversities of masks presented to her on these occasions.'

Elizabeth may have overlooked the possibility that, for some of Frances's guests, the Trollope soirées were a two-way process, and that character-collecting may have been their sole reason for attending: what we might call 'networking' today. I have long suspected that Dickens reincarnated Frances Trollope as the character Mrs Jellyby in *Bleak House*; a woman for whom charity begins anywhere but at home, and who, at the expense of her family life, dedicates every hour of her existence – and those of her long-suffering husband and children – to some vague resettlement project 'on the left bank of the Niger' that she calls 'my African project'.

One literary occupant of the English Cemetery who certainly became a Dickens character in his own lifetime was the larger-than-life aptly named English poet, Walter Savage Landor. Ferociously republican, boisterous and thorny, Landor became Mr Boythorn in *Bleak House*. Landor's lifelong handicap was an uncontrollable temper, and if he should ever feel slighted, he was inclined to assault his protagonist, challenge him to a duel, or both. He was expelled, first from Rugby School, then from Oxford University, for insolence, and was reputed, following some culinary mishap at his Villa Gherardesca in Fiesole, to have thrown his Italian chef out of a first-floor window, showing contrition only on remembering that he had recently planted a bed of violets beneath the same window.

From being an admirer of Napoleon as a young man, Landor later changed sides and at his own expense took a troop of militia to Spain, to fight against the French in the Peninsular War. On becoming heir to his father's fortune, he purchased the estate of Llanthony Priory, a former Augustinian priory in Monmouthshire, but because of his financial ineptitude and total lack of people management skills, he was in trouble from the start. Within a few months he had lost the property to creditors and lawyers, and decided to move to Italy. He arrived in Florence with his family in 1821 and they spent their first four years there in the Medici Palace on the Borgo degli Albizi, just south of the cathedral. The family then moved to the Villa Gherardesca, a large villa in San Domenico di Fiesole in the hills above Florence with a magnificent view of the Arno Valley and with what Landor called 'a central turret, round which the kite perpetually circle in search of pigeons or smaller prey'. He remained there until 1835 when, after a particularly acrimonious domestic tiff, he decided to return to England. He stayed in Bath for the next 22 years, until, as a result of yet another neighbourhood squabble, he was charged £1,000 damages for libel and decided to return to the refuge of Tuscany.

Landor was advised to protect his estate from his creditors by transferring it to his eldest son, Arnold. Once again he demonstrated his financial naivety: unlike Somerset Maugham, who, when a similar suggestion was put to him, said, 'Thank you – I have read King Lear,' Landor agreed. When he returned to the Villa Gherardesca in 1858 after his 22-year absence, Arnold turned him out, penniless. Landor walked the two miles into Florence, where he was rescued from destitution by the kindness of Robert Browning, who found him in the street, helped him financially and found him lodgings near to the Casa Guidi with Elizabeth's former maid, by then married to an Italian.

Whatever Landor's social eccentricities, his sensitive poetry was much admired by poets such as Browning, Robert Southey and Algernon Charles Swinburne, and eminent critics such as William Hazlitt, but he is best remembered for his prose *Imaginary Conversations of Literary Men and Statesmen*, which began appearing in 1824 and continued for five years, and provided an outlet for his erudition and eccentricities. 'Poetry was always my amusement,' he once wrote, 'prose my study and business.' *Imaginary Conversations* eventually comprised 150 eloquent conversations between historians, philosophers, artists and politicians from different countries and eras. Most critics agree that in Landor's *Imaginary Conversations*, every protagonist, whatever his theme, spoke with the voice of his author.

Landor died in Florence in 1864 at the age of 89, and is buried in the English Cemetery. One of the last visitors to his bedside was his friend and admirer, the poet Swinburne. Despite Landor's request for an unadorned gravestone, the following lines from Swinburne's 'In Memory of Walter Savage Landor' now appear on his tombstone:

> AND THOU, HIS FLORENCE, TO THY TRUST
> RECEIVE AND KEEP,
> KEEP SAFE HIS DEDICATED DUST,
> HIS SACRED SLEEP.

Landor may well be thought to have already written his own epitaph, however, with the memorable closing lines of his poem, 'Dying Speech of an Old Philosopher':

> I strove with none, for none was worth my strife;
> Nature I loved, and, next to Nature, Art:
> I warm'd both hands before the fire of Life;
> It sinks, and I am ready to depart.

The Villa Gherardesca is now a Roman Catholic orphanage.

A few metres away from Landor's grave is that of Arthur Hugh Clough, a Liverpool-born poet and former pupil of the educationalist

Dr Thomas Arnold at Rugby School. Clough first visited Florence at the age of 24 and later spent much of his life there. Like James Fenimore Cooper 30 years earlier, Clough lived in the Hotel York in the Via Cerretani. He married a cousin of Florence Nightingale and moved to the Casa Fabriani in the Piazza Pitti, which, six years later, would be the home of Dostoevsky. Clough's uplifting poem 'Say Not the Struggle Naught Availeth' was quoted by King George VI in a speech at one of the darker moments of the Second World War, many claiming that its last line, 'But westward, look, the land is bright,' was a veiled, if vain, attempt to encourage America to enter the war against Fascism. The epitaph on Clough's gravestone contains lines from 'Thyrsis', written by his Rugby schoolmate and fellow poet, Matthew Arnold, son of the headmaster and another frequent visitor to Florence over much of his life.

A visitor to the poets' corner of the cemetery in 1908 was another ex-Rugby boy, the newly graduated poet, Rupert Brooke, one of the First World War 'war poets' who, apart from his presence in Antwerp during the German siege, was not able to play a significant role in the war. He died, not in some corner of a foreign field, but in a French hospital ship – from a septic mosquito bite – on his way to the Gallipoli landing. When he was travelling in Florence, he reported to his aunts in England: 'Today I went in state with an armful of flowers which I placed on Landor's and Clough's graves. I felt I represented Rugby, and ought to! I spared one rose for E. B. Browning.'

Harriett Beecher Stowe, the American author of *Uncle Tom's Cabin*, was a regular visitor to Frances Trollope's Villino Trollope during her stays in Florence in the late 1850s. She had recently been received and 'honoured' by Queen Victoria, and had come to Florence, like George Eliot, to study the life of Savonarola as background to a planned novel. Stowe's book, *Agnes of Sorrento*, published in 1862, and Eliot's, *Romola*, in the following year, were both about a virtuous young woman torn between romance and a dedication to furthering the good work of Savonarola, whom both authors saw as an emissary sent to save Italy from Catholicism – Stowe called him the 'Italian Luther'. The fact that Italy is 88 per cent Catholic today would indicate that their literary quests were more successful than their theological ones. Thomas Trollope was less than enthusiastic about *Romola*: 'In drawing the girl Romola, [Eliot's] subjectivity has overpowered her objectivity. Romola is not – could never have been – the product of the period and of the civilisation from which she is described as having issued'. Eliot would have found Henry James's criticism even more harsh: *Romola*, he thought, was scholarly but cold: 'The great defect is that it does not seem positively to live. It is overladen with learning, it smells of the lamp, it tastes just short of pedantry.'

During her stay in Florence, Stowe, a tireless dropper-in, also befriended Elizabeth Barrett Browning, who congratulated her on the international success of *Uncle Tom's Cabin*. Denying all credit, Stowe said that the book was the work of the Lord: 'I was but the humblest instrument in His hand.' The two women were also deeply interested in spiritualism, Stowe believing that she had received messages from her dead son, Henry. Sophia Hawthorne, wife of Nathaniel, was another convert, noting that 'Mr Browning cannot believe, and Mrs Browning cannot help believing.'

Elizabeth had been introduced to spiritualism by Seymour Kirkup, an artist born in London in 1788, who spent much of his life in Florence. He came to Italy in his late twenties for his health, with evident success, for he died in Livorno at the age of 92. His many friends among the expatriate literati included the Brownings, Landor, Swinburne and Hawthorne, who described him thus: 'He has a high, thin nose, of the English aristocratic type; his eyes have a queer, rather wild look, and the eyebrows are arched above them, so that he seems all the time to be seeing something that strikes him with surprise. I judged him to be a little crack-brained, chiefly on the strength of this expression.' Crack-brained or not, Kirkup was a good friend to many writers: he was present at the funeral of Keats in Rome in 1821 and at the cremation of Percy Shelley at Viareggio the following year. He also probably saved Walter Savage Landor's life: when the hot-headed poet challenged a neighbour to a duel, Kirkup managed to have the matter settled in court with no casualties. A passionate scholar of Dante, Kirkup achieved immortality in the art world with his remarkable discovery (shared with an American writer, Richard Henry Wilde) of the now-famous fresco of Dante, painted by the poet's friend Giotto. The painting was found under whitewash on a wall in what later became the Bargello Museum in Florence. Kirkup bribed a guard to leave him with the painting and drew a copy of it that has become almost as famous as the original.

The eccentric Kirkup married late in life – twice. In 1854, at the age of 68, he married his landlady's 17-year-old daughter, described by Thomas Trollope as 'a clever, worthless hussy', with whom he had a daughter – perhaps the reason for his surprised expression. After the child's mother died, he moved to Livorno to be near his daughter's lover, and in 1878, at the age of 90, married the clever hussy's equally clever sister, thus securing her inheritance. She was just in time: Kirkup died two years later.

The English Cemetery was officially closed in 1877, when the medieval walls of Florence came down, making burials within the city boundary illegal, and for a century and a quarter the mini-necropolis remained locked and neglected.

Ten years ago, Julia Bolton Holloway, a literary scholar specialising in the works of Elizabeth Barrett Browning – whose Penguin Classic *Anthology* she co-edited – took on responsibility for the cemetery. It was reopened to the public in 2003 for the reception of ashes but not bodies, and Holloway is actively raising restoration funds. When I called, she was re-lettering a gravestone, and she has set up a number of charitable institutions to ensure its future maintenance. Today, with the gardens replanted and well-maintained and the memorials inscribed and re-erected, it is a pleasure to visit, and well worth the slalom through the traffic – safe in the knowledge that if you don't make it to the cemetery, there is a hospital next door.

The River Arno

On an impetuous river in the heart of the Italian peninsula there stands
a city whose past seems to imitate that river in its violence and contrasts.
(E.-R. Labande, *Florence*)

Some would say that Florence's river is appropriately named: phonetically, it sounds like a negative. Alexandre Dumas, in his *Une Année à Florence*, wrote of it, 'After the Var [the river at Nice that separated France from Italy at the time], the Arno is the biggest waterless river I have ever known. It barely moves for nine months of the year.' The river flows – or more often, trickles – from east to west through the city at such a leisurely pace that there is all the time in the world for algae to collect and for mosquitoes to breed. Looking at its placid surface, it is hard to imagine the floods that have devastated the city in years past: most recently in 1966. Mark Twain, a former river pilot, no doubt thinking of his mighty Mississippi, disparaged it:

> It is a great historical creek with four feet in the channel and some scows floating around. It would be a plausible river if they would pump some water into it. They all call it a river and they honestly think it *is* a river, do these dark and bloody Florentines. They even help out the delusion by building bridges over it. I do not see why they are too good to wade.

Sinclair Lewis's hero in *World so Wide*, Hayden Chart, changed his impression of Florence while looking at the river: 'in the bright morning of late autumn he looked from his hotel and began to fall in love with a city. He saw the Arno, in full brown tide after the mountain rains, with old palaces along it and cypress-waving hills beyond. . . . with old passageways, crooked and mysterious, arched over with stone that bore carven heraldic shields.'

In the Florence of today, the Arno is ochre-coloured, becoming only slightly less so on its arrival at Pisa, 30 kilometres downriver,

8 *The River Arno from the Piazza Michelangelo, Florence*

where it is reminiscent of curried chicken. It is so yellow that some people, misled by the blue sky reflected in it, think it is emerald green. The old buildings along its banks tend to have the same distressed, antiquated look. 'On the north side', said Henry James,

> is a row of immemorial houses that back on the river, in whose yellow flood they bathe their sore old feet. Anything more battered and befouled, more cracked and disjointed, dirtier, drearier, poorer, it would be impossible to conceive. They look as if fifty years ago the liquid mud had risen over their chimneys and then subsided again and left them coated for ever with its unsightly slime.

The French novelist André Gide's view was more lyrical: 'along the shores of the Arno – setting sun; water losing itself in golden sands; in the far distance, some fisherman; the smoke arising from the roofs, at first grey, becomes gilded when the sun touches it . . . the white walls of the villas become the colour of unripe apricots; the cypresses around them seem all the darker.' In Florence the Arno's best-known features are the bridges that cross it, especially the Ponte Santa Trinità and the Ponte Vecchio.

Ponte Santa Trinità

Ammannati's bridge, the most beautiful in Florence, the most beautiful perhaps in the world. (Mary McCarthy, *Stones of Florence*)

In 1557, after the existing Ponte Santa Trinità had been washed away by a flood, Cosimo I de' Medici, then Grand Duke of Tuscany, decided to build a new bridge as a triumphal arch to commemorate his victory over the Sienese two years earlier. Such notable artists as Michelangelo and Vasari were consulted in earlier design discussions, but the challenge of building the bridge eventually fell to Bartolomeo Ammannati. The bridge, linking the Via Maggio on the south side of the river to the Via Tornabuoni to the north, would become the busiest and most important bridge in the city. Seen from along the Arno, it shimmers in the setting sun. Frances Trollope wrote, in *Italy and the Italians*, 'The short twilight sank almost into darkness, and as we drove over the beautiful bridge of La Trinità its statues looked like ghosts in the starlight.'

Those statues and the bridge were innocent casualties of the Second World War. In 1945, in the closing stages of the war, the retreating German armies, in the hope of slowing the advance of the Allied forces, blew up all the bridges across the river except one. As they destroyed the Ponte Santa Trinità, the four statues – representing the four seasons, one at each corner – that had stood at the entrances to the bridge since they were added to celebrate Cosimo II's wedding in 1608, were blown into the river.

After the war, the rebuilding of the Ponte Santa Trinità became a symbol of Florence's revival. The four-hundred-year-old plans of

Ammannati were found, and the bridge was rebuilt using the same plans and many of the original stones. It was paid for by public subscriptions and donations from an international fund set up by the wealthy American art dealer, Bernard Berenson. The missing statues were retrieved from the riverbed and put in place at the entrances to the bridge, the approach roads of which were widened to cope with modern traffic. 'The rebuilders', wrote Mary McCarthy in *Stones of Florence*, 'became conscious of the mystery attaching to the full, swelling, looping curve of the three arches – the slender bridge's most exquisite feature – which conforms to no line or figure in geometry and seems to have been drawn, freehand, by a linear genius, which Ammannati was not.' In 1833, the American poet Ralph Waldo Emerson had declared the bridge's 'elegant curves' to be 'one of the most satisfying sights in the city'.

There remained one more problem: the statue on the north-eastern corner, Primavera – the one representing Spring – which was

9 The Ponte Santa Trinità, Florence

decapitated in the demolition, had stood headless since the bridge reopened in 1958. Thinking that her head might have somehow left the country in some soldier's kit-bag, the Parker Pen Company advertised internationally, offering a reward of $3,000 for its return, but as the deadline passed, Primavera remained headless, so the money was given to the poor. It was not until 1961 that a dredger brought up the long-submerged head from the riverbed, and, after spending a week displayed on a velvet cushion in the Palazzo Vecchio, the head was returned to its rightful shoulders. Now, proudly headed but with a necklace of mortar, Primavera stands at the northern end of the bridge, gazing up at the lofty statue of Cosimo I in the Piazza Santa Trinità.

In this same piazza stands the Palazzo Buondelmonti, once the home of the Gabinetto Vieusseux Library, a nineteenth-century Mecca for expatriate writers, attracted by its assortment of foreign books, newspapers and magazines, and frequented by so many literati that the American author and consul J. D. Howells called it 'the place where sooner or later you meet everyone you know among the foreign residents at Florence'. Its visitors' book was a literary *Who's Who*, including Americans Henry Wadsworth Longfellow and James Fenimore Cooper, and an assortment of Europeans: Heinrich Heine, Stendhal and Dostoevsky, and Britons John Ruskin and Robert Browning.

Hunter Davies, a prolific English financial and business journalist and ghost-biographer of an eclectic range of celebrities that includes the Beatles, road transport tycoon Eddie Stobart, politician John Prescott and footballer Wayne Rooney, made his own version of the Grand Tour in style, on the Orient Express, recording it in his *Grand Tour* in 1986. For Davies, though, the Ponte Santa Trinità was an anticlimax; he had heard so much about it that he promised his family that he would drive them across it as their dramatic entrance to Florence. But it was a bridge too far: at first he could not find it, and when he did, he had failed to realise that, like most bridges, the Santa Trinità is best viewed in profile, and not from a rented Fiat in a Florentine traffic jam. He judged the bridge 'utterly ordinary'.

From the Piazza Santa Trinità northwards, the Via Tornabuoni leads to the Piazza Santa Maria Novella. The Via Tornabuoni has been called Florence's Bond Street, either because, like London's Bond Street, it features the top brand boutiques, or perhaps because it is one of the few streets in Florence on which two people can pass on its pavements without one having to step into the road. It is a good quarter to stay in because it is near the main railway station, and as close to the river and main city piazzas as one can get without paying their prices. Nearby were the Hotels Arno, in which Henry James began his Florence-based *Portrait of a Lady*, and du Nord, favourites with Dickens and other writers, especially Americans, who included Ralph Waldo Emerson, Herman Melville, James R. Lowell and Fenimore Cooper.

A more recent literary tenant of the piazza, at Via Tornabuoni 3, was the Nobel Prize-winning novelist, John Steinbeck. Steinbeck came to southern Italy in 1943 as a war correspondent for the *New York Herald Tribune*. He returned from the war with a shrapnel wound, clinical depression and an obsession that J. Edgar Hoover's FBI was 'stepping on my heels'; to avoid its attentions, he took to travel. Sadly, despite the evident compassion of his earlier, successful 'California' novels: *Of Mice and Men* and *The Grapes of Wrath*, he came to be seen by his government less as a champion of the common man than as an incipient threat to American capitalism, especially after his travels in the Soviet Union in 1948 that produced his *A Russian Journey*. It is evidence of Steinbeck's later success that his hotel of choice in Florence should be, not the du Nord, but the elegant Hotel Tornabuoni Beacci, which still enhances the upper floors of the magnificent Renaissance Palazzo Strozzi.

The hotels of the Piazza Santa Trinità were also the Florentine haunts of Sir George and Lady Ida Sitwell, progenitors of the literary dynasty of that name. The most productive author of the Sitwell clan, their older son Osbert, would, as a young man, visit them at their Florence hotel: 'I found I could be happy all day, visiting galleries or walking round the streets.'

In the Piazza Santa Trinità, facing the northern end of the Ponte Santa Trinità, stands a beautifully preserved medieval castle with crenellated battlements, the Palazzo Spini-Feroni. Here Oscar Wilde stayed in 1895 as a guest of his eventual nemesis, Lord Alfred Douglas, who had an apartment in the palazzo. Wilde enjoyed the Anglo-Saxon social scene in Florence – and it him. When André Gide met the tragic pair in a Florence café, he reported discreetly that he had met Wilde 'in the company of another poet of a younger generation'. Wilde's interest in Tuscany had been aroused many years earlier by the lectures of John Ruskin at Oxford. Wilde found Florence especially inspiring and had written the poem 'On the Arno' on his first visit there twenty years earlier. These were Wilde's last months of freedom before his disastrous trial and imprisonment in Reading Gaol for homosexual practices. After his release, his friend and biographer, the American writer Frank Harris – to whom Wilde had dedicated his play *An Ideal Husband* as 'a slight tribute to his power and distinction as an artist, his chivalry and nobility as a friend' – helped him to move to the French Riviera in the hope of encouraging him to start writing again, but after being insulted in a Nice hotel by some English tourists, Wilde left the coast for the less restrictive ambience of Paris, where he died in 1900, having produced little of note since his trial, other than his *Ballad of Reading Gaol*. Close friends claimed that it was the spiritual elements of Renaissance painting that inspired Wilde's deathbed wish to enter the Roman Catholic faith. In 1938, the Palazzo Spini-Feroni was bought by the shoemaker to the stars, Salvatore Ferragamo, and became a shoe factory.

In this same square, beneath the lofty statue of Justice, stood the foreigners' café in which expatriate writers gathered for breakfast or afternoon tea: Doney's. Charles Lever's two-volume novel, *One of Them*, starts in it, and in Somerset Maugham's short story, *Woman of Fifty*, it was the 'happy hunting-ground' in which titled but impoverished Italian men tracked down wealthy American widows – and vice versa. Sadly, Doney's is now closed: replaced, like many of its contemporaries, by a different type of hunting-ground: a branch of some global haute couture chain. In the 1920s the Via Tornabuoni was a writers' rendezvous: a long-term resident of Florence, Harold Acton, wrote in his *Memoirs of an Aesthete*, 'there was a plethora of writers, and you were bound to meet them on the Via Tornabuoni; D. H. Lawrence with his Rubens *frau* and his string bag after marketing . . .' Carinthia 'Kinta' Beevor, mother of the historian Antony Beevor, wrote a memoir of her early years, *A Tuscan Childhood*, in which she reflected on the changes in the quarter since the Second World War: 'In Florence, we wandered down the via Tornabuoni, past Procacci, which still makes its delicious little sandwiches, and Parenti, where the best wedding presents come from. But most of the shops, such as Gucci and Ferragamo, even if Florentine in origin, are now glaringly international.'

The Ponte Vecchio

The most enchanting feature of the scene.

(Charles Dickens, *Pictures from Italy*)

The Ponte Vecchio is aptly named: there has been a bridge at this point since pre-Roman times. The picturesque, slightly arched bridge, lined with shops on both sides, has been there since 1345, and replaced an eleventh-century bridge that was washed away by floods in 1333. In 1593, Grand Duke Ferdinando I decreed that the mixture of traders on the bridge should be replaced by only jewellers and goldsmiths. By 1644, when John Evelyn crossed the bridge, he confirmed that it was occupied exclusively by jewellers, and so it is today; some of the shops hanging precariously over the sides of the bridge seemingly in danger of falling off.

In 1740 Horace Walpole saw the river in flood: 'Yesterday, with violent rains, there came flouncing down from the mountains such a flood, that it floated the whole city. The jewellers on the Old Bridge removed their commodities, and in two hours the bridge was cracked'; while a century later, during yet another flood, Thomas Adolphus Trollope, looking down from the Campanile, 'saw a cradle with a child in it, safely navigating the tumbling waters! It was drawn to the window of a house by throwing a line over it, and the infant navigator was none the worse.'

To Dickens, the Ponte Vecchio was 'the bridge which is covered with the shops of Jewellers and Goldsmiths – the most enchanting feature of the scene,' and Longfellow let it speak in the first person in his sonnet 'The Old Bridge at Florence':

> Florence adorns me with her jewellery;
> And when I think that Michael Angelo
> Hath leaned on me, I glory in myself.

Being free of traffic, and narrow, the bridge attracts shoppers in their hordes. There is a convenient gap in the shops – described by Dickens in his *Pictures from Italy* as 'The space of one house, in the centre, being left open, the view beyond is shown as in a frame; and that precious glimpse of sky, and water; and rich buildings,

10 The Ponte Vecchio, Florence

shining so quietly among the huddled roofs and gables on the bridge, is exquisite'. This central gap of the bridge is a popular spot for photographers. A bronze bust in the middle of the gap surveys the jewellery-seeking crowds with the delight of a former goldsmith. He is Benvenuto Cellini, a leading sixteenth-century sculptor whose work is seen in many parts of the city, most famously in the bronze Perseus in the Piazza della Signoria. The Ponte Vecchio was the only bridge not destroyed by the retreating Germans in 1945, a reprieve shrewdly negotiated by the commune on condition that the bridge's southern approaches were made unusable.

On the southern end of the Ponte Vecchio, running parallel to the river is the ancient Via de' Bardi, where, in 1921, D. H. Lawrence and his wife Frieda lived at number 32, a house lent to them by a friend. Before the Bardi family built their palazzo there, the Via de' Bardi, being in one of the poorer parts of town, was called Borgo Pidiglioso, or the street of fleas. In the thirteenth century, number 30, next-door to the Lawrences' lodgings, was a hospital in which Petrarch's mother was born. It was later largely rebuilt into a Renaissance palazzo by another branch of the Bardi family.

Lawrence found the Via de' Bardi too noisy for writing: 'I want to get away from this infernal noise.' On other occasions he was the dutiful travel writer: 'On the Arno many boats with lovely lanterns . . . On the Ponte Vecchio the windows of the little houses shine yellow, and make golden points on the water.' He and Frieda left Florence again the following year after what was a relatively long stay for him, and it would be three years, seven countries and four continents later before the restless pair returned to Florence.

George Eliot describes the Via de' Bardi in her *Romola*, a novel set in late fifteenth-century Florence, as extending:

> from the Ponte Vecchio to the Piazza de' Mozzi, . . . its right-hand line of houses and walls being backed by the rather steep ascent which in the fifteenth century was known as the hill of Bogoli, the famous quarry whence the city got its pavement; . . . its left-hand buildings flanking the river, and making on their northern side

a length of quaint irregularly pierced façade, of which the waters give a softened, loving reflection as the sun begins to decline.

Five centuries later, little has changed: the name of the hill has become Boboli, and the 'irregularly pierced façade' now contains an Indian restaurant. Although George Eliot installed her heroine in the Via de' Bardi, Eliot herself chose to live across the river on the Via Tornabuoni in the presumably flea-free Hôtel Suisse.

One evening in 1858, Nathaniel Hawthorne walked with his family on the Lungarno – the road along the riverbank. His wife Sophia was ecstatic: 'The Lung-Arno was lighted with gas along its whole extent, making a cornice of glittering gems, converging in the distance, and the reflection of the illuminated border made a fairy show. No painting, and scarcely a dream, could equal the magical beauty of the scene.' The same evening walk had been taken by Alexandre Dumas a decade earlier, and is described in his *Une Année à Florence*: 'Florence is a magnificent sight by moonlight: the columns, churches and monuments take on a grandiose aspect which puts the modern edifices to shame.'

Facing the river on the Lungarno Guicciardini, its Left Bank, is the former palazzo that today houses the British Institute, a home-from-home for British travellers and residents. It was founded in 1917 by a writer: English resident Lina Waterfield, who for many years between the wars was the *Observer*'s Italian correspondent. Her daughter, Carinthia ('Kinta'), who was brought up in Florence, would also become a writer, but not until she was in her eighties, when she wrote the memoir, *A Tuscan Childhood*, published two years before her death in 1995. In it, 'Kinta' Beevor graciously acknowledges the contribution of her son, the historian Antony Beevor, 'who worked with me and helped me write it all down'.

From the Grand Tour era onwards, many of the old palazzi along the left bank were converted into travellers' *pensioni*. One of them was the Widow Vanini's, on the Piazza Sauro, near the Ponte alla Carraia, where Tobias Smollett lodged in 1764: the fastidious Smollett found Mary Vanini 'very obliging', the villa 'an

English house delightfully situated on the bank of the Arno', and the rooms comfortable and reasonably priced. Another converted palazzo was the Locanda Carlo, on the Lungarno Guiccardini near the Ponte Santa Trinità, which the biographer James Boswell gave as his address. 'Carlo' was an Englishman (or possibly an Irishman), Charles Hadfield. On his own Grand Tour, Hadfield had been enchanted by the city but appalled at the poor quality of the accommodation, and decided to stay and open an up-market hotel. Locanda Carlo became a favoured residence for many foreign – mainly English – writers and artists. It was, according to Sir Lucas Pepys, descendant of the diarist Samuel, and physician to King George III, one of the best hotels in all Italy.

Hadfield was an ideal host in the style of the English innkeeper. His portly figure is pictured in *The Punch Party* of 1760, painted by the Devon-born portraitist, Thomas Patch, one of Carlo's regular customers. In the picture, Hadfield is seen serving punch to a group of guests, including Patch himself. Other artist customers included the young Swiss painter Angelica Kauffmann, later a founder member of the Royal Academy, and the Georgian painter, Johan Zoffany. Edward Gibbon stayed at Carlo's on his way to Rome in 1764, where he began his monumental *History of the Decline and Fall of the Roman Empire*, and James Boswell was a returning guest the following year. Boswell did not stay long in Florence; he found the Florentine women 'very proud and very mercenary' – and moved quickly on to Siena, where he fared better. The depressive German philosopher, Arthur Schopenhauer, who visited Florence in 1818 at the age of 30, was equally scathing about Florentine women. After a number of rejections, he decided that 'only the male intellect, clouded by the sexual impulse, could call the undersized, narrow-shouldered, broad-hipped, and short-legged sex "the fair sex".' Undeterred, he returned a year later to find his success rate greatly improved, to the extent that he became engaged 'to a lady of noble family', but he broke it off when he learned that she had tuberculosis.

✢

In the same year in which Thomas Patch painted *The Punch Party*, Signora Hadfield gave birth to a daughter, Maria – her fifth child, and the first to survive infancy. Surrounded on a daily basis by the classical delights of Florence, and growing up steeped in the conversation of visiting painters, architects, writers and musicians, it is not surprising that Maria acquired a deep appreciation of the arts. She was admitted to the Academy of Arts of Florence at 18 – the minimum age for entrance – and went to Rome to continue her studies, but her father died soon afterwards and her mother decided to move the family to England, in the hope of exploiting Maria's artistic talents. Signora Hadfield may have had a different type of exploitation in mind, for she was quick to accept, on Maria's behalf, the proposal of the successful miniaturist Richard Cosway, 18 years her daughter's senior. As Maria wrote when in her seventies, 'I made the acquaintance of Mr. Cosway, my mother's wishes were satisfied, and I married before I was 21.'

After Maria and Richard Cosway were married in London in 1781, the new Mrs Cosway began to hold musical soirées at their fashionable Carlton House Terrace home, at which a neighbour, the Prince of Wales – the future George IV – was a frequent guest, thereby ensuring a suitable level of well-heeled potential clients for Richard. They included distinguished writers of the day, such as Oliver Goldsmith, Dr Samuel Johnson and his biographer-to-be, James Boswell, who was another of Maria's conquests, and once offered to take her to see some performing dogs, 'because, since you treat your men like dogs, you may like to see dogs being treated like men'.

In the summer of 1786, Richard Cosway was commissioned to paint the portraits of the family of the Duke of Orleans, and the couple moved to Paris for several months. It was there that she met the then American Minister to France, the newly widowed Thomas Jefferson, the future third President of the United States.

The two immediately fell in love, and although their tempestuous affair covered a period of no more than a month, during that period the pair were inseparable, and business between two burgeoning republics – the United States and France – was put on hold. The idyll ended with the Cosways' return to London, but Maria's correspondence with Jefferson continued until his exquisitely timed death forty years later, on 4 July 1826, the fiftieth anniversary of the Declaration of Independence, of which he had been the author.

Despite the often flirtatious tone of their letters, the couple did not meet again. Either Jefferson's freedom was restricted by the arrival from America of his teenage daughter Polly, or his interest in Maria had waned because Polly was accompanied by her 13-year-old nurse – Jefferson's slave Sally Hemmings – by whom he was secretly to father six children. Or did the passions that had flared in Paris in the hot summer of 1786 cool just as quickly?

A nearby riverside residence, the Pensione Simi, at 2 Lungarno delle Grazie, was the home in 1901 of the novelist E. M. Forster and his mother. They had originally stayed at the nearby Albergo Bonciani, which Forster had liked, but his mother insisted they move because she wanted a room with a view. The Simi had a cockney landlady, who, according to Forster, 'Scatters Hs like morsels'. Forster's letter from there in 1902 epitomises the lifestyle of the *pensione* resident: 'Oh what a viewpoint is the English hotel or Pension! Our life is where we sleep and eat, and the glimpses of Italy that I get are only accidents.' In Forster's *A Room with a View*, the Simi becomes the Pensione Bertolini, the landlady of which appals the snooty Miss Lucy Honeychurch: '"And a Cockney, besides!" said Lucy, who had been further saddened by the Signora's unexpected accent. "It might be London."' It would take a murder, a broken engagement, and an elopement before a more mature Lucy would return to the Pensione Bertolini and her room with a view – with her new husband, George Emerson. Forster returned to the Pensione Simi in each of the next two years and spent a further six years planning *A Room with a View*, during which time he wrote another Tuscany-based novel, *Where Angels Fear to Tread*, set in San Gimignano.

The early twentieth century was a high season for Grand Tourists: in 1912 yet another Anglo-Italian *pensione* on the Lungarno, the

Pensione White, in the Piazza dei Cavallagieri, was home to the young poet, Rupert Brooke, who complained to a fellow graduate that his aunts had asked for his impressions of Florence, and that 'a local guide-book has proved invaluable'. Brooke was followed at the same *pensione* by the novelist Arnold Bennett, presumably on the recommendation of Brooke, with whom he had had tea in Cannes on the French Riviera earlier in the year. Bennett decided that the loveliest of Florence's many churches was the San Lorenzo, but it was not a happy or fruitful six weeks for him: he was writing his novel *Edwin Clayhanger* at the time and in his mind was associating the character's reaction to his father's death with the slow, painful death of his own father.

In the maze of narrow streets to the north of the Lungarno della Grazie is a small square, the Piazza Mentana, in what used to be the dyers' quarter, to which wool, cloth and dyes arrived by river, and from which richly coloured fabrics were shipped all over Europe by the same route. It was given its present name, Mentana, much later, to commemorate a Garibaldi victory near Rome during the unification of Italy. The Pensione Balestra, at number 5, was the first of many Florence residences of D. H. Lawrence in 1919. Fellow boarders included at least two other writers: English novelist Norman Douglas and American Magnus Maurice, both fugitives from homosexuality laws and both later fictionalised in Lawrence novels.

In December of that year, Lawrence's wife Frieda, who had eloped with him in 1912, leaving her husband and children behind, arrived from Germany. After a week of sight-seeing in Florence, they were soon on the road again in search of warmth – a perpetual Lawrence quest – this time to Rome, Capri, Malta and Sicily, by which time Lawrence could no longer endure the summer heat and they moved on; Frieda to Bavaria and Lawrence to Florence. On Frieda's return to Italy they went back to Sicily, but by the spring they were back in Florence, at their friend's apartment near the Ponte Vecchio.

The Oltrarno

Fair Florence on her peaceful shore.　　　　(Horace Walpole, *Letters*)

The Oltrarno – literally, across the Arno – is on the south or left bank of the river. It is the nearest Florence comes to a Bohemian quarter on the lines of Rome's Trastavere or the Rive Gauche of Paris. Being apart to some extent from the busy piazzas of the right bank, it is relatively peaceful – at least for Florence – which may be the reason for its appeal to writers and artists from the seventeenth century onwards.

With its friendly neighbourhoods, quiet squares, classical Italian gardens and Renaissance churches, it is to me the part of the city where I could most easily live. The Via di Santo Spirito runs through it, parallel to the river, ending at its western end in the heart of the Oltrarno, the Piazza di Santo Spirito, in which John Evelyn stayed in 1644. By day it is a quiet square ringed with restaurants, with a local market in the middle, but in the evenings it can be lively. On its northern side is the magnificent Church of Santo Spirito, originally a thirteenth-century convent, whose nave and cloisters were built by Brunelleschi in the fifteenth century. His plans were altered during the construction, which could explain the almost windowless western façade, which is rather like the silhouette of a man's head and shoulders. Vasari claimed that, if the building had been completed according to Brunelleschi's original plans, it would have been 'the most perfect temple in Christianity'. When I was last there, a coffee bar in the piazza had the idea of holding a competition among local schoolchildren for a suggested design for a more interesting new façade for the church. The entries were posted around the walls of the café: I never found out which design was the winner, but I doubt if it was the one proposing a church-sized fresco of Michael Jackson.

Two hundred metres or so west of the Piazza di Santo Spirito is another, larger, piazza, the Piazza di Santa Maria del Carmine. Like the Santo Spirito, it is dominated at one end by a church, the Church of Santa Maria del Carmine (Carmelites), famous for its fifteenth-century frescoes and their disputed provenance. They are said to be by the Tuscan painters Masaccio and Masolino, but both died before the frescoes were finished – the former at the unreasonably early age of 26 – and the work was completed by Filippino Lippi. Or so it is said, but the question of who painted which frescoes has been a matter of debate for half a millennium. That they are there at all is because of a book: the portraitist Thomas Patch, having moved from Hadfield's *pensione* Locanda Carlo to the Via di Santo Spirito, became, like Vasari, a painter-turned-author. In 1765, to obtain illustrations for his book, *The Life of the Celebrated Painter, Masaccio*, Patch visited his local church, the Santa Maria del' Carmine, and took meticulous copies of its 'Masaccio' frescoes, which he etched onto copper. The book, published in 1770 and still in print, is dedicated to another Englishman, Sir Horace Mann, by then Patch's neighbour and procurer of clients from among the Grand Tour gentry. In the famous painting by Johan Zoffany, *The Tribuna of the Uffizi*, now in the Royal Collection at Windsor Castle, Patch is seen chatting to Mann.

The following year, the Church of Santa Maria del' Carmine caught fire, and all of its frescoes were either destroyed or seriously damaged. The frescoes in the church today, which are still advertised as the 'Masaccio' frescoes, were reconstructed from Patch's precise copies – so now no one can tell who painted them. Whoever it was, the paintings look fresh and colourful, and for me are among the most moving frescoes in Florence.

The most famous writer to have been associated with the Santo Spirito quarter was Niccolò Machiavelli, playwright, poet, historian and farmer, who was born here on 3 May 1469. He claimed to have been born in poverty, but his father was a well-connected notary in the city and his mother owned large vineyards in the southern hillsides. The excommunication and death of Savonarola, together with a number of his fellow priests and acolytes in 1498, created a career opportunity for the ambitious young lawyer, then employed by the city, and he made the most of it, rising to a senior position in the city chancellery, in which capacity he was sent on a number of diplomatic missions on behalf of the city. Unfortunately, he lasted only 13 years in the job before being suspected of conspiracy against the Medici dynasty and sent into exile. He went to his family farm at nearby San Casciano, to the south of the city, where he used his banishment as an opportunity to record his political philosophy. Machiavelli would work with the peasants in the fields during the day and write in the evenings. He described his new lifestyle in a letter to a friend:

> I am living in the country since my disgrace. I get up at dawn and go to the little wood to see what work has been done. . . . When evening comes I return to my house and go into my study. Before I enter I take off my rough mud-stained country dress. I put on my royal and curial robes and thus fittingly attired I enter into the assembly of men of old times. I dare to talk with them, and ask the reasons for their actions. From these notes I have composed a little work, *Il Principe.*

Il Principe – *The Prince* – was not the only work of Machiavelli to come out of San Casciano, but it is by far the best known. First published in 1532, five years after his death, it has been in print ever since. It was a collection of his thoughts on statecraft and political science, much of which are as appropriate today as when they were written. A guidebook for anyone wishing to acquire or increase political power, its principles have since been applied to subjects ranging from corporate management to warfare: it is claimed to have influenced political leaders from Henry VIII to Stalin. Henry Kissinger denied its influence on him with excessive vigour, but Mussolini selected it as the subject for his doctoral thesis.

George Eliot gives a fictional outline of Machiavelli's character in her novel *Romola*, and he was the equestrian hero of Somerset Maugham's maudlin novel, *Then and Now*: 'There it was, the city he loved more than his soul: Florence, the city of flowers, with its campanile and its baptistery, its churches and palaces, its tortuous streets, the old bridge he crossed every day to go to the palazzo . . . his birthplace and the birthplace of his ancestors.'

After *The Prince*, possibly because of its praise of the infamous Cesare Borgia, Machiavelli's name became a synonym for treachery and cunning, a connotation supported by authorities as respected as Shakespeare and *The Oxford English Dictionary*. The use of the term 'Old Nick' as a name for the devil is also claimed to have been derived from the name of Niccolò Machiavelli. He died in 1527 at the age of 58 and is buried beside his father and within a few feet of Michelangelo and Galileo in the Church of Santa Croce.

The Englishman who was probably the greatest authority on late eighteenth-century Florence lived in the Via di Santo Spirito, at the Casa Manetti, now number 23. He was Horace – later Sir Horace – Mann, the British chargé d'affaires at the court of the Grand Duke of Tuscany. His duties as the representative of the British Crown included looking after the interests of the British resident nobility and keeping a watchful eye on the activities of the man who would – if he could – be King of England, the exiled Charles Edward Stuart, who, as the son of the Old Pretender, James Edward Stuart, and self-styled King Charles III of England, was known as the Young Pretender. Between 1775 and his death in 1788, he spent most of his time in Florence, living much of it in the Palazzo San Clemente on the Via Gino Capponi, north of the river. It now houses the Faculty of Architecture of the University of Florence and is in serious need of care and attention. There is no plaque outside to indicate the former residence of a would-be Roman Catholic King of England, but in the main lobby of the university there hangs a large tapestry, which is the only English royal coat of arms in Florence.

Another of Mann's tasks was to welcome, and accommodate in the Casa Manetti, the 22-year-old Horace Walpole, son of the British Prime Minister, Sir Robert Walpole. As already mentioned, Walpole junior travelled through France and arrived in January 1740, accompanied by the poet Thomas Gray. Unlike Gray, Walpole was not yet a published writer, although he went on to publish essays and poetry, and, in 1764, what is now recognised as the first Gothic novel, *The Castle of Otranto*. That he may have nurtured hopes of literary recognition is indicated by the fact that he asked his correspondents to return his letters when read, presumably with an eye to future publication – and that on his return to England he bought a printing press. The two friends stayed in Florence for 15 months, Gray avidly studying art and architecture, while Walpole enjoyed the many social diversions. When Gray suggested they visit other Tuscan cities, such as Lucca or Pisa, Walpole would decline, but lend his carriage to the less-affluent Gray so that he could go alone, while Walpole stayed with Mann. Walpole found Florence 'infinitely the most agreeable of all the places I have seen since London', and he settled in quickly. 'I am lodged with Mr Mann,' he wrote to another old Etonian classmate: 'the best of creatures. I have a terrace all to myself, with an open gallery on the Arno.'

Since their schooldays at Eton, the shy, unassuming Gray had been in awe of the urbane son of the Prime Minister – a homage that Walpole readily accepted. Unlike Walpole, Gray was from a middle-class background and broken home: in the absence of a father, he was his mother's idol, a passion he fervently returned, the more so since he was the sole survivor of her 12 children. He was a committed bachelor whose only known heterosexual inclinations were short-lived and centred on women considerably older than himself. He went on to Cambridge University and studied Italian literature, with a special interest in Dante, whom Walpole likened to 'a Methodist parson in Bedlam'.

The gay *ménage à trois* remained together until Gray and Walpole left Florence for Bologna and Reggio in northern Italy in April 1741. On the day they left, a devastated Mann wrote to Walpole, 'One thing alone makes me really happy, which is that I am sure you love me and are convinced of my most sincere and tender affection for you.' Within two weeks, Gray and Walpole had quarrelled and parted, and did not see each other for three years. It is tempting to suppose that Gray may have hoped for more of his relationship with Walpole and resented his attachment to their host. Walpole and Mann never met again, but wrote to each other almost daily for the next 45 years. Walpole later accepted full responsibility for the quarrel with Gray: 'I have since felt my finite inferiority to him . . . with the dignity of his spirit, and the obstinate carelessness of mine.' He went on to print and publish collections of Gray's poems.

The eastern end of the Via di Santo Spirito joins the Via Maggio, which runs south into the Piazza San Felice. Here, at number 8, stands the fifteenth-century Palazzo Guidi, in which Robert and Elizabeth Barrett Browning lived from April 1847, following their six-month stay in Pisa. They had left Pisa, with Elizabeth's dog, Flush, and their maid, Elizabeth Wilson, on a proposed tour of Italy, but fell in love with Florence on sight, Elizabeth saying it was 'the most beautiful of the cities devised by man'. She wrote to a friend in England:

> Florence is beautiful, as I have said before and must say again and again, most beautiful. The river rushes through the midst of its palaces like a crystal arrow, and it is hard to tell, when you see all by the clear sunset, whether those churches, and houses, and windows, and bridges, and people walking, are the real walls and windows, and bridges, and people, and churches.

She would declare her love for the city with ever-increasing fervour: 'I love it with somewhat of the kind of blind, stupid, respectable, obstinate love which people feel when they talk of "beloved native lands". . . . Florence is my chimney-corner, where I can sulk and be happy.' A further attraction, she discovered, was that it was 'cheaper by half' than Pisa.

Elizabeth was a prolific letter-writer, and, despite her fragile health, she involved herself deeply in the Italian politics of the day, of which the key issues were independence from Austrian occupation and the Risorgimento, and she supported both causes obsessively. She lived just long enough to see both of them achieved.

The egalitarian Elizabeth, thinking that 'Palazzo' sounded pretentious, called their home the 'Casa Guidi', and so it has remained. The Brownings lived there, in the first-floor suite, 'as happy', as Robert wrote in that first year, 'as two owls in a hole', until Elizabeth's death 14 years later, and it was there that they produced some of their finest works, including Elizabeth's *Casa Guidi Windows* in 1851. In the heat of the summer they would move up to the Villa Montauto, in the Bellosguardo hills – later the home of the American author Nathaniel Hawthorne and family. The Brownings always worked separately, never reading work to each other until it was finished. Their only joint production, in 1849, was their son, christened Robert but known as Penino or Pen. The boy was adored by his mother, who dressed him in the finest embroidery and kept his hair in long, flowing ringlets. Nathaniel Hawthorne was there in 1858, fresh from his job as American consul in Liverpool, and recorded that Elizabeth was, 'of that quickly appreciative and responsive order of women, with whom I can talk more freely than with any men. . . . I like her very much – a great deal better than her poetry.'

Because of Elizabeth's ill-health, most of the Brownings' social contact was with visitors to Casa Guidi, many of them English and American writers, including Alfred, Lord Tennyson and his musician brother, Frederick; John Ruskin; novelist Frances Trollope and her son Thomas; the ubiquitous Henry James and the American poet James Russell Lowell, who, while the Brownings were away, would rent Casa Guidi from them. Lowell, like Elizabeth, was an enthusiastic campaigner for Italian independence: his poem 'Freedom', called it the 'pearl beneath the feet of Austrian swine'. He returned to the USA to take up the post of professor of languages at Harvard and later became American ambassador to Britain.

The description of the Casa Guidi apartment by Hawthorne's wife, Sophia, is as accurate today as it was in the nineteenth century: 'a spacious staircase and ample accommodation of vestibule and hall, the latter opening onto a balcony where we could hear the chanting of priests in a church close by'. Pen used to keep his pet rabbits on the balcony.

Alfred Tennyson had arrived in Florence in the autumn of 1851, staying with his brother Frederick in the Villa Torrigiani, in Doccia, north-east of the city in the hills above Fiesole. The previous year Alfred had won acclaim with his 'In Memoriam', and on Wordsworth's death early in 1851 had succeeded him as poet laureate. He was fluent in Italian and liked to read Italian works in the language – and location – in which they had been written. Robert Browning liked to tell of Tennyson arriving in Florence, but, on finding that he could not buy the famously noxious pipe tobacco which he claimed was his 'inspiration', turning around and going home.

Another friend of the Brownings in Florence was the novelist, poet and playwright Edward Lytton, formerly Edward Bulwer-Lytton, author of the successful novel *The Last Days of Pompeii* and the less well-known *Paul Clifford*. The latter work, with its ominous opening words: 'It was a dark and stormy night,' has

11 The drawing-room of the Casa Guidi, home of the Brownings, Florence

inspired an international literary award of dubious distinction. The Bulwer-Lytton Fiction Contest is an annual competition sponsored by the State University of San Jose, California since 1982, in which contestants are required to 'compose the opening sentence of the worst of all possible novels'.

Because of maintenance work being carried out on the Casa Guidi apartment, I was able to see only three of its six rooms: Robert's study, the dining room and the drawing room, now restored in early Victorian style, mimicking as closely as possible the painting by Mignaty that Robert commissioned soon after Elizabeth's death. Above the fireplace hangs an ornate baroque mirror supported by two chubby cherubs bearing gilded candlesticks. It carries a handwritten notice: 'Please do not light the candles'. This is surely the mirror described by Elizabeth in a letter to her sister as having 'the most beautiful carved gilt frame I ever saw in my life. Two cupids hold lights at the lower part'; Robert also described it in his poem, 'The Ring and the Book':

> 'Neath the twin cherubs in the tarnished frame
> O' the mirror, tall thence to the ceiling top.

In June 1861, Elizabeth was well enough to go out in their carriage, but when she arrived back at the Casa Guidi, she had developed a cold and had difficulty breathing, and, while still telling Browning that he was making 'an exaggerated case of it', suffered a relapse and died, 'her head on my cheek', as the ever-attentive Robert put it. She was buried in the English Cemetery on the Piazzale Donatello. Unable to find Elizabeth's grave, I was helped by the custodian, Julia Bolton Holloway, who explained that it is marked discreetly with the initials E. B. B. because Browning did not want his wife's full name on the tomb, fearing that it might become a place of pilgrimage for her readers. Soon after the funeral, Robert Browning and his son Pen – now with hair cut short and boyishly attired – left Casa Guidi and Florence, never to return: Robert died in Venice 28 years later.

A stone plaque above the front door of Casa Guidi, placed there by the city of Florence in recognition of Elizabeth's support for Italian independence, bears in Italian the following tribute:

HERE WROTE AND DIED
ELIZABETH BARRETT BROWNING
SHE WHO IN HER WOMAN'S HEART COMBINED
A SCHOLAR'S LEARNING WITH A POET'S SPIRIT
AND WHOSE POEMS FORGED A GOLDEN RING
BETWEEN ITALY AND ENGLAND

MEMORIAL PLACED BY A
GRATEFUL FLORENCE
1861

'The Golden Ring' has since become a metaphor for Anglo-Florentine friendship, in acknowledgement of which Robert dedicated *Last Poems*, a posthumous collection of Elizabeth's works, to the people and city of Florence.

The suite of rooms in which the devoted couple lived for almost the whole of their brief but happy marriage is now owned by Eton College and managed by the Landmark Trust, from whom it can be rented as self-catering accommodation for six people for a mere £366 a night, the only inconvenience being that, on three afternoons per week in the summer, tenants may expect to encounter members of the public on a tour of the apartment – and, of course, they must not light the candles.

A few hundred yards to the north of the Casa Guidi, still on the Via Guiccardini, is the fortress-like Pitti Palace, its rusticated stonework a traditional feature of Renaissance Florence. Arnold Bennett called it a 'rather expensive barracks', but it was originally built as a residence for the wealthy Pitti family and, from the mid-sixteenth century, was the home of the grand dukes of Tuscany, from the Grand Duke Cosimo I onwards. Bartolomeo Ammannati, the builder of the Ponte Santa Trinità, added two wings and a gallery.

It is still known as the Palazzo Pitti, but it is now a public gallery, housing huge collections of paintings and sculptures, porcelain and costumes. The English essayist and critic William Hazlitt said of it in his *Notes of a Journey through France and Italy* in 1826: 'The pictures in the Pitti Palace are finely preserved, and have that deep, mellow tone of age upon them which is to the eyes of a connoisseur in painting as the rust of medals or the crust on wine is to connoisseurs and judges of a different stamp.'

James Fenimore Cooper, a pioneer of the 'Western' novel, came to Florence in 1828 at the age of 40. His books were well known in Italy in translation: even the Prussian Grand Duke of Tuscany, Leopold II, was a fan. He welcomed Cooper to the palace on both official and private visits, as Cooper records in his *Excursions in Italy*:

> The Grand Duke was standing alone, at the upper end of a long table that was covered by some drawings and plans of the Maremme, a part of his territories in reclaiming of which he is said to be just now much occupied. As I entered, he advanced and gave me a very civil reception. I paid my compliments, and made an offering of a book which I had caused to be printed in Florence.

The Grand Duke 'spoke of [George] Washington with great respect, and evidently felt no hostility to him on account of his political career'. Cooper was surprised to find that 'the Grand Duke was disposed to view us [Americans] kindly – a thing so unusual among political men in Europe as to be worthy of mention'. The Cooper family left for Sorrento in the autumn of the following year.

After the Risorgimento in 1861 the Pitti Palace was the residence of the Italian royal family, and later, on the establishment of the Italian Republic at the end of the Second World War, it became, thanks to the bequest of accumulated works of the Medici family, one of the city's most important showcases of Italian art.

Almost opposite the palace, on the wall outside number 22, there hangs another literary memento, a sign in Italian that reads:

IN THIS HOUSE,
BETWEEN 1868 AND 1869
FEODOR MIKHAILOVICH DOSTOEVSKY
FINISHED THE NOVEL *THE IDIOT*

Dostoevsky and his wife Anna arrived early in November 1868. He had been in Florence five years earlier and was hoping once again to avoid the severe St Petersburg winter and to finish *The Idiot* in relative warmth. He was desperately short of money and suffering from an ailment not unknown among authors – that of anxiously awaiting payments promised by his publisher. They stayed in a hotel for a week before renting two rooms at 22 Via Guicciardini. One of Dostoevsky's first actions was to join the international Vieusseux Library to have access to Russian newspapers. Anna, who had already begun to learn Italian, continued her studies, and Dostoevsky, although anxious to finish the book, took some time off to show her the sights.

The nearest attraction was just across the street, behind the Pitti Palace: the vast Boboli Gardens. Dostoevsky wrote home, 'Florence is beautiful but too humid, the roses are still flowering in the open air in the gardens of the Boboli. And what treasures in the galleries!' In the Pitti Palace, Dostoevsky was particularly taken with Raphael's circular painting, *Madonna della Seggiola – The Madonna of the Chair*, which, eight years earlier, had left George Eliot 'impressed only by the grave gaze of the infant'. Dostoevsky wrote, 'How many wonderful things there are, even aside from this painting. But I postpone everything till the end of the novel [*The Idiot*]. I have closed myself off.'

One of the many autobiographical events in *The Idiot* recalls an occasion in 1849 when Dostoevsky was arrested for having published a criticism of the Orthodox Church and the Supreme Powers, a crime for which he was sentenced to death. It was not until he stood facing the firing squad that his sentence was reduced to four years' hard labour. Conversely, his life was soon to mirror his art when, like *The Idiot*'s main character, his epileptic fits started:

'the climate of Florence is perhaps even more unfavourable to my health than that of Milan or Vevey,' he wrote, 'the epileptic attacks return more frequently. Besides, it rains too much in Florence; though in fine weather it is real Paradise.'

In January the Dostoevskys were overjoyed to find that Anna was pregnant again – she had lost their previous child – but the joy was tempered by their continuing poverty. Poor and homesick, they were lonely in Florence, with little knowledge of Italian and no friends. 'Around us', wrote Anna, 'all were strangers and sometimes hostile ones; and this total isolation was sometimes difficult to bear.'

In addition, the climate did not suit Dostoevsky's medical condition: 'the guide-books may say that Florence, by reason of its position, is the coldest town in winter of all Italy (that is to say, the whole peninsula); but in summer, it is the hottest town in the peninsula, and even in the whole Mediterranean region.' In the 1950s, Sinclair Lewis agreed: 'The Florentine winter lasts only from mid-December to March – jeeringly cold nights and days together when the *tramontana* wind comes devastatingly down from the Alps three pinched days at a spell, blowing pitilessly, playing rowdy with the tiles and shutters,' and a few decades later, another American Nobel Prize-winner, Saul Bellow, encountered the Tuscan *tramontana:* 'it forced open our windows at night and scoured our faces by day.'

With *The Idiot* finished, the Dostoevskys had hoped to return home by the spring, but could not afford to go because by the time one of Dostoevsky's advances finally arrived, it was insufficient to pay their debts plus the cost of the journey, and he was forced to ask a friend for money. They finally left Florence in July 1869 for Prague. It was as far as they could afford, but they were on their way home at last.

The Boboli Gardens were also a favourite of John Evelyn. A dedicated gardener himself, he noted in 1644, 'every variety of hills, dales, rocks, groves, aviaries, fontaines, especially one with five jettos'. The gardens, which were built in the space from which stone for the palace had been quarried, climb steeply to a belvedere with a panoramic view over the Arno and central Florence that is well worth the climb even if, like me, you find the belvedere itself locked. Of the gardens, Henry James wrote, 'You wonder how compact little Florence finds room for [the gardens] within her walls. But they are scattered . . . over a group of steep undulations between the rugged and terraced palace and a still-surviving stretch of city wall, where the unevenness of the ground much adds to their apparent size.'

Goethe's journal entry in 1786 was cryptic, 'The Boboli Garden has a choice location. I hurried out of it as fast as I went in'; a century later, Sigmund Freud put in a plug for his home city of Vienna, calling the gardens 'a kind of Schönbrunn for the Medici' – although the two locations have little in common.

The Algerian novelist, philosopher and footballer, Albert Camus came to Florence for the first time in September 1937. He was only 23 years old, and, despite having shown great promise as a goalkeeper, had had to give up his football career when, at 17, he was diagnosed as having consumption. He was already a dedicated writer and had decided to spend the last of his holidays – and money – on a trip to Florence, Siena and Pisa, via Marseilles. He spent most of this time in Florence, where, as he later wrote, he 'found himself' as a writer, calling it 'one of the only places in Europe where I understood that underneath my revolt, a consent was lying dormant'. His stay in Florence was shorter than intended because his funds ran out, and he had just enough money left for a third-class boat ticket from Marseilles to Algiers, where he took a job as a teacher in Sidi-bel-Abbès, a small town about 80 kilometres south of his home in Oman, as an undemanding source of income to finance his writing. He had early success with *L'Etranger*, and at the age of only 44 he was awarded the Nobel Prize for Literature. Just three years afterwards, in a wry comment on the injustice of life, he was killed in a car accident while taking a book manuscript to his publisher.

Bellosguardo

I like my present residence immensely.

(Nathaniel Hawthorne, *Notes in Italy*)

In the heat of summer, the outskirts of Florence, being much higher than the city itself, tend to attract writers and repel mosquitoes. Following the Via Guicciardini south from the Pitti Palace, you will come to the Porta Romana, the old gateway towards Rome, and beyond it the Via Senese, from which, to the right, runs the Via Colombaia, where, in the villa of that name, a famous Englishwoman was born in 1820. Like her older sister, she was named after the city in which she was born – in which respect she was more fortunate than her sister, who was born a year earlier in Parthenope – the Greek name for Naples. Parthenope Nightingale may not be a name that falls readily from the tongue, but Florence's fame as a campaigning nurse, while giving her name a special significance for Victorian parents, has tended to overshadow her reputation as a writer. Her written works covered a range of subjects, including not only nursing, but theology, child care, military health, travels in Egypt and India, and women's rights. The Villa Colombaia is now a private Roman Catholic school, but it is well maintained, as are its gardens with their view over Florence, and its owners treasure its association with Florence Nightingale, A sign on the wall in Italian reads:

WE REMEMBER THE GREAT HEART
OF
FLORENCE NIGHTINGALE
THE 'LADY WITH THE LAMP'
WHO WAS BORN ON 12 MAY 1820
WHO FROM THE TORTURE OF WAR
AND FROM HEROIC DEDICATION TO PATIENTS
DREW THE DETERMINATION TO CREATE
A SERVICE OF HEALTH ASSISTANCE
WORTHY OF THE MODERN WORLD

To the south and east of Florence lie the suburbs of Arcetri, where Milton was greeted by the exiled and ailing Galileo in 1638, and the hill of Bellosguardo, where, in 1858, Nathaniel Hawthorne rented the Villa Montauto to escape the summer heat of the city. Its altitude made the area popular with foreigners: James Fenimore Cooper had lived there 30 years earlier. Thirty years later, Henry James lived in the nearby Villa Bichieri – previously the home of Frederick Tennyson, brother of the poet laureate. This and many other villas and palaces in the locality come to life in James's fiction: the Villa Castellani is a prominent setting in both *Roderick Hudson* and *Portrait of a Lady*. It was in the Villa Bichieri in 1886 and 1887 that James wrote his novella, *The Aspern Papers*, a story about a dead poet, Jeffrey Aspern, and his would-be biographer's attempts to prise some documents from an old woman, only to find that she had burned them all, one by one. It is a fictionalised version of a true story: Claire Clairmont had made surreptitious attempts to secrete papers and other material relating to the lives of her brother-in-law, Percy Bysshe Shelley and her lover Lord Byron. Mark Bostridge, the English biographer of Florence Nightingale, had the opposite problem: 'she left enough papers lying about', he lamented, 'to cover Australia'.

Nathaniel Hawthorne said of his Bellosguardo home, the Villa Montauto:

> The house stands on a hill overlooking Florence, and is big enough to quarter a regiment, insomuch that each member of the family, including servants, has a separate suite of apartments, and there are vast wildernesses of upper rooms into which we have never yet sent exploring expeditions. At one end of the house there is a moss-grown tower, haunted by owls and by the ghost of a monk [allegedly Savonarola] who was confined there in the thirteenth century, previous to being burnt at the stake in the principal square of Florence.

Hawthorne rented the villa, tower and all, including linen and silver, for $28 a month – 'but I mean to take it away bodily and clap it into a romance, which I have in my head, ready to be written out.' The romance into which the Villa Montauto was 'clapped' during the summer of 1858 was *The Marble Faun* (published in England as *Transformation*), Hawthorne's fictional memoir of his sojourn in Florence, in which the villa, complete with tower, became the Castello di Monte Beni. Hawthorne's introduction begins: 'This Romance was sketched out during a residence of considerable length in Italy.' To Hawthorne, who had spent his first fifty years in small New England towns, and whose residences abroad had been restricted to Rome – which he hated – and Liverpool, on which he withheld comment, the impact of Tuscany must have been overwhelming. His friend Henry James wrote later,

> Out of his mingled sensations, his pleasure and his weariness, his discomforts and his reveries, there sprang another beautiful work. During the summer of 1858, he rented a picturesque old villa on the hill of Bellosguardo, near Florence, a curious structure with a crenellated tower, which, after having in the course of its career suffered many vicissitudes and played many parts, now finds its most vivid identity in being pointed out to strangers as the sometime residence of the celebrated American romancer. Hawthorne took a fancy to the place, as well he might, for it is one of the loveliest spots on earth, and the great view that stretched itself before him contains every element of beauty. Florence lay at his feet with her memories and treasures; the olive-covered hills bloomed around him, studded with villas as picturesque as his own; the Apennines, perfect in form and colour, disposed themselves opposite, and in the distance, along its fertile valley, the Arno wandered to Pisa and the sea.

James was so moved by the tower of Montauto that he mentions it as 'looming vaguely above' the Villa Pandolfini in his novel, *Roderick Hudson*. It was in this tower, on a September evening in 1858, that Hawthorne wrote, as he was about to return to New England, 'The nights are wonderfully beautiful now. When the moon was at the full a few nights ago, its light was an absolute glory, such as I seem only to have dreamed of heretofore . . . and it makes the Val d'Arno with its surrounding hills, and its soft mist in the distance, as beautiful a scene as exists anywhere outside Heaven.' Some time later, Hawthorne's son Julian said it was a pity that they went back to the United States, 'for had he [Nathaniel] continued in an atmosphere which so admirably suited him, there might have been not just one more romance to be published but a whole series'.

Knowing of James's taste for grand residences – he lived at Windsor Castle as an infant – I confess to a frisson of vicarious pride when I look across the street from my home in Windsor at the gabled mock-Tudor mansion, now broken up into apartments, in which he and Edith Wharton lodged in the early years of the twentieth century.

Another American writer to favour the southern heights of the city was the satirical novelist Sinclair Lewis, who in 1930 was the first American to be awarded the Nobel Prize in Literature – 'for his vigorous and graphic art of description and his ability to create, with wit and humour, new types of characters'. In his acceptance speech he complained that 'in America most of us are still afraid of any literature which is not a glorification of everything American' – which seems at variance with the fact that his success derived almost exclusively from books based in small-town America: *Babbit*, *Main Street*, *Dodsworth* and others. Some of the characters from these early works reappear in his last novel, written and set in Florence: *World so Wide*. Sam Dodsworth, the red-neck auto engineer, becomes Samuel, now grown worldly wise and living in Florence. Although the book satirises what Lewis called 'the Florentine American Colony – some of whom had even met an Italian', Lewis was very much a member of it, and a regular visitor to the Villa I Tatti in Fiesole, the home of the American art dealer Bernard Berenson, whose faint praise for Lewis was that he found him 'more presentable than I expected'. In *World so Wide*, Lewis classified the colony's members by length of residence: 'the colonists who had been there for forty years looked down on the settlers of ten years' standing, who looked down on the one-year squatters who looked down on the newcomers of one month who were extremely lofty and informative with the one-week horrors'.

Another American author, David Leavitt, in his light-hearted *Florence: A Delicate Case*, presents a unique, if jaundiced, view of the long-term residents: 'As Florence became more and more like a museum, its foreign residents – many of whom started off as observers – came to be regarded, increasingly, as part of the exhibit. . . . The paradise of exiles revealed itself for what it really was: the most elegant, interesting and comfortable of prisons.'

The English writer and art collector Sir Harold Acton published three novels and some non-fiction works about art and Florence, and was the ringmaster of the Anglo-Florentine social circus. He was born in the Villa La Pietra, on the north-west perimeter of the city, in 1904, and – with the exception of seven years in China, followed by service in the RAF in the Second World War – spent most of his life in Florence. His other travels, mostly to Paris and London, were largely devoted to artistic pursuits, and his visitors at La Pietra included many English writers, from fellow Etonians such as Cyril Connolly and Ian Fleming to former Oxford University contemporaries such as Graham Greene and Evelyn Waugh. Acton, who was best man at Waugh's first marriage, believed that he was the Anthony Blanche of Waugh's novel, *Brideshead Revisited*, but Waugh denied it. On the honeymoon of his second marriage in May 1937, Waugh again stayed overnight at La Pietra, noting in his diary, 'Filthy luncheon, filthy dinner'.

Acton's guest at La Pietra in the spring of the following year was yet another English novelist, W. Somerset Maugham. He had recently disembarked at the port of Naples after a voyage from Bombay, and was making a leisurely return, accompanied by his companion Alan Searle, to his Villa Mauresque on the French Riviera. Within a year, the villa would be occupied by German troops and Maugham would be evacuated to Liverpool in the hold of a coal ship.

When the English journalist Hunter Davies visited La Pietra in 1986, he was impressed by the statues in the gardens, but could not help noticing that the male nudes were strangely incomplete. Sir Harold explained that the missing genitalia had been removed by German troops as war trophies during the German occupation of the villa in the Second World War. David Leavitt, in *Florence: A Delicate Case*, refers to Sir Harold's compulsive references to homosexual men, without specifically 'outing' himself. Acton died in his natal home in 2004 at the age of 90, having, as discreet obituary writers say, 'never married'. He bequeathed La Pietra as a study and conference centre to the University of New York – one of the more than thirty American universities represented in the city.

Harold Acton could never have been called a fan of Sinclair Lewis: he described Lewis as 'lean and lanky, with a parboiled complexion and prominent blue eyes', and considered the American's rented home in the Via del Pian dei Giullari 'a tasteless modern villa'. 'He seemed', Acton wrote in his *More Memoirs of an Aesthete*, 'aggressively self-satisfied. According to him, only America produced a galaxy of talent in the art of fiction: he thought that "the English novel had decayed with the nineteenth century".' 'Even sober', continued Acton, 'he could be incredibly gauche: he once addressed the American Consul, Mr. George Waller, an old-fashioned southern gentleman, as "George". Mr. Waller's response was "Only the Duchess of Luxembourg, Winston Churchill and Franklin Roosevelt call me by my Christian name"' – thus revealing Waller to be as much a snob as Sir Harold. Acton's repeated claim that Lewis did not appreciate the works of British novelists seems inconsistent with the fact that Lewis took the title of his book *World so Wide* from a Rudyard Kipling poem, and named his only son Wells, after the English novelist H. G. Wells. Lieutenant Wells Lewis was killed in northern France in the Second World War.

Lewis's life was a constant battle with alcoholism. According to his biographer, Richard Lingemann, in *Rebel from Main Street*, drinking was Lewis's attempt 'to confront the demons of his own life: his sexual failure with women, his inability to look into himself, and his rootlessness'. Lewis suffered from chronic myocarditis, an inflammation of the heart lining caused by too much alcohol and nicotine: after one heart attack the cardiologist who was called to his bedside noted that the water carafe was filled with whisky. In 1937, Lewis's doctors had warned him that he would have to choose between living without alcohol, or dying with it. Fourteen years later he had clearly chosen the latter course, for he died in a Rome hospital from alcoholic poisoning. *World so Wide*, which Lewis had promised his publisher would be 'one of my major novels and have a chance for big sales' was published posthumously, but did not live up to his expectations: Lingemann called it 'a shadow of a novel'.

Confirming the American writers' preference for Bellosguardo, Gertrude Stein, poet, novelist, mentor to many Paris-based American writers in the 1920s and 1930s and author of her own biographical memoir, *The Autobiography of Alice B. Toklas*, stayed there with her lifelong companion of that name, at the Villa Curonia in the Via San Matteo.

A long-term resident of the hill of Bellosguardo was Mrs Alice Keppel, the last mistress of King Edward VII. She evidently fared much better than his first, poor Mary Robinson, to whom, as the young Prince of Wales, he had promised a home and income when he came of age, but changed his mind. Too proud to sue, Mary died in Old Windsor in poverty and anonymity. Alice Keppel, on the other hand, was wealthy enough to buy the Villa dell'Ombrellino, a spacious house, high on the hill of Bellosguardo, with panoramic views across the city and mountains beyond. The snooty Acton called it 'gloomy in spite of its splendid view'. While many expatriate British residents in Florence returned home on the devaluation of the pound in 1932, Alice remained a loyal Bellos-guardian – except for a period during the Second World War when the house was commandeered by occupying German troops – and lived there until her death in the summer of 1947. Alice Keppel's great-granddaughter, Camilla Parker-Bowles, enjoyed an equally intimate association with royalty, becoming the second wife of Charles, Prince of Wales, at Windsor in 2005.

Alice's daughter, the novelist Violet Trefusis, inherited dell'Ombrellino on her mother's death. Violet once wrote of her mother, 'I wonder if I shall ever squeeze as much romance into my life as she had in hers'. Violet certainly did, in her fashion: a devoted admirer of Vita Sackville-West from the age of 10, their later overt lesbian affair became the gossip of sedate London society.

On inheriting the Villa dell'Ombrellino, Violet became a Florentine socialite, entertaining the elite of Italian and French society, politicians – Winston Churchill painted the view from her terrace – and minor royalty. In old age, Violet repeatedly claimed to be the illegitimate daughter of King Edward VII, despite the fact that Edward did not meet her mother until four years after Violet was born. She was awarded the French Légion d'Honneur for her broadcasts on Radio France Libre during the Second World War, and in 1971 her friend François Mitterrand, later to be President of France, came to tea at the Villa dell'Ombrellino. Violet died there the following year at the age of 78.

An earlier resident of the southern heights was the English novelist William Makepeace Thackeray. Although never a professional artist, Thackeray had studied art in Paris and occasionally illustrated his own novels. In Paris, he worked in Galignani's bookshop – now on the rue de Rivoli – for 10 francs a day ('and very happy'), and was a sub-editor on *Galignani's Messenger*, the first English-language magazine in France. It was suspended during the 'Hundred Days' following Napoleon's escape from Elba, but restarted after his defeat at Waterloo and ran for a further 80 years, being popular also with Anglo-Florentines. Thackeray gave the magazine a plug in his novel *Vanity Fair*, referring to *Galignani* as 'the exile's friend'. He came to Florence early in 1854 and lived with his friend, the Irish novelist Charles Lever, at the Villa San Leonardo in the hills between the Boboli Gardens and the Chiesa di San Miniato, where he finished his satirical work *The Rose and the Ring*, a moralistic tale still popular with children. Thackeray did not like biographers, and did all he could to thwart them, going so far as to instruct his daughter:

'There is no life to be written of me; *mind this*, and consider it my last testament and desire'. It was a literary vanity that has since been ignored by a number of biographers – including his daughter and his close friend Anthony Trollope.

Scandicci

It's very picturesque, and many a paintable bit.
(D. H. Lawrence, *Letters of D. H. Lawrence*)

D. H. Lawrence and his wife Frieda returned to Florence at the end of April 1926 from their three-year Odyssey, and settled at Scandicci, a half-hour walk from the tramway terminus 10 kilometres south-west of Florence, where they rented the upper floor and garden of the Villa Mirenda. Lawrence described it as an 'old square whitish villa on a little hill all of its own, with the peasant houses and cypresses behind it and vines and olives and corn on all the slopes.' To a neighbour, it was 'a handsome antique villa . . . one of those large summer villas, rising with its peasant house and church out of a misty grey sea of olive trees'. Lawrence's Florentine publisher, Pino Orioli, called it 'a distant and dilapidated place among the hills with no water supply and only one fireplace'. Their landlord was an officer in Mussolini's Fascist cavalry, Captain Angelo Ravagli, who was later to play a significant role in the Lawrences' lives.

The most obvious change that had taken place in Italy during their absence abroad was the accession to power of Mussolini's Blackshirts. 'It is queer, this Fascist movement,' wrote a strangely detached Lawrence. 'One wonders what the end will be. Interesting, in its way.' Lawrence found the gardens of the Villa Mirenda calming and inspirational. He had missed floral Tuscany on his travels, and wrote a long essay called 'Flowery Tuscany': 'The spring that first year was a revelation in flowers, from the first violets in the woods . . . Carpets of them we found.'

Lawrence spent much of the spring and summer studying Etruscan history and painting, which he found 'a much more amusing art than writing . . . costs are less, amuses one more'. In the autumn he made a trip to England to see his family, and on his return to the Villa Mirenda the couple welcomed his biographer and friend, Richard Aldington, and Aldous and Maria Huxley joined them in Florence over Christmas. It was at the Villa Mirenda that Lawrence began to write his most famous and controversial work, *Lady Chatterley's Lover*. Lawrence's recent trip to the Nottingham coalfields had reminded him of the poverty of his home community and the rigidity of England's class divisions: 'labouring under a queer, savage weight of dismalness and acquiescence'. Other autobiographical references are not hard to find: an aristocratic but affection-starved wife; an impotent, semi-invalid husband who wrote fiction; an uneducated man from a mining background.

The following summer, Lawrence started to write the essays that he intended for the book that he described to his publisher as 'half a travel book and half a book about the Etruscan things, which interest me very much'. But although he added more essays later, progress was delayed by his having a severe haemorrhage. The illness resulted in the couple's decision to move to Frieda's home in Bavaria, and on Lawrence's return to Italy in November 1927, assuming that he would never get *Lady Chatterley's Lover* published in England, he decided to publish it privately in Florence and rewrote it, this time with even more four-letter words than before. This raised a further difficulty – that of finding a typist who would be willing to type the manuscript after the first walked out in disgust. The problem was resolved by the more worldly Maria Huxley. A collection of the essays was published posthumously as *Sketches of Etruscan Places*.

As Lawrence's health continued to deteriorate, he accepted the advice of his doctor – and his friend and fellow tubercular, Katherine Mansfield – and moved to Bandol on the French Riviera, never to return to Tuscany. During this period, Frieda would take the occasional trip back to Scandicci, ostensibly to complete their removal, but more probably to continue her Chatterley-esque dalliance, begun during Lawrence's trip home, with their Italian landlord. In October 1928 the couple arranged to meet as Aldington's guests at a villa on the Riviera island of Port Cros, but Lawrence arrived alone: Frieda was delayed in Scandicci and arrived 10 days later.

Early in 1930, an English doctor in Bandol told Lawrence that he should live at a higher altitude, and he was transferred to the aptly named Ad Astra, [To the Stars] opposite the cemetery in Vence, in the hills above Nice, where he died on 2 March 1930. He was buried in Vence Cemetery, the small funerary group including Frieda, her daughter Barby, and Aldous and Maria Huxley. Lawrence always claimed that his work would result in greater freedom for future writers, but he may not have expected it to take so long. *Lady Chatterley's Lover* was not cleared for legal distribution in Britain until the famous *Regina v. Penguin Books* trial in 1960, 30 years after his death, marked the end of literary censorship in Britain.

Lawrence in death was to prove as peripatetic as in life: it had been his dream to return to the Indian encampment he and Freida had loved in Taos, New Mexico, and Frieda set about fulfilling it. With the help of Angelo Ravagli, their former landlord, she had built a small mausoleum there in Lawrence's memory – a friend called it a 'station toilet'. Ravagli was given the job of transporting Lawrence's remains to Taos to complete the shrine, and five years after Lawrence's funeral, the same small group, minus Frieda, reconvened in Vence for his exhumation.

Discouraged by the complications of exporting a long-dead body, Ravagli had the remains burned and urned in preparation for their 5,000-mile journey. In New York, Ravagli and the ashes boarded a train to New Mexico, but Ravagli carelessly left the incinerated Lawrence on the train. No one knows the ultimate fate of the ashes: some say that locals in Taos, suspecting that Ravagli had built the mausoleum with a view to charging admission to tourists, cast them to the desert winds; a view supported by a leading necrophile website is that Frieda, hearing of this plan, tipped the ashes into the concrete mixer and that they are now part of the altar stone in the chapel. Many years later, a drunken Ravagli admitted that the ashes had never left Vence, and that he had filled an urn with a similar substance.

In 1950, 20 years after Lawrence's death, Frieda and Angelo were married. Frieda died in Taos six years later, on her seventy-seventh birthday. Conveniently for Ravagli, Italian law did not recognise his American divorce, or marriage, so he was able to rejoin his first wife in Florence without further ceremony, and share with her the Lawrence royalties to which American law entitled him.

Twenty years after the Lawrences left, another British poet came to live in Scandicci, this time a Welsh one. In May 1947, the Society of Authors awarded a young poet named Dylan Thomas a travelling scholarship of £150, with the recommendation that he spend the time in Italy – possibly because the chairman of the approvals committee was Dame Edith Sitwell, who had family connections there. Dylan's patron, the wife of historian A. J. P. Taylor, offered the Thomases the loan of the Villa Beccaro, near to the Lawrences' Villa Mirenda at Scandicci, in the hills to the south-west of Florence. Thomas described the Villa Beccaro on a postcard to his parents:

> This is our house. Really, it's a hundred times nicer than this, which gives little idea. It's on the hills above Florence, some five miles from the centre, from the great Cathedral Dome that we can see from the sunbathing terrace above the swimming pool. It's a very big villa, with huge rooms and lovely grounds, arbours, terraces, pools: we have a pinewood and a vineyard of our own. Our garden is full of roses. Nightingales sing all night long. Lizards scuttle out of the walls in the sun. It is lovely.

It may have impressed his parents, but, unlike Lawrence, Thomas was not inspired by Scandicci – he hated it. He wrote to a friend, 'I am awfully sick of it here, . . . drinking chianti in our marble shanty, sick of vini and contadini and bambini'.

Eight years earlier, he had refused an invitation from Lawrence Durrell in Corfu on the grounds that 'a bucket of Greek sun would drown in one colour the crowds of colour I like to try to mix for myself . . .' In the heat of July, he found Florence 'sizzling' – which meant he could write only in the early morning – and the wine 'overpowering'. As a serious beer drinker, he found the local brew unpalatable, he had no Italian, and, lonely for conversation, wrote to a friend in England, 'Do you know anybody in Florence to have a drink with?' After two months at the Villa Beccaro, during which he spent much of his time indoors listening to the cricket Test Matches and cursing the 'pick-axed and pneumatic-drilled mosquitoes', Thomas and his family moved to Rio Marina on the island of Elba.

Fiesole

Where the Florentines go to look down on the lazy river gleaming in the sunset. (Guglielmo Amerighi, *The City of Florence*)

The road from Florence winds its way up the wooded hill from the Piazza San Marco, past the Villa Medici and Bernard Berenson's I Tatti, through the village of San Domenico, in whose monastery the fifteenth-century painter Fra Angelico had prayed and painted; through the Valle delle Donne, and up the Via Vecchia Fiesolana to the cypressed skyline of Fiesole, 7 kilometres north-east of the city. The reward for the climb is a panoramic view of the Arno Valley spread out below, with Florence in the foreground and, as a backdrop, the southern hills of Alcetri and Bellosguardo. Leading from the main square, the Piazza Mino, the Via Giuseppe Verdi continues the climb, the view becoming ever more spectacular – and the legs more fatigued – with every step. A plaque on the wall says that the Chicago architect Frank Lloyd Wright lived there in 1910. Fiesole is a true Etruscan town: its antiquity, dating from millennia before Christ, and its part-Etruscan, part-Roman temple (now an archaeological museum) make the city of Florence a relative latecomer. Fiesole's faithfully preserved first-century AD Roman amphitheatre is today a summer venue for concerts and festivals.

Etruscan artefacts excavated in the area included the black-figured porcelain that so inspired the eighteenth-century English potter Josiah Wedgwood that his company would reproduce the designs for much of the next two centuries in the town that he named Etruria after this region. The profits from the enterprise, inherited by Josiah's granddaughter, helped to finance the important work of her husband, Charles Darwin, in writing *On the Origin of Species*.

Fiesole, like its surrounding villages, is rich in Etruscan and Roman remains, a pre-Christian heritage that made it inspirational to writers such as Thomas Hardy and D. H. Lawrence. The area is equally abundant with literary associations. In about 1345, some years before his more famous *Decameron*, Boccaccio wrote there what many think his greatest poem, *Ninfale Fiesolano* (*Nymphs of Fiesole*), the story of a young man transformed from somnolent simpleton to fearless warrior by the love of a nymph he meets in the woods.

The adventure novelist Sir Henry Rider Haggard stayed in an ancient villa in Fiesole, the history of which could be traced back to the tenth century, and claimed that the well in its garden was the very one around which Boccaccio's 'gay gallants and their ladies whiled away the heat of a summer day by telling each other stories'. Fiesole left Haggard with a lasting impression: 'my most pleasing recollection of Florence and its neighbourhood is this white and ancient villa and the marvellous landscape which lies beneath and around it for miles and miles.' Walter Savage Landor, a later Fiesole resident, paid tribute to the *Decameron* in a poem beginning:

> Here by the lake Boccaccio's fair brigade
> Beguiled the hours and tale for tale repaid

The view south from Fiesole has enchanted many writers: the English banker, art collector and poet Samuel Rogers visited Florence in 1814, and, although much travelled, decided that this was where he would like to live, 'beyond all the cities of the world'. His journal entry after walking with his sister from Fiesole back to his lodgings in the city, reads: 'An evening mist, like the bloom of a plum, had overspread the mountains & the distant parts of the valley. Fiesole behind us, with its tower, and in front, seen over cypresses, the towers & dome of Florence! A heavenly dream. In the sky a red streak so often in Italian paintings; & which I used to think unnatural.' Rogers's last – and longest – published work was his poem *Italy*.

Leigh Hunt came to Florence in 1822 at the instigation of his friends Shelley and Byron. Hunt, who had spent two years in prison for disclosing details of the Prince Regent's private life, had originally been attracted to Tuscany by their invitation to help to set up an English-language magazine, *The Liberal*, but with the death of Shelley soon after his arrival, and with Byron on the point of leaving for Greece, the magazine project fell through after only four issues. Hunt, his wife and their six, later seven, children, lodged first in Pisa and Florence, and finally in the village of Maiano, on the hills between Fiesole and Florence, where, as he wrote in his *Autobiography*, he would walk almost every day through the woods 'looking through the pines down to Florence'. While at Maiano, Hunt tried to start his own monthly English-language magazine, but that project also fell through, this time because the over-cautious government censors could not read it in English and did not trust his (Italian) publisher's own translations – and he eventually returned to England.

The essayist William Hazlitt visited Fiesole in 1824, which he describes in his *Notes of a Journey through France and Italy* as 'a place of the highest antiquity and renown, but it does not bear the stamp of anything extraordinary upon its face. You stand upon a bleak, rocky hill, without suspecting it to have been the centre of a thronged population, the seat of battles and of mighty events in eldest times.'

Frances Trollope's impressions in her *Italy and the Italians* were less restrained: '. . . beautiful in its isolated elevation . . . beautiful in its bold outline . . . beautiful by the convent that crowns its summit, and the fine tower beneath it, . . . and doubly, trebly beautiful by the poetic halo that has settled round it, and which can never fade'; while her friend Charles Dickens was more intrigued by Fiesole's historical and scientific associations than poetic halos. 'Beyond the walls,' he wrote, 'the whole sweet valley of the Arno, the convent at Fiesole, the Tower of Galileo, Boccaccio's house, old villas and retreats; innumerable spots of interest, all glowing in a landscape of surpassing beauty steeped in the richest light; are spread before us.'

While sitting in the Roman amphitheatre on the Fiesole hill, Thomas Hardy was so moved when a child showed him a Roman coin that he wrote his sonnet 'In the Old Theatre' on the spot:

> I traced the Circus whose grey stones incline
> Where Rome and dim Etruria interjoin,
> Till came a child who showed an ancient coin
> That bore the image of a Constantine.

D. H. Lawrence was a regular visitor to Fiesole on research for the essays that he intended to call 'Etruscan Places', and gathered Etruscan elements into his poem 'Cypresses', written there in 1920; but he could not avoid mentioning the view of Florence, 'So clear and beautiful in the sun, the Lily town',

> Among the sinuous, flame-tall cypresses
> That swayed their length of darkness all around.
> Etruscan-dusky, wavering men of old Etruria:
> Naked except for fanciful long shoes.

Fiesole has many fictional associations. Its Franciscan monastery is the setting for Henry James's novel *Roderick Hudson* and the town and its surroundings feature in Sinclair Lewis's *World so Wide*:

On the northern rim of Florence, towards the mutely watching mountains, Fiesole perches on its hill-top like a monstrous eagle, with its bell-tower for upstretched neck. It looks down on the flood plain of the Arno, which is Florence, and remembers it was a ponderous-walled Etruscan city twenty-five hundred years ago, when Florence was a nameless huddle of mud huts.

Fiesole's wealthiest resident at the beginning of the twentieth century was Lady Sybil Cutting, the Anglo-Irish widow of a fabulously rich New Yorker, William B. Cutting. Their daughter Iris was born in 1902. In 1910, following the early death of her husband, Lady Sybil bought the sumptuous Villa Medici, in the Via Fra' Giovanni di Fiesole, formerly a palazzo that had been built for Cosimo I de' Medici, the first Grand Duke of Tuscany. A near neighbour, in the upmarket Villa I Tatti, was the equally affluent Bernard Berenson, American author, art historian and dealer. He had bought the villa in 1900 after his marriage, and remained there until his death 59 years later, including the years of the Second World War. Less well-heeled neighbours were the Welsh-born novelist Eric Linklater and his wife, whom he had brought to Italy to await the birth of their

12 The Roman Arena, Fiesole

first child. Lady Sybil took a fancy to the couple and housed them in what Linklater called her 'enormous villa'. Her hospitality did not end there: she also related to the author the story of a local peasant who had shown great courage in the First World War. The story became *Private Angelo*, the most successful of Linklater's 26 novels, and was made into a successful film starring a young Peter Ustinov. Regular literary visitors to I Tatti included fellow Americans Edith Wharton and Sinclair Lewis, and the philosopher Bertrand Russell, who was also Berenson's brother-in-law. On his death, Berenson left I Tatti to Harvard University and it is now the Harvard University Center for Italian Renaissance Studies.

Iris Cutting described her first sight of the villa that her newly widowed mother Lady Sybil had just bought:

> I am not certain how it came about that my mother bought the Villa Medici, on the southern slopes of the Fiesole hill above Florence, but I do remember the spring day on which . . . she took me for a drive up a long hill, first between high walls over which yellow banksia roses tumbled and a tangle of wisteria, then through olive groves opening to an ever wider view; and finally down a long drive over-shadowed by ilex trees. At the end of the terrace stood a square house with a deep loggia, looking due west towards the sunset over the whole valley of the Arno. 'This is where we are going to live', she said.

Lady Sybil was already the owner of a luxurious apartment in Rome and a seaside retreat, Gli Scafari, in Lerici on the Gulf of La Spezia. Lady Sybil, doyenne of the wealthy Anglo-Florentine set, then married Berenson's secretary, the English architect, Geoffrey Scott, but divorced him eight years later because of his affair with the sexually adaptable Vita Sackville-West, and in 1926 went on to marry Berenson's equally opulent friend and biographer, Percy Lubbock. Fortunately, before Lady Sybil divorced Geoffrey Scott, he had redesigned the Villa Medici's terraced gardens, and today Cosimo's palazzo, now known as the Villa Medici of Fiesole, is a luxurious holiday rental home, the immaculate gardens of which are open to the public on weekday mornings.

In her autobiographical *Images and Shadows*, Iris Cutting tells part of the palazzo's iniquitous history:

> It was at this villa that Cosimo's grandson, Lorenzo [the Magnificent] gave a party every year on Plato's birthday. One of these evening parties, however, on the night of April 25, 1478, nearly had a tragic ending, for the bitter rivals of the Medici, the Pazzi, having been invited to a banquet at Fiesole by Lorenzo and his brother Giuliano in honour of Cardinal Riario, planned to take this opportunity of murdering their hosts at their own table.

The assassination was thwarted by Giuliano having a sudden attack of gout, but it was only a temporary reprieve. The next day, a Sunday, the murderers struck again in the infamous Pazzi Conspiracy, when Bernardo Bandi and Francesco de' Pazzi attacked the Medici brothers in the Duomo during High Mass. Giuliano de' Medici was stabbed 19 times and bled to death in the cathedral, while his brother Lorenzo escaped. Angry Florentines captured and killed the conspirators, Giuliano de' Pazzi being stabbed beside the high altar, and Jacopo de' Pazzi, the instigator of the conspiracy, thrown from a window and his body dragged naked through the city and thrown into the Arno.

Lady Sybil and Iris remained at the Villa Medici together – through Lady Sybil's affair with their neighbour, Bernard Berenson – until 1924, when Iris married Antonio Origo, becoming the Contessa Origo, Marchesa of Val d'Orcia. The newlyweds bought a typically decrepit Tuscan farmhouse, La Foce (The Mouth), in remote Chianti countryside, and after their honeymoon, set about a lifetime task of restoring it. Iris wrote a memoir of her life in La Foce during the Second World War, *War in the Val D'Orcia*, which was so successful that she went on to write 12 more books.

In 1950, one of Berenson's Fiesole properties was the temporary home of a multi-talented writer, playwright, actor, lyricist and singer to whom he had lent a *villino* on his estate. Noël Coward's journal entry explains the brevity of his stay:

> Woke feeling lousy. Bathroom *frigorifico* and no hot water. Just my dish. . . . It is filled with priceless *objets d'art* and pictures – a great number of immensely famous Madonnas simpering in gold leaf. . . . I made my great decision and told [my host] that I was leaving his bed and board in favour of the Excelsior Hotel on account of not wanting to catch pneumonia.

There is no evidence that Noël Coward ever returned to Fiesole.

Iris Origo was not the first author to begin a writing career in Florence. Ever since Chaucer's visit six centuries earlier, Florence, more than almost any other city in the world, has attracted writers from abroad and inspired new ones. The literary migration has been compared with the influx of authors to Paris between the two world wars, but the comparison is unfair. Paris attracted its literati over decades; the allure of Florence has endured for centuries, and shows no sign of abating. The reason is not hard to find: Eve Borsook called it 'a city that is at once immensely attractive and intimidating'. Florence has all that is needed to inspire and challenge the itinerant artist: mountains, an historic river with elegant bridges, the best of architecture from any era and art in abundance; and it stands amid cultured Tuscan countryside. Florentines have led the world in art, science and literature. Who would not want to write about them?

❧ 3 ❧

LA SPEZIA

The Gulf of Poets

Thence we came forth to see the stars again.
(Dante Alighieri, *Divine Comedy: Inferno*)

My first impression of La Spezia was that it did not look very Tuscan. Having decided to travel through Tuscany in a roughly north-to-south direction, using second-class rail as a way of meeting as many locals as possible, the obvious place to start my journey seemed to be the most northern railway station on my map, La Spezia. Unfortunately, my map did not distinguish the provinces: it was not until I was corrected by a kindly taxi driver that I discovered that La Spezia is not in Tuscany, but in the province of Liguria, on the Italian Riviera.

My authority for including part of Liguria in a book about Tuscany could be called poetic licence. The Gulf of La Spezia, in recognition of its ancient poetic associations, has long been known as 'Il Golfo dei Poeti' (the Gulf of Poets). Like Tuscany's Etruscan heritage, its literary patrimony also extends beyond its geographic borders: culturally, the Gulf of La Spezia belongs in Tuscany.

I drew solace from the fact that, more than seven hundred years earlier, Dante Alighieri had made the same mistake. A Florentine Guelph, he was hounded from Florence, then Bologna, by Ghibelline sympathisers, and was given a job as lawyer to the Malaspina family and took refuge in their castle in coastal Sarzana. He mentions the gulf specifically in his *Inferno*, lamenting the vertiginous descent from Turbia (now the French La Turbie) to Lerici, the Gulf of La

Spezia's main seaside resort. Dante's 'craggiest way' is now the treacherously steep and winding D37 – the road on which Princess Grace had her fatal car accident. At the road's 500-metre peak, lines from Canto III of Dante's *Inferno* are engraved in stone:

> Meanwhile, we'd reached the mountain's foot – and dead
> Upright it rose, a cliff so steep and sheer
> 'Twould make the nimblest legs seem dull as lead.
> The craggiest way, the most remote and drear
> Between Turbia and Lerici, you'd call,
> Compared with that, a broad and easy stair.

Petrarch, like Dante, was a poetic Guelph exile, and spent time in the area in the fourteenth century, but it is not known if he thought he was in Tuscany. Charles Dickens also arrived on the wrong side of the border in 1845, and was forced to wait in La Spezia – 'a good place to tarry at; by reason of its beautiful bay' – until the waters of the River Magra had subsided enough for him to cross into Tuscany: 'The passage is not by any means agreeable,' he wrote in *Pictures from Italy*.

Lerici is about 15 kilometres north of the Tuscan border. My first objectives were the seaside villages of San Terenzo, a kilometre north of Lerici, and Fiascherino, the same distance south. They were once the homes, respectively, of Percy Bysshe Shelley and D. H. Lawrence, both of whom were linked romantically and geographically with Il Golfo dei Poeti. To find their homes I sought the advice of a local real estate agent, who directed me to a bus stop. I was not asked for a fare, which seemed strange; it seemed even stranger when the packed bus wheezed up a steep, winding hill, because I knew that both objectives lay on the coast. Finally the bus stopped and everyone got out, and I asked a fellow passenger where we were. 'Here,' he said. I thanked him for his help, having by then realised that we were in a vast car park. I stayed on the bus and went back to Lerici.

The young Shelley was looking, in 1821, for a cottage by the sea where he could settle with his family and sail his new 8-metre schooner *Ariel*, and he found it in the Casa Magni at San Terenzo. The family included his wife Mary and her half-sister Claire Clairmont. Mary Shelley was the daughter of the early feminist writer Mary Wollstonecraft, who had died giving birth to Mary. The Casa Magni was the perfect realisation of Shelley's Italian dream: a two-storey cottage on the sandy beach at San Terenzo. The fourth member of the Shelley ménage was Claire's daughter Allegra, the consequence of a brief affair with Lord Byron.

It was at the Casa Magni that Shelley wrote much of his best work in Italy, including *Adonaïs*, 'Ode to the West Wind' and 'Lines Written in the Bay of Lerici', and it was to there that he was sailing on his final voyage.

In June 1822, Shelley sailed from San Terenzo in *Ariel* with a friend, Ned Williams, to the port of Livorno, 90 kilometres south, to welcome his old friend, Leigh Hunt and his large family on their arrival from England. Shelley, who had already established Byron in the magnificent Palazzo Lanfranchi on the banks of the Arno in Pisa, now installed the Hunts in the ground floor of the same palazzo, then set off back to Livorno, intending to return to the Casa Magni with Williams, who, with his wife, was living with the Shelleys.

They sailed out of Livorno harbour on 8 July, but they never arrived at San Terenzo. The distraught Mary, recovering from a painful miscarriage, and Williams's wife, Jane, raced to Pisa to see if the Byrons had any news of their husbands, thinking that they may have decided to stay overnight in Pisa because of bad weather. Being told that the two men had left for Livorno, the wives assumed, correctly, that the men must have decided to sail back to San Terenzo. They made their way back there, where they waited for two agonising weeks before the body of Shelley was washed ashore on the beach at Viareggio, about halfway between Livorno and San Terenzo, and that of Williams was recovered a few kilometres away.

Local health laws required that bodies washed ashore must be cremated within 24 hours, a task that was undertaken by a friend of Shelley, Edward Trelawny, who had a special furnace made by a shipbuilder in Livorno. Attended by his family and his friends Byron and the Hunts, Shelley's body was cremated on the beach at the spot where it was found, in a Greek-style funeral pyre. In Trelawny's record of the event, published 36 years later as *Recollections of the Last Days of Shelley and Byron*, he claimed that, as the fire died down, 'the corpse fell open' and he saw Shelley's heart among the smouldering ashes.

> What surprised us all was that the heart remained entire. In snatching this relic from the fiery furnace, my hand was severely burnt; had anyone seen me do the act I should have been put into quarantine. . . . As I undertook and executed this novel ceremony, I have been thus tediously minute in describing it.

Tediously minute he certainly was, but of the differing accounts of Shelley's funeral, none supports that of Trelawny. The biographer Richard Holmes, in his radio play about Shelley's death, *To the Tempest Given*, describes Trelawny as a myth-maker: 'nothing he ever says is ever quite reliable, ever quite serious.' Trelawny's similarly romanticised version of the distribution of the remains was that he gave the ashes and bones of the atheist Shelley to the British consul in Rome, to be buried in the Protestant cemetery there, and gave the heart to Mary, who kept it until she died. On Mary's death 29 years later, an unmarked envelope was found, containing some ashes. On the assumption that they were Shelley's, they were buried with her in the cemetery of St Peter's Church, Bournemouth, in 1851. The little family was reunited 39 years later with the burial there of the body of the Shelleys' only son, Sir Percy Florence Shelley, in 1889.

There was considerable speculation over the cause of the sinking of the *Ariel*. Shelley had initially called the boat *Don Juan* as a tribute to Byron, but Mary, probably thinking of Byron's treatment of Claire, had insisted on his changing it. Theories ranged from the suggestion that a suicidal Shelley, who could not swim, had scuttled the boat himself, to assassination in reprisal for his outspoken atheism. Mary Shelley claimed simply that the boat had been unseaworthy, but some years later there was a bizarre sequel: a local fisherman made a deathbed confession admitting that he had deliberately rammed the *Ariel*, thinking it was Byron's boat, in the hope of robbing its crew. Richard Holmes, whose biography *Shelley: The Pursuit* won the Somerset Maugham Award in 1974, records that both Shelley and Mary had premonitions of the disaster. The diary entry of Edward Williams, Shelley's sailing colleague, on 23 June 1822, was, 'Shelley sees spirits and alarms the whole house,' and on 1 July Mary had written to Hunt in Livorno warning, 'let me entreat you to let no persuasions induce you to come . . . it would be complete madness to come.' Mary recalled, 17 years later, 'During the whole of our stay at Lerici, an intense presentiment of coming evil brooded over my mind, and covered this beautiful place and genial summer with the shadow of coming misery.'

In the Piazza Shelley in Viareggio, not far from the beach on which he was cremated, stands a bust of Shelley, bearing an inscription in Italian which, translated, reads:

TO P. B. SHELLEY,

HEART O' HEARTS

WHO IN 1822,

DROWNED IN THESE WATERS

AND WAS CREMATED ON THIS SHORE,

ALONG WHICH HE CREATED *PROMETHEUS UNBOUND*

A FINAL PAGE

OF WHICH EACH GENERATION

WILL REMEMBER HIS

STRUGGLES, TEARS, REDEMPTION

The line 'Heart o' hearts' is from *Prometheus Unbound*, which was in fact completed in Florence in 1819, two years before Shelley moved to Lerici.

13 The P. B. Shelley memorial, Viareggio

Shelley's house, the Casa Magni, still stands near to, but no longer quite *on*, the family-friendly beach of San Terenzo; a coastal road now intervenes. On either side of the house, in rusting metallic letters, are extracts in English from Shelley's letters: on the north-facing side: 'I still inhabit this Divine Bay, reading dramas and sailing and listening to the most enchanting music'; and on the south: 'A lonely house close by the soft and sublime scenery of the Bay of Lerici'; while on the wall of the terrace from which Mary Shelley and Jane Williams gazed anxiously out to sea awaiting their husbands' return, hangs a more recent plaque, placed there in 1992, bearing the cryptic inscription in Italian:

> Poets are mirrors of the gigantic shadows
> that the future casts on the present.
>
> A force that is not moved but which moves.
> Poets are the unrecognised
> legislators of the world.
> Percy B. Shelley
> Bicentenary of his birth:
> 1792–1822

The Casa Magni, now renamed the Villa Shelley, is uninhabited but well maintained, and geraniums bloom on its balcony. Lerici township shows its impartiality by having both a Hotel Byron and a Hotel Shelley.

I am not by any means the only writer to have visited Shelley's monument in Viareggio and the Casa Magni in San Terenzo: they have become romantic shrines to which many itinerant writers have come to pay their respects, including, in 1887, the novelist and poet, Thomas Hardy, and in 1935, Virginia Woolf and her husband Leonard.

Behind the monument in the Piazza Shelley, and built in the year of Shelley's death, is a Baroque gem, the Villa Paolina, the summer residence of Napoleon's younger, and reputedly favourite, sister,

14 The Casa Magni, home of P. B. Shelley, San Terenzo

Pauline, after her marriage to the Prince Camillo Borghese. By the time she moved in, in 1821, Napoleon had died as a prisoner on St Helena. The villa is now a community art museum.

Ninety years after the death of Shelley, another English poet arrived, having heard of the delights of the Gulf of La Spezia. In March 1912 D. H. Lawrence eloped with his lover Frieda Weekley (née von Richthofen), taking her away from her husband and their three children. They made for Italy because they could not afford to live anywhere else, and stayed on the tiny isolated bay of Fiascherino, near the mouth of the river Magra, the border between Liguria and Tuscany. There they found a cottage on the beach from which they could put out their rowing boat and bathe. Lawrence described it as 'Perfect. There is a little tiny bay half shut in by rocks and smothered by olive woods that slope down. . . . You run out of the gate into the sea, which washes among the rocks at the mouth of the bay. At evening all the sea is milky gold and scarlet with sundown. It is very pretty.'

It was at Fiascherino that Lawrence finalised *Sons and Lovers* and started to plan the book that, 40 years later and after many trials – literary and litigious – was to make his name. He was, although he never acknowledged it, chronically tubercular, and, finding the outdoor life beneficial to his health, was able to take the occasional trip down the Tuscan coast to visit old friends from his Bloomsbury days, writer Aldous Huxley and his wife Maria, then living in Forte dei Marmi on the Tuscan coast.

Lawrence and Frieda returned to England, where they were married in London on 13 July 1914. Just two weeks earlier, Serbian nationalists had killed the Archduke Ferdinand in Sarajevo, and for the next few years pan-European travel was out of the question. It would be five years before the Lawrences could return to Italy, and when they did, it was to Scandicci, on the southern hills near Florence. Fiascherino today is little changed: there are a few more cottages, a coastal road and a bus service, but the rocks still deter all but the hardiest of swimmers, and the sea at twilight is still 'milky gold and scarlet with sundown'.

In 1933, Lerici was the home of yet another British writer, the Scottish poet, playwright, novelist and biographer Eric Linklater – or at least he claimed throughout his life to have been a Scot born in the Orkneys, but confessed when in his seventies that he had been born and brought up in Cardiff. He was already famous, having hit the bestseller lists with his novel *Juan in America*, a pastiche of the Byronic character's adventures in prohibitionist America, but he was not yet rich. Linklater chose the Villa San Carlo, which he described as a 'very diminutive and somewhat chilly villa' as the ideal retreat in which to continue work on his biography of Robert the Bruce, and to await the appearance of his novel *Magnus Merriman*, and his first child. One of his guests at Lerici was fellow novelist, Scottish Nationalist and *true* Orcadian, Compton Mackenzie.

The Linklaters passed the winter quietly and frugally, living a simple life: 'we see no one, we walk a little, when the winds do not blow too sheer and bitter off the hills,' Eric wrote to a friend, 'We're on a steep, precipitous slope, with olive trees all round and the sea just below us, coming into a tiny and almost private bay . . . We live on spaghetti, minestrone, pinocchi, ravioli, iron-hard rolls and floods of Chianti.' As the winter became more severe, a wealthy neighbour, Lady Sybil Cutting, an occasional resident at her nearby seaside villa, took pity on the impoverished pair, as already mentioned, and it was at her palazzo in Fiesole that their daughter Alison was born in the spring of 1934.

Looking back before crossing into the real Tuscany, I was reminded of the author who called this gulf 'the most beautiful of all the spots I have ever seen'. He was the Dublin-born novelist Charles Lever, who became so attached to the area that he stayed for 10 years – nine of them as the British vice-consul in La Spezia – and wrote his novel *One of Them* here. His recreation while here was to gamble heavily at the casino of Bagni di Lucca, contributing so generously that in 2006 the city held a conference on the bicentennial of his birth to celebrate his stay.

❧ 4 ❧

LUCCA

The Romantic City

A city overflowing with everything that makes for ease, for plenty, for beauty, for interest and for good example.

(Henry James, *Italian Hours*)

As the train approached Lucca, I was looking for typical Tuscan flora – vineyards, olive trees and sunflowers – but the approach to Lucca is not typically Tuscan. If I could reach a hand out of the window, I would grab handfuls of the tall maize that brushes the train. Yet the city itself is all that one expects of a truly Tuscan city, sheltering behind its 4 kilometres of unscalable ramparts. Etruscan relics abut Roman remains; medieval columns support Gothic buildings and Renaissance palaces. It is a city of open squares and Romanesque churches – the city that Henry James, who loved it, described as 'pre-eminently a city of churches; ecclesiastical architecture being indeed the only one of the arts to which it seems to have given attention'.

In the vast Piazza Napoleone stands the statue of a toga-clad Maria Louisa, the Habsburg second wife sought by Napoleon Bonaparte after he divorced his first, Josephine de Beauharnais, for failing to give him a son and heir. Maria Louisa did produce a son, whom Napoleon pronounced King of Italy at birth, but he was a frail lad whose pampered life ended with his death from tuberculosis at the age of 21.

Lucca became an independent state in the twelfth century and prospered, not just from its abundant crops, but also from early trading – mostly with England – first in wool and fine silks and later in olive oil and wine. The city also had military links with England: in 1364, during the long wars against Florence, Sir John Hawkwood, the mercenary leader from Essex, contracted to dedicate his troops to the defence of Lucca against any forces except those of the King of England. The arrangement must have suited the commune, because in 1375 a grateful Lucca awarded Hawkwood a generous honorarium and made him a freeman of the city.

The first literary migrant to visit Lucca was the French philosopher and essayist, Michel Eyquem de Montaigne, who came to Lucca seeking relief in the nearby thermal baths from the inherited complaint of kidney stones. He had set off from home in 1580 and had visited the watering places of France, Germany, Austria and Switzerland without success, so the following year, leaving no stone unturned, he came to Bagni di Lucca – the Baths of Lucca – a popular watering resort some 20 kilometres north-east of the city. Montaigne preceded the first English writer in Lucca, the poet John Milton, by half a century. Milton addressed the academy there in 1639, and established academic links between Tuscany and Britain that exist today in such organisations as the British Institute of Florence.

Many years later, after the Second World War, the English travel writer Eric Newby and his wife came to Lucca and took the opportunity to taste its waters: 'whenever we visited it', said Newby, 'and it was a fascinating place, we steeled ourselves to drink a glass of the beverage, which was so horrible that we both felt that it must have been doing us good'.

Percy Bysshe Shelley was Lucca's first famous English publicist. With his second wife, Mary, the poet first came to Italy shortly after their marriage in 1818 and chose Bagni di Lucca as the first of their many Italian homes. Shelley was enchanted; a better poet than he was astronomer, he wrote to an English friend

the nights are forever serene, and we see a star in the east at sunset – I think it is Jupiter – almost as fine as Venus was last summer:

but which belongs, I suppose, to the latter planet by virtue of its at once divine and female nature. In the middle of the day I bathe in a pool or fountain, formed in the middle of the forests by a torrent. . . . My custom is to undress and sit on the rocks, reading Herodotus, until the perspiration has subsided, then leap from the edge of the rock into this fountain.

A non-swimmer, he thus revealed an incompatibility between his passions and his capabilities that was to prove fatal.

The Shelley ménage – Percy, Mary, her half-sister Claire Clairmont and the Shelleys' two children, Clara and William – left Lucca in the spring to begin a trek around Italy with the main objectives, it seems, of enabling Claire to see her daughter Allegra, who was then living with her father, the perfidious Lord Byron – who had long since lost interest in Claire – and to support Claire in her relentless pursuit of him. It was a pointless and eventually tragic trek that took them to Padua, Venice, Este, Naples and Rome.

Within a year the Luccan idyll was over for the Shelleys. In the course of their travels after leaving Lucca, they lost their two children through illnesses: Clara in Venice from dysentery and William in Rome. The three adults moved on to Livorno, where Shelley had a productive period, during which he worked on his tragedy, *The Cenci*, and was inspired by local birdsong to write his 'Ode to a Skylark'. Their placid stay in Livorno ended when the river flooded and they had to be rescued by boat from an upstairs window of their house. The Shelleys were on the road again, this time to Pisa.

Lucca is one of the quieter cities in this tranquil and fertile region. In the heat of the day, in tiny squares away from the tourist cafés and luxury shops, the town's elders, complexions wrinkled by sun and time, meet to rediscuss the matters they discussed the day before, their movable feast rotating slowly around the square to follow the shade. Cars are allowed into the old town, but for delivery purposes only, otherwise they must be left at the entrance gates, beyond which the only acceptable vehicles are invalid chairs and bicycles. Not only do the locals ride bicycles, but there are rental stations at each gateway to the city, where visitors can hire one for €2.50 an hour. The bikes are scantly equipped, and do not offer such luxuries as lights or warning bells, which is seldom an inconvenience to the cyclist, but can be a hazard for pedestrians, who, in leaping to avoid one, are liable to jump into the path of another. In *Italy: The Places in Between*, the Polish-American travel writer Kate Simon suggested one reason for Lucca's calm. 'A few of the churches are justly famous,' she wrote, 'and there is an impressive museum that absorbs the treasures of those decayed and abandoned, but with Florence nearby, Pisa around the corner and Siena not too far away, these don't call for studious attention, and that can be a great relief and Lucca's greatest asset.'

Lucca is a city of many moods. In the cool of early evening it bursts into noisy life as the shops reopen and residents assemble, like the cast of a play, for the twilight *passeggiata*, the evening stroll along Via Fillungo and adjoining streets; chatting, laughing, walking the children and dogs, shopping, flirting or just sitting, according to ancient laws of generation and gender. If city walls kept people out, they can also keep them in, and the sense of community is intense: Henry James, ever partial to a participle, wrote,

> If Pisa is dead Tuscany, Lucca is Tuscany still living and enjoying, desiring and intending. The town is a charming mixture of antique 'character' and modern inconsequence; and not only the town, but the country – the blooming romantic country which you admire from the famous promenade on the city-wall. The wall is of superbly solid and intensely 'toned' brickwork and of extraordinary breadth, and its summit, planted with goodly trees and swelling here and there into bastions and outworks and little open gardens, surrounds the city with a circular lounging-place of a splendid dignity.

The *passeggiata* ends as quickly as it began, as if someone had rung a curfew, and soon the streets are void of everything but the fragrant whiff of garlic, fried onions and simmering Bolognese sauce.

Lucca is a city of music: the violinist and operatic composer Giacomo Puccini was a Lucchese. The English novelist Osbert Sitwell tells in his autobiography, *Left Hand, Right Hand!*, of having watched his first opera, *Madame Butterfly*, in Lucca, and recalls seeing its composer walking the ramparts: 'As he strolled under the flowering chestnuts with their pallid torches showing ivory among the thick leaves, he was treated as if he were an Emperor. People went bare-headed in his presence.' Puccini's bronze figure sits, relaxed, bronze cigar in hand, outside the house of his birth, and the town honours his memory with a festival of his music every summer. It was in Lucca also that Kate Simon spotted a stone plaque that seems the ultimate in musical name-dropping: 'Here Niccolò Paganini was a guest in 1809 of the family Bucchianeri. Love and poetry tormented the genius but the musical city gave his magical violin the wings of glory.'

In 1961 another tormented genius lived in Lucca: one of the world's great jazz musicians, Chet Baker. The funny valentine who thought he could live unnoticed and undisturbed in peaceful Lucca spent a year as a guest of the Carcere di San Giorgio, the town's ancient prison, for possessing heroin. Every evening, while his red Ferrari collected dust outside, the pie-eyed piper drew fans old and new to gather on the city walls outside the prison to listen to him practise. Local jazz musicians would join in, to entertain what was truly a captive audience. Baker promised his Lucchesi fans a concert when he got out, and they were amazed at his proficiency in the Italian he had learned in prison – but then this was a musician with an infallible ear, who was never seen with a sheet of music. Baker's appeal against his 22-month sentence was eventually successful and it was reduced, enabling him to be released in time for Christmas, as was his album, *Chet is Back*, containing some Italian songs he had written in Lucca's gaol. When Lucca held a concert to celebrate Chet Baker's release, its opera house was filled to bursting, so his fans from the prison wall did finally hear him in concert – free.

The last time I saw him was in a small jazz club in Nice, but I didn't hear him play a note. Arriving on stage hours late, he was led by the arm towards a chair; he sat, and put his trumpet to his lips. No sound came, but no one moved, and when a few people started to murmur, they were immediately shushed by their neighbours. He tried again, several times, but produced no more than a few squawks and some mumbled words, and I wondered if I would ever see him again. I never did: the remaining weeks in the tragic life of the world's greatest jazz trumpeter – the musician who had played alongside the likes of Gerry Mulligan, Charlie Parker and other jazz legends – were spent in the backstreets of the city to which he had always turned in search of his needs: Amsterdam. His twisted body was found in the cobblestoned street beneath his hotel window. In Lucca, in the birthplace of Puccini, there is no bronze statue outside Chet Baker's custodial home, no annual festival celebrates his music and no commemorative plaque records his passing. But there is a plaque in a cobbled street in Amsterdam. It reads: 'Chet Baker died here on May 13, 1988. He will live on in his music for everyone willing to listen and feel.'

Lucca is a city of churches: the Romanesque Church of San Michele, with its Gaudí-esque jumble of twisted columns and loggias, was described by John Ruskin, very much a hands-on art critic, in a letter to his father in 1845, as 'white marble, inlaid with figures cut an inch deep in the green porphyry, and framed with carved, rich, hollow marble tracery'. More poetically, Kate Simon said of its outrageous charm: 'It has no caution or restraint or modesty but, like a child dressing up out of a trunkful of clothing and costume jewellery, puts on everything.' It reminded me of some lines from E. M. Forster's *Where Angels Fear to Tread*: 'There is something majestic in the bad taste of Italy; it is not the bad taste of a country which knows no better; it is not the nervous vulgarity of England, or the blinded vulgarity of Germany. It observes beauty, and chooses to pass it by.'

The old town – La Città Vecchia – is laid out like a Roman camp, and is encircled by what seems to be a magnet to Lucchesi

15 The Church of San Michele, Lucca

joggers and strollers: a circular wall topped with lines of oleander and chestnut trees: a memento of Lucca's brief period of French occupancy. Old Lucca is also a city of romance, particularly for this writer, for it was in La Città Vecchia some years ago, in its mandorla-shaped Piazza dell'Anfiteatro, that my wife and I plighted our respective troths.

The watering resort of Bagni di Lucca is famous for its 19 natural spas, supposedly rich in calcium, sulphates and bicarbonates. Its thermal waters were first harnessed by the Romans, but rediscovered in the thirteenth century, and their alleged curative powers have been celebrated by successive rulers ever since, in particular during the French occupancy by Napoleon's sister Elisa, on whom, as with all his grasping siblings, he bestowed lavish titles. She was Princess of Piombino and head of the Duchy of Lucca, in which capacity she made her home in Bagni di Lucca.

More recent literary bathers have included the German poet Heinrich Heine, who while there wrote a book, *Die Bäder von Lucca* (*The Baths of Lucca*) that maliciously 'outed' a rival author as homosexual. Byron and Shelley were also Bagni bathers, as were the Italian composers Puccini and Mascagni, who called Bagni 'the Switzerland of Tuscany'.

Montaigne was one of the most influential of French Renaissance writers, famous for his volumes of *Essays* on a wide range of topics and for interspersing his scholarly writings with casual personal asides. Montaigne directly influenced many writers, British and foreign, from Shakespeare to present day authors. When criticised by contemporaries for his tendency to digress into personal anecdote, his response was, 'I am myself the subject of my book; it is not reasonable to expect you to waste your leisure on a matter so frivolous and empty.' However, modern non-fiction writers have found inspiration in Montaigne, and many of today's historians and biographers garnish their works with personal advocacy.

Montaigne was born in the family home, the Château de Montaigne, near Bordeaux, in 1533. His lawyer father had bought the château and changed the family name to match it. His father had some idiosyncratic ideas on how his son should be brought up: although the family were wealthy, having made their fortune in herring fishing, the baby Michel was fostered with a peasant family for the first three years of his life, to avoid his taking his accustomed wealth for granted, or, as his father put it, 'to know the conditions of the people who need our help'. It is doubtful if, in later years, Michel remembered much of his early hardship. Afterwards, to ensure his son's fluency in Latin, Michel's father instructed the entire household to speak only Latin in the lad's presence – which, if stressful for the family, must have been even more arduous for the domestic staff. Montaigne senior also believed in the therapeutic powers of music, so from his son's waking moments he was shadowed constantly by a zither player. The results of these strategies are not recorded, but he certainly became an industrious student, graduating at 13, and becoming a successful lawyer.

From the age of 45, Montaigne suffered from kidney stones, and, as mentioned earlier he visited various European spas, still hoping for a cure. Bagni di Lucca was his last resort: he was still in Bagni – and still suffering from abdominal pains – when he heard that he had been elected mayor of Bordeaux, and returned immediately to the Château de Montaigne to take up the position. His detailed record of his travel experiences, *Journal de Voyage*, was published much later, in 1774, and gives a highly personal account of his travels. He does not flatter Italy: with the exception of Florence, he knew of no other country with so few beautiful women; its hotels were worse than those in Germany and the food served in them was not only half of the quantity served in France, but much less well prepared. A true Bordelais, groomed from birth to be sniffy about Italian wine, he thought the glasses were too small and the wines 'insipid'.

Montaigne was followed, two centuries later, by another resolutely unimpressed French traveller. 'You cannot enjoy the company of the Lucchesi', wrote Stendhal in 1800, 'because they are all, even the children, continually occupied at their business and in acquiring goods by means of trade. Therefore the city is somewhat tiresome and disagreeable for strangers.' There is still no evidence that Lucca's waters cure kidney stones, but we know that Montaigne served the city of Bordeaux with distinction for four years, and lived a further seven years after that.

Collodi

Beyond the stream, a mosaic and an obelisk constitute a monument to the puppet Pinocchio, hero of the famous book of that name. It is a production in somewhat dubious taste . . .

(Archibald Lyall, *The Companion Guide to Tuscany*)

In the town of Collodi, about 15 kilometres east of Lucca, is a memorial to a Florentine writer, Carlo Lorenzini. Born in Florence in 1826, he was a successful author of children's books and chose the pen name of Carlo Collodi, after the town in which his mother was born. It is now the home of the Carlo Collodi Foundation, a cultural institution dedicated to children's literacy, and comprises a Children's Library and the International Study Centre for Children's Literature. But the highlight of the Foundation is Pinocchio Park, featuring Collodi's best-known puppet and his anthropomorphic cricket.

Pinocchio Park is not so much a theme park in the homogenised Disney sense as an animated morality tale for children: a homily for the indolent and untruthful. The park is a dynamic work of art: a literary ramble marked out by mosaics, buildings and sculptures, and set amid art and nature. The winding path threads through dense vegetation, so that every stage on the route comes as a surprise, the plants and trees contributing to recreate episodes in Collodi's stories. The park holds various cultural activities throughout the year: exhibitions of art and illustrations inspired by children's literature and the story of Pinocchio, puppet-making workshops, puppet and marionette shows and minstrels.

❧ 5 ❧

PISA

City of Miracles

Pisa is a fine old city.

(Tobias Smollett, *Travels through France and Italy*)

Having decided to use public transport, Pisa seemed the obvious
hub from which to reach northern and coastal Tuscany: its railway
station is on direct lines to Livorno, La Spezia, Viareggio, Lucca
and Florence, and its international airport is 1 kilometre from the
station. It also has a magnificent cathedral, baptistery, and a bell
tower that is one of the wonders of the world. Like Florence, it is on
the Arno, and its literary credentials are impeccable: Shelley, Byron,
Smollett, the Brownings, Dickens, James, Twain, Landor – and
many more – lived there.

Its main visitor attraction is one of the most famous monuments
in the world. As I walk up the Via Nicola Pisano, the domes and
pinnacles of the Campo dei Miracoli – the Field of Miracles –
appear, disappear and reappear like a mirage. Eventually, a cluster of
eleventh- to fourteenth-century buildings set in green lawns comes
into view: Pisa's Duomo, Baptistery and the most visited tower in
the world. Externally, the three buildings are a mix of Romanesque
and Gothic architectures with a touch of Moorish – yet the whole
harmonises as if planned. Of the Duomo, Henry James said, 'Of
the smaller cathedrals of Italy I know none I prefer to that of Pisa;
none that, on a moderate scale, produces more the impression of a
great church.' It is small outside but appears larger inside.

A young Mark Twain saw its political potential:

The Duomo, close at hand, is one of the finest cathedrals in Europe. It is eight hundred years old. Its grandeur has outlived the high commercial prosperity and the political importance that made it a necessity, or rather a possibility. Surrounded by poverty, decay and ruin, it conveys to us a more tangible impression of the former greatness of Pisa than books could give us.

He was also somewhat indifferent to the whole city and found Pisa an enigma: 'Pisa is believed to be about three thousand years old. It was one of the twelve great cities of ancient Etruria, that commonwealth which has left so many monuments in testimony of its extraordinary advancement, and so little history of itself that is tangible and comprehensible.'

The Duomo's most striking feature, the one to which the green Michelin guide gives its highest accolade, is Nicola Pisano's pulpit. The Pisans were renowned for their relief sculpture: their work is seen as far south as Monreale in Sicily. Nicola worked in the Pisa Baptistery for a decade in the early fourteenth century, and his masterpiece, the hexagonal pulpit, with its porphyry columns and interwoven statues, was so famous that when the city of Siena commissioned him to create one for its own Duomo, it demanded a pulpit similar to that of Pisa. He died before this task was completed and his son Giovanni completed the work. John Ruskin saw the Pisanos' work in the Duomo of Pisa as 'native Etruscan – the race has held its own to this day; one of them drove me last night, with the same black eyes that are inlaid on the font of Pisa.'

But the miracle that most visitors have come to see is neither the Duomo nor the Baptistery, for all their beauty: it is the Campanile – the bell tower. Everyone knows what it looks like, but the real thing is not at all like the postcards: Dickens, having formed his impression from a shop window in St Paul's Churchyard, was disappointed. 'The moon was shining when we approached Pisa, and for a long time we could see, behind the wall, the leaning tower, all awry in the uncertain light; the shadowy original of the old pictures in school books and schooltimes, it was too small. I

16 *The Leaning Tower, Pisa*

felt it keenly.' Like Dickens, the American writer Henry James was familiar with the image of the tower from childhood, as he describes in circumlocutory Jamesian:

> Few of us can have had a childhood so unblessed by contact with the arts as that one of its occasional diversions shan't have been a puzzled scrutiny of some alabaster model of the Leaning Tower under a glass cover in a back-parlour. Pisa and its monuments have, in other words, been industriously vulgarised, but it is astonishing how well they have survived the process.

The most striking difference between the real thing and the picture postcards is that the photographs were taken when the Field of Miracles was deserted. Today – and every day – it is full of people.

The Torre Pendente, Pisa's Leaning Tower, is by far the city's main tourist attraction – and among the world's – not for its inherent beauty, although it is beautiful, but because its top leans almost 4 metres to the south-east. Whilst the revenue in admission fees and sales of plaster replicas must delight its managers, the Opera Primaziale Pisana, it must surely be frustrating for lovers of Renaissance architecture to see the tourist hordes queueing to pay €15 for the disorienting experience of climbing its 296 steps – or 294, depending which side you climb – while, barely 100 metres away across grassy lawns, one of the world's most magnificent cathedrals stands gleaming in the sunshine, relatively ignored.

It is now generally accepted that the white marble bell tower, the building of which began in 1173, was already leaning when its construction was less than half finished. Tobias Smollett, who climbed it in 1765, almost six hundred years after it was built, goes as far as to say, in his *Travels through France and Italy*, not only that the tower was built aslant from the vertical, but intentionally so. 'I should never have dreamed', he wrote, 'that this inclination proceeded from any other cause than an accidental subsidence of the foundation on this side, if some connoisseurs had not taken great pains to prove it was done on purpose by the architect'.

The angle of lean of the tower depends on which author you read. Smollett claimed that the variance from the vertical was 16 feet (4.9 metres); to Dickens, 80 years later, it was 'barely apparent'; yet, 22 years on, the journalist Mark Twain reported it as 13 feet (3.96 metres). The variance is now officially 12 feet 9½ inches (3.89 metres), thus proving either that the tower has grown straighter since Smollett's visit, or that journalists tend to be more reliable witnesses than novelists.

In October of the year of Smollett's visit, Pisa was the penultimate stop in Italy of biographer James Boswell, when he left for Livorno and Corsica. On seeing the tower, he was moved to make what was his only recorded comment on the architecture of Italy: 'with great modesty [I] proposed doubt if the wind had bowed it'.

The tower had a narrow escape in 1945, during the last weeks of the war in Europe, when a group of soldiers from the US Army passed through and found themselves under fire from German snipers, who they thought were hiding in the tower. The Americans' group commander, deciding that the appropriate retaliation would be to destroy the tower, ordered up the necessary heavy artillery, but either by chance or thanks to some sense of history on the part of his superiors, before his plan could be carried out, he was ordered to another position and the tower survived undamaged – as did the commander. The only war injury suffered by the tower was to have one of its marble columns destroyed by Italian anti-aircraft fire. No aircraft were damaged.

It was not until the 1970s that experts began to worry that, with the tower moving a millimetre or two every year, unless something were done, it would fall flat on its south-eastern face, and that, while a tower with a tilt of 5 degrees might be one of the world's wonders, a horizontal one was unlikely to pull in any tourists.

In the 1980s a worldwide call was made for solutions to the problem, eliciting hundreds of proposals, ranging from the inspired to the bizarre, and in 1990 the tower was closed while the alternatives were considered. After three years' deliberation, the authorities chose the most mundane and least aesthetic solution: to attach huge lead weights to the north-west side of the tower, in the hope of lowering the tower's centre of gravity. It did not take the Opera Primaziale Pisana long to notice that several tonnes of lead stuck half-parenthetically on one side of the tower detracted from its beauty, and it was decided that the only acceptable solution had to be below ground, and the unleaded tower reopened in 2001.

The tower is now more popular than ever in all its Romanesque splendour, appearing to be held securely at 4.8 degrees from the vertical by those thousands of public-spirited people who stand in profile beside it with their hands raised, palms outwards, while their friends photograph them in the pretence of holding the tower upright.

Pisa was Percy and Mary Shelley's next stop – except for a brief stay in Florence – after they were flooded out of Livorno. The rains that drove them out were followed by frosts and snow in the severe winter of 1818/19, Tuscany's worst in 70 years. The couple found a villa beside the Arno, in the Tre Palazzi di Chiesa, which overlooks the river by the Ponte alla Fortezza. 'Our roots were never struck so deeply as at Pisa,' wrote Shelley afterwards.

The English poet Walter Savage Landor, who was in Pisa at this time, refused to meet Shelley because of his treatment of his first wife. Landor, who first arrived in Pisa in 1818 at the age of 43, was no lover of the city: 'Pisa has the advantage of a river, 200 feet wide, running through its principal street, but it is infested with English and Irish moschitos.' He left soon afterwards for Florence, where, except for a 22-year period in England, he remained until his death 46 years later. Of his snubbing of Shelley in Pisa, he wrote later, 'I blush in anguish at my prejudice and injustice.'

One of Shelley's more urgent tasks in Pisa was to get rid of Claire Clairmont. Mary had begun to feel that Shelley's relationship with her half-sister had become rather more than that of a brother-in-law, and it was decided that Claire should go to live in Florence. Shelley took her there, staying overnight – a matter of some conjecture among his biographers – and returned, not with Claire, but with a new guest: his cousin, the poet Thomas Medwin, with whom he was planning a joint project to translate Dante's *Divine Comedy* into English – Shelley having long felt that no good translation yet existed.

Byron had left England in 1816 because, he said, he could no longer bear its 'puritan conventionalism', but more probably because of mounting debts and the scandal of an incestuous affair with his half-sister. Landor once wrote of him, 'Whenever he wrote a bad poem, he supported his sinking fame by some signal act of profligacy: an elegy by a seduction, a heroic by an adultery, a tragedy by a divorce.' After many more affairs, Byron began an assignation in Venice with a 20-year-old Italian countess, Teresa Guiccioli, recently married to a wealthy 60-year-old landowner. Byron had promised that when Teresa and her strangely compliant husband returned from Venice to their home in Ravenna, he, Byron, would return to England, but at the Count's invitation he finally changed his mind and followed the couple to Ravenna, complete with his usual entourage of carriages, servants, horses, monkeys, cats and dogs.

At first, affections between Byron and Teresa were less than equal: Teresa wrote many years later that he was 'noble and exquisitely beautiful. His voice, his manners, the thousand enchantments that surrounded him, rendered him so different and so superior a being . . . that it was impossible he should not have left the most profound impression on me.' Byron's patronising appraisal of Teresa was that she had 'talent enough to value mine, but not sufficient to be able to shine herself'.

Having joined Teresa, her husband and his family in the Palazzo Guiccioli in Ravenna, Byron received a further request from Claire – already back living with the Shelleys in Pisa – that she might come and collect their daughter Allegra, and take her to spend the summer with them in Bagni di Lucca. Byron had little confidence in the Shelley ménage's ability to look after Allegra: they had, after all, already lost two children of their own, and he felt that Shelley's other-worldliness, combined with his atheism, tended to cast some doubt on his foster-parenting capabilities. Not that Byron offered much better for his daughter, having left her with nuns in Venice.

In August of 1821, Shelley came to visit Byron in Ravenna, and tried to resolve the Allegra problem by persuading him and Teresa to leave Ravenna and move to Pisa. Shelley rented for the pair a magnificent Renaissance palace, Palazzo Lanfranchi, on the north bank of the Arno, diagonally opposite their Tre Palazzi di Chiesa, from where Shelley wrote to a friend, 'We expect Lord Byron here in about a fortnight. I have just taken the finest palace in Pisa for him and his luggage, and all his train are, I believe, already on their way hither. I dare say you have heard of the life he led at Venice, rivalling the wise Solomon almost, in the number of his concubines'.

The Palazzo Lanfranchi is the only building on that side of the river with its own stone landing-steps cut into the river wall, cut there centuries ago to allow English wool to be unloaded. The steps made it convenient for Shelley, once Byron was installed, to come and call, crossing the river in his skiff; nightly crossings that may have inspired his poem 'Evening: Ponte al Mare, Pisa':

> Within the surface of the fleeting river
> The wrinkled image of the city lay,
> Immovably quiet, and forever
> It trembles, but it never fades away

Byron's Palazzo Lanfranchi is still extremely well preserved – appropriately, since it now houses the Tuscan State Archives. A plaque in Italian on the outside of the building reads:

GEORGE GORDON NOEL BYRON
LIVED HERE FROM AUTUMN 1821 TO SUMMER 1822
AND WROTE SIX CANTOS OF DON JUAN

Although Byron wrote much of *Don Juan* when he was only 33 years old, so much of it reveals his fear of advancing age that one wonders if he, like Shelley, might have had some premonition of early death:

17 *The Palazzo Lanfranchi, home of Lord Byron, Pisa*

> My days of love are over; me no more
> The charms of maid, wife, and still less of widow,
> Can make the fool of which they made before.

The Shelleys' own apartment, across on the southern side of the river, carries no plaque: the building was destroyed by Allied bombers in 1944.

Further downriver on the same side is a perfect miniature Gothic church with its feet in the water: the white marble Santa Maria della Spina (Maria of the Thorn, representing the thorn in the crown of Jesus), built in 1230 and raised in the nineteenth century to prevent further intrusion by the river. Ruskin called it 'the Gothic spirit at its greatest'.

Another literary guest in the Palazzo Lanfranchi was Byron's and Shelley's friend, the critic, essayist and poet Leigh Hunt. Hunt, newly arrived from England with his tubercular wife and their children, occupied the ground floor. Hunt lost no time in recording his impressions of Pisa:

> Let the reader imagine a small white city, with a tower leaning at one end of it, trees on either side, and blue mountains for the background. Add to this, in summertime, fields of corn on all sides, bordered with hedgerow trees and festoons of vines hanging from tree to tree, and he may judge of the impression made upon an admirer of Italy who is in Tuscany for the first time. . . . On entering the city, the impression is not injured. What looked white in the distance remains as pure and fair on closer acquaintance.

Hunt's enjoyment of Pisa leaps out with every word of his journals: 'the first novelty that strikes you . . . is the singular fairness and new look of houses that have been standing hundreds of years. Antiquity refuses to look ancient in Italy.'

Hunt also commented on his host's working habits: 'Lord Byron used to sit up at night writing *Don Juan* (which he did under the influence of gin and water), and rose late in the morning. He breakfasted, read; lounged about, singing an air, generally out of Rossini; took a bath, and was dressed; and coming downstairs was heard, still singing, in the courtyard'.

Because of some violent capers in Ravenna by the more unruly members of her husband's family, Teresa's brothers-in-law needed to make themselves scarce until the legal proceedings were over. The ever-resourceful Byron provided them with yet another villa, this time on a coastal hillside in Montenero, just south of Livorno. Today, the Villa Byron, like the Palazzo Lanfranchi, is still in excellent condition. To reach it you have to catch a *funiculare*, then climb the Via Byron to the very top of the hill, where a delightful cream and white villa gazes west towards the sea, looking much too elegant for a fugitives' hideout.

In May of 1823, less than a year after Shelley was drowned, Byron, despite his deteriorating health, decided to go to Greece with Teresa's brother, Count Pietro, but could not bring himself to break the news to her, so left without doing so. He never returned. A year later, he caught a chill while riding in the rain in Missolonghi and died of the ensuing fever. Teresa returned briefly to her husband, but then married the French Marquis de Boissey, who died, leaving her a villa at Settebello. Angered by what she saw as biased or sensationalised biographies of Byron, Teresa spent the last seven years of her life writing her own version. She put it away with all their letters and souvenirs, and died. The fact that her book, *The Life of Lord Byron in Italy* is still in print indicates that Byron was wrong: her talent was more than 'sufficient to be able to shine herself' – how sad that neither of them ever knew.

Two decades later, Pisa was the first Italian home of Robert and Elizabeth Barrett Browning after their marriage at London's St Marylebone Parish Church and their famous elopement to escape from Elizabeth's tyrannical father. Their stay in Pisa turned out to be brief: they arrived in October 1846 with Elizabeth's maid and her dog, the literary cocker spaniel whose autobiography, *Flush*, was ghost-written by Virginia Woolf and published in 1933 – 'to stem the [financial] ruin we shall suffer from the failure of *The Waves*'. Browning was 34, small and dapper, Elizabeth was 40, even smaller and frail. The following spring they set off on what was intended to be a tour of Italy, with the intention of returning to Pisa to live, but reached only as far as Florence because Elizabeth fell in love with that city and, as we know, they remained there until her death 14 years later.

Tobias Smollett almost chose Pisa as his Tuscan home: 'Pisa is a fine old city,' he wrote in his *Travels through France and Italy*, 'the number of inhabitants is very inconsiderable; and this very circumstance gives it an air of majestic solitude . . . and the solitude that reigns in Pisa would with me be a strong motive to choose it as a place of residence – not that this would be the only inducement for living at Pisa.' In the end, however, he chose to live in Livorno.

One writer came to Pisa, not from choice, but under armed guard. The expatriate American poet Ezra Pound was born in Hailey, Idaho in 1885 and raised in Philadelphia, Pennsylvania. He moved to London in 1908, where he lived for 16 years, and in 1924 he and his English painter wife, Dorothy, moved to Rapallo, on the Italian Riviera. Pound was a leading figure in the modernist movement, and edited and promoted the work of many of his contemporaries, in particular James Joyce, W. B. Yeats, Ernest Hemingway and T. S. Eliot. Eliot once said of him, 'Pound suffers from being seen as objectionably modern and objectionably antiquarian at the same time.' Nevertheless, Pound's astute but ruthless editing was a vital contribution to the success of such works as Eliot's *The Wasteland*. In beautiful Rapallo, writing and producing plays and concerts, Pound became a popular but eccentric local character, even as an enemy alien during the Second World War.

On 3 May 1945, two days before the end of the war in Europe, Pound was visited by two armed local ex-partisans, who, having heard that the Americans were offering a reward of half a million lire for Pound's 'capture', had come to arrest him. On 24 May, two weeks after Germany had surrendered unconditionally, the 60-year-old Pound was taken, under heavy military police guard and handcuffed to a burly military policeman, to the US Army Disciplinary Training Centre – a euphemism for a punishment camp – near the village of Metato, a few kilometres north of Pisa. Ezra Pound had had no trial; he had been given access to a lawyer, but the lawyer failed to mention that he was working for the prosecution. The instructions from Washington were concise: 'Afford no preferential treatment' – and they were carried out to the letter. Pound's 'cell' was one of those reserved for the most dangerous criminals or those under sentence of death by execution. It was a 2-metre-square wire cage with a concrete floor, open to the elements on all sides: from photographs it looked like a prototype for those in Guantánamo Bay. He was the only civilian out of almost four thousand military prisoners in the camp; he had no bed and was allowed no exercise or verbal communication; he was fully exposed to the Tuscan sun by day, and by night was watched under floodlights.

Pound's crime was that not only had he criticised his government, but that he had done so on (Fascist) Italian state radio. The content of his talks, which were monitored by the FBI, was both anti-war and anti-Semitic, and the fact that he had agreed to do the talks solely on condition that each broadcast would be preceded by a statement that he would not say anything 'contrary to his own conscience or his duties as an American citizen' was not taken into account. The American playwright Arthur Miller, hearing the broadcasts, denounced Pound in articles and speeches, saying, 'a greater calamity cannot befall the art than that Ezra Pound, the Mussolini mouthpiece, should be welcomed back.' Miller's wish was granted; but 11 years later he apologised for his earlier 'excitement'.

After more than two weeks under these conditions, Pound finally cracked: 'the raft broke and the waters came over me,' as he later wrote. He was taken to Washington to be tried for treason, the penalty for which was execution. His breakdown was probably a blessing, because psychiatrists decided he was mentally unfit to stand trial and he was transferred to a medical compound and given a bed, table and writing materials, and allowed exercise. Five months later, he was permitted a visit from his wife and daughter before being committed to St Elizabeth's Psychiatric Hospital in Washington DC. The Nuremburg trials were taking place and the national mood was unforgiving; Pound languished in St Elizabeth's for the next 12 years, still without trial. It was during this time that he completed his much-acclaimed *Pisan Cantos*, published in 1969.

In 1958, following a sustained campaign by fellow writers, including T. S. Eliot and Ernest Hemingway – who, in his speech of acceptance of the Nobel Prize for Literature in 1954, asked why Pound was still a prisoner – he was released from the hospital. He returned to Italy, living first in Rapallo and later in Venice, where he died in 1972. The English novelist P. G. Wodehouse made several voluntary trips to Berlin during the war to speak on German Fascist radio. Shrewder than Pound, Wodehouse claimed he had done it to greet his American fans. In 1975, shortly before his death at the age of 94, Wodehouse was knighted by the Queen.

❧ 6 ❧

LIVORNO

The Gateway City

A kind of polite Wapping, with a square and a theatre.
(Leigh Hunt, *The Liberal*)

Livorno is the port on Italy's western coast that has for many years been the visitors' seaboard gateway to Florence and Tuscany. John Milton arrived there by felucca from Genoa in 1638, and the city is still the entry point for many cruise passengers on their way to visit Florence and the many tourist attractions of Tuscany. Following the silting of the Arno below Pisa, which cut off Florence from the sea, the port of Livorno was established in the late sixteenth century, on the orders of the Grand Duke Ferdinando I, to whom a grateful city built the huge marble monument that overlooks the port. The statue is named *I Quatro Mori*, after the statues of four larger-than-life Moorish slaves in bronze struggling against their chains at its base, and was described by a cautious John Evelyn on his arrival in 1644 as 'in the judgement of most artists, one of the best pieces of modern work'.

In the eighteenth century, Livorno, known to the British as Leghorn, was important to the Royal Navy as a free port and supply centre, and when war broke out with the French in 1793 Captain Horatio Nelson was based there in command of a 64-gun man-of-war that later blockaded Toulon and attacked the Corsican port of Calvi (in which Nelson lost an eye). The literary history of Livorno, however, began, not in Tuscany, but in France – or a part of France that was Italy at the time: Nizza, now Nice. Until the late eighteenth century, the 120 miles of coastline in south-eastern France that is known today as the French Riviera was rarely visited, even by the French. It did not even feature in the Grand Tour.

Today, Nice and its surrounding regions welcome more than ten million visitors a year. One of the first of them, almost two-and-a-half centuries ago, was the 42-year-old Tobias Smollett. Asthmatic, consumptive and hypochondriac, he hoped that the Mediterranean climate would ease his respiratory problems. This objective achieved, he stayed in Nizza from 1763 to 1765, using the city as a base for journeys into Provence and Italy, visiting Lucca, Pisa, Florence, Livorno and Rome. His account of these journeys, *Travels through France and Italy*, published in 1766, became a bestseller of its day.

Two years later Smollett's reputation was tarnished by the publication of *A Sentimental Journey through France and Italy*, in which a rival novelist, Irish-born Laurence Sterne, author of *Tristram Shandy*, lampooned Smollett as 'the learned Smellfungus', whose journey was 'nothing but the account of his miserable feelings'. The charge stuck, as did adjectives such as 'cranky' and 'curmudgeonly', despite the claims of Smollett's admirers – among them this writer – that, in *Travels*, Smollett was not only heralding the then almost unique epistolary style of his next novel, *The Expedition of Humphry Clinker*, but introducing the persona of its principal character, the cantankerous but honest Matthew Bramble. In the end, Smollett had the last laugh. *Travels through France and Italy* is still in print, its most recent edition being published in 2010. Praised by George Orwell, who called Smollett Scotland's best novelist, for their 'intellectual honesty', Smollett's works have taken two centuries to achieve their rightful place in popular literature.

Two years after the publication of *Travels through France and Italy,* Smollett and his wife returned to Tuscany to live, staying first in Pisa, then at the Villa Giardino, high on the crepuscular hillside of Montenero, a few kilometres south of Livorno, close to where the Shelleys and Lord Byron chose to live half a century later. It was there that Smollett wrote, 'I am at present rusticated on the side of a mountain that overlooks the sea, in the neighbourhood of Leghorn, a most romantic and salutary situation,' and it was there also, three years later, on 17 September 1771, that his succession of illnesses finally took their toll and he died, only 50 years old, still within sight of his much-loved Mediterranean. The English writer and Tuscany resident, Olive Hamilton, for her *Paradise of Exiles: Tuscany and the British*, obtained the reports of Smollett's Italian doctor: his account of Smollett's death translates thus: 'Mr Smollett, a man of historical talent . . . suffers from colic, diarrhoea, convulsions, fever. . . . He died asthmatic and consumptive without trying to help himself.' Having earned his living solely by writing, Smollett left no fortune, and his widow, Ann, lived for a further 20 years in comparative penury, supported by faithful friends.

A century later, a Smollett admirer, Alexander Malcolm, made a pilgrimage in Smollett's footsteps and was shown over his house. Olive Hamilton quotes his words:

> There is none to be compared in point either of situation or elegance with the last abode of Smollett. . . . You may guess the feelings of a countryman and an ardent admirer of his genius, when I was shown the very bed where the poet's eyes were closed forever upon all terrestrial things, and also when the identical stadium was pointed out in which his last and most humorous work [*The Expedition of Humphry Clinker*] was begun and finished.

The importance of Smollett's contribution to the English novel has been attested by many writers who came after him, but none has done so more emphatically than Charles Dickens, who, as a boy, read and reread Smollett's works in his father's library, acknowledging their influence both in his journal and through the words of his own favourite character, David Copperfield: 'My father had left a small collection of books in a little room upstairs, to which I had access (for it adjoined my own) and which nobody in our house ever troubled.' Through Copperfield, Dickens lists his favourite characters from his childhood reading: the 'heavenly host who kept alive my fancy'. The first three names on the list were Smollett creations, some of which found their way into Dickens's works; Smollett's biographer Jeremy Lewis describes Emilia, in Smollett's *The Adventures of Peregrine Pickle* as 'all of Dickens's heroines: . . . a saccharine embodiment of goodness'.

Dickens's first view of Livorno was 'from the summit of a lofty hill beyond Carrara'. He saw it as 'a purple spot in the flat distance. Nor is it only distance that lends enchantment to the view; for the fruitful country, and the rich woods of olive-trees through which the road subsequently passes, render it delightful.' He called Livorno 'a thriving, business-like, matter-of-fact-place, where idleness is shouldered out of the way by commerce'. Seventy-four years after Tobias Smollett's death, Dickens diverted from his own Grand Tour to pay his tribute in the city that he described in *Pictures from Italy* as 'made illustrious by Smollett's grave'.

My own attempts at finding Smollett's tomb 160 years later were less successful: the lock of the cemetery gate was rusted over. I asked the only person I could see – a fireman at the nearby Misericordia – how to get inside, and he told me to stand beneath an open window that overlooked the cemetery and shout 'Antonio'. The large key that narrowly missed me was as rusty as the lock, and when I asked Antonio how I might return it, he said to leave it with the *pompiere*.

It was a hard-hat zone, with mosquitoes. Inside, monuments lay mangled by tree roots, and cracked tombstones, their inscriptions covered in moss, leaned drunkenly against each other for support. Deciding that I would never find Smollett's tomb without a bull-dozer, I returned the key to the fireman. It did not seem to have been in great demand: the cemetery had not been used as such for many years. Olive Hamilton, 40 years before me, had fared better: she found a 'gray marble pyramid with a Latin inscription'.

As I left the cemetery, I noticed on the inside wall a lichen-covered marble slab whose message was barely readable:

THIS BURIAL PLACE OF THE BRITISH NATION RESIDING
IN LEGHORN WAS SURROUNDED WITH A LOW WALL AND
RAILD WITH IRON RAIL IN THE YEAR OF OUR LORD
1746.

Back in Livorno a year later, I thought I might have one more try at finding Smollett. This time the *pompiere* recognised me and opened the gate – with pride, for there were signs of restoration: the mosquitoes still waited in anticipation, but the tombstones had been re-erected in orderly rows, the unruly vegetation had been cut back, and there, in the farthest corner of the cemetery, stood a tall, narrow obelisk, on the base of which were hewn in Latin some words, of which I could understand only a name, but which translated as:

IN MEMORY OF
TOBIAS SMOLLETT,
WHO DIED IN LIVORNO ON
16 SEPTEMBER 1773 [SIC]
THIS TOMB WAS ERECTED BY FRIENDS
AND FELLOW CITIZENS

Like this memorial, erected on the second anniversary of his death, Smollett's old home, the Villa Giardino, still stands, looking out over the islands of the Tuscan archipelago and a cluster of quiet, oleander-lined streets, one of which carries a sign reading: 'Via Tobia Smollet, Scrittore Inglese, 1721–1771'.

Another cemetery in Livorno houses the remains of 'Baron' Seymour Kirkup, who was born in London in 1788. A painter more than a writer, he had many friends in the literary community, and came to Livorno after his first marriage in Florence at the age of 68. He died at the age of 92, and his remains now lie buried alongside those of his daughter Imogene in Livorno's 'new' Protestant cemetery – built to replace the one in which Smollett's remains had been buried more than a century earlier.

For a jaded Mark Twain, about to sail for home after his Mediterranean cruise, Livorno was one Tuscan city too many: 'We shall not go ashore in Leghorn. We are surfeited with Italian cities for the present, and much prefer to walk the familiar quarter-deck and view this one from a distance.'

The poet Percy Bysshe Shelley and his wife Mary came to live in Livorno in 1820 from Bagni di Lucca, following the deaths in infancy of their children, and lived in the Villa Valsovana in the southern hills near to Smollett's old house. Mary described it later as,

> situated in the midst of a *podere* [smallholding]; the peasants sang as they worked beneath our windows during the heat of a very hot summer, and at night the water-wheel creaked as the process of irrigation went on and the fire-flies flashed from among the hedges; nature was bright, sunshiny, and cheerful, or diversified by storms of a majestic terror such as we had never before witnessed.

On Shelley's advice, his and Byron's friend, the English writer Leigh Hunt, travelled to Tuscany by sea. It was a nightmare voyage. They embarked in London on 15 November 1821, but the ship, damaged by storms in the Channel, had to put in to Plymouth for repairs. There, Hunt's wife became seriously ill, and they did not leave until May 1822, arriving at Livorno in June 1822. It was the same port from which, a few days later, Shelley, with his friend Ned Williams, sailed his schooner *Ariel* on their last tragic journey, just weeks before Shelley's thirtieth birthday.

The Scottish biographer James Boswell spent some days in Livorno in 1765 and caught up with his mail while waiting for a boat for Corsica, where, on the recommendation of Swiss-born philospher Jean-Jacques Rousseau, he was hoping to meet the island's leader, General Pasquale Paoli, who, 10 years earlier, had won the island's independence from Genoa. Boswell wrote to Rousseau with his usual histrionics: 'In half an hour I embark for Corsica. I am going directly to the territories of Paoli. I am all vigour, all nobility. If I perish on this expedition, think of your Spanish Scot with affection, and we shall meet in the paradise of imaginative souls. If I return safely you will have a valuable account. Death is nothing to me.' The 'valuable account' was Boswell's *The Journal of a Tour to Corsica and Memoirs of Pascal Paoli*, published in 1768, which both established Boswell's credibility as a diarist and biographer and raised awareness of Corsica in England before it became, temporarily, a British colony.

Henry James did not find enough of architectural or artistic value in Livorno to lure him away from his usual Tuscan haunts.

> The most striking fact as to Leghorn, it must be conceded at the outset, is that, being in Tuscany, it should be so scantily Tuscan. The traveller curious in local colour must content himself with the deep blue expanse of the Mediterranean. The streets, away from the docks, are modern, genteel and on a rectangular plan; Liverpool might acknowledge them if it weren't for their clean-coloured, sun-bleached stucco. Of interesting architecture, Leghorn is singularly destitute. It has neither a church worth one's attention, nor a municipal palace, nor a museum, and it may claim the distinction, unique in Italy, of being the city of no pictures.

The normally precise James seems to have overlooked at least seven museums and twenty churches, of which the most striking is the octagonal Santa Caterina in the Venetian Quarter, with its Baroque interior and its Renaissance treasure, Giorgio Vasari's altarpiece, *The Coronation of the Virgin*. James's visit appears also to have preceded the reconstruction of the city's fifteenth-century Duomo. More recently, the city has enjoyed a reputation for contemporary art as a result of having been the birthplace in 1884 of the famous modern Italian painter and sculptor, Amedeo Modigliani. Since Modigliani, it is no longer a city of no pictures.

The descriptions by both Dickens and James are to some extent true: the Livorno of today is unashamedly a post-war city. Its pavements, tastefully lined with modern loggias, are sheltered from sun and rain, and the city has a clean, modern look; the result of thoughtful reconstruction following the damage inflicted in more than ninety air raids by Allied bombers during the Second World War.

18 *The Duomo, Livorno*

༂ 7 ༂

AREZZO

The Roman City

Think you, if Laura had been Petrarch's wife,
Would he have written sonnets all his life?   (Byron, *Don Juan*)

Arezzo is Tuscany's Tuscany; it lies in the region's south-eastern corner, so is close to the heart of Italy. It ticks all the archaeological boxes: Etruscan remains dating back seven centuries before Christ; a Roman amphitheatre, medieval ramparts, Gothic churches and Renaissance palazzi. All it seems to lack is evidence of its brief period of French occupation, Napoleon having left hurriedly on forced retirement to another part of Tuscany – the island of Elba.

Arezzo's museums house many relics showing that the city was an important centre for the Etruscans – that mysterious race that gave Tuscany its name – to be followed by the Romans in the fourth century BC. Many Roman ruins remain, but the historic quarters are still predominantly medieval. Arezzo's most prosperous period was before the town was taken over by Florence in 1348. Its wealth came not just from its abundant crops, but from trade, first in wool and textiles and later in olive oil and wine. It continued to prosper through the exploitation of a traditional Tuscan skill, becoming an internationally known centre for the manufacture of jewellery – literally the city's golden age. Its tourism industry is profitable, but not to the same extent as for package-tour leaders such as Florence and Pisa.

The highlight of a visit to Arezzo is the old town, which surrounds the sloping Piazza Grande, where the Romans had their forum.

It is a warren of narrow, winding streets and palaces, dominated by a sixteenth-century Medici fortress built by Cosimo I, the first of the Medici rulers, as a watchtower. It now provides impressive views of the surrounding countryside: rolling hills, vineyards and olive groves, punctuated by tall cypresses. Like most ancient Italian towns, the historic part of the city was built, defensively, on top of a hill, which means it is almost invisible on arrival by train. Rail engineers did not like hills, so the town came down to the railway, building new wide streets named, not after saints by this time, but with nineteenth-century names such as Piazza Risorgimento and Piazza della Repubblica.

I had special reasons to come to Arezzo. Not only has it strong literary associations – it was the birthplace of Francesco Petrarca – but it has generated, for its size, a disproportionate share of famous progeny, especially in the arts, and it honours them in its street names. In addition to the Via Petrarca, the Via Giorgio Vasari and the Via Piero della Francesca (who lived and died in nearby Sansepolcro),

19 The Piazza Grande, Arezzo

there is the Via Mecenate, recalling Maecenas, a Roman of Etruscan descent who was born here in 70 BC and rose to become a sort of culture minister to the Emperor Augustus and an entry in *The Oxford English Dictionary* meaning enlightened patronage of the arts. In the middle of the Piazza Guido Monaco on Arezzo's main street stands an impressive statue honouring the eleventh-century Benedictine monk who invented musical notation and identified the notes by the initial syllables of a favourite hymn: do-re-mi . . . I have not yet found a Via Michelangelo, which seems fair, since only 13 kilometres away there is a whole village named after him.

The three greatest writers in Italian history were all Tuscans, and the natal homes of all three were on my 'must see' list. One of them, the poet Francesco Petrarca – known to us as Petrarch – was born in Arezzo in 1304. Petrarch's poetry was esteemed and imitated by many writers who followed him. His English contemporary, Geoffrey Chaucer, in his *Canterbury Tales*, rather generously credits Petrarch with the Oxford Clerk's tale. The story actually came from Boccaccio, but Chaucer could not think how that name might be written – or read – in Chaucerian English.

> As preved by his wordes and his werk
> Fraunceys Petrak, the lauriat poete.

Chaucer was a Petrarch admirer, and came to Florence in 1373 in the hope of meeting him, but there is no evidence that they met. I have found Petrarch the more difficult and less joyful of the two, but perhaps he had less to be joyful about: he left Arezzo with his parents at the age of 9 to follow the papacy to Avignon, as many good Tuscan Catholics did at the time. He studied law in Montpellier and entered the Church, but was more interested in writing. The family returned to Florence, but in 1326 the 22-year-old Petrarch went back to Avignon, and on Good Friday of the following year, caught sight of the beautiful Laura on her way out of church after the Easter Mass, and fell hopelessly in love. He gave up the Church so that he might marry her, but she refused him, presumably because she was already married. We are not sure who Laura was, or even if that was her real name, but like Dante and his Beatrice, Petrarch's love for Laura became his inspiration, and her rejection of it his literary spur. While most men have a Laura or two in their lives and recover, Petrarch felt it necessary to immortalise his unrequited passion in over three hundred sonnets. As the sceptical Roxy, in Sinclair Lewis's *World so Wide* puts it: 'all about a girl he never even made'. In his early thirties Petrarch managed to suspend his grief for long enough to father two illegitimate children, one of whom died in the plague, but after Laura's death in 1348 – probably also from the plague – he confessed, in his 'Letter to Posterity',

> In my younger days I struggled constantly with an overwhelming but pure love affair – my only one, and I would have struggled with it longer had not premature death, bitter but salutary for me, extinguished the cooling flames. I certainly wish I could say that I have always been entirely free from desires of the flesh, but I would be lying if I did.

On his own death in 1374, at his house in the town of Arquà, near Padua, on the eve of his seventieth birthday, he bequeathed to his old friend and fellow poet Boccaccio 50 gold florins 'to buy a warm winter dressing gown'. Sadly, Boccaccio was able to snuggle in it for only one winter: he died the following year in his own natal home in Certaldo.

Having visited the birthplace of Dante, and made plans to see that of Boccaccio, La Casa del Petrarca became a key target for my stay in Arezzo. To miss the house where one of Italy's literary trinity was born would be like *The Three Musketeers* without Aramis. The little house in the Via dell'Orto seemed in keeping with Petrarch's lifestyle: it was austere and humble enough, but was it really the house in which Petrarch was born in 1304? The brochure says that it is, 'according to tradition'. I pay my €4 and am directed into a room lined floor-to-ceiling with books – mostly tattered paperbacks with hand-written spines, untouchable behind chicken-wire. This room leads to a similar room, then another, then another, then the exit. I estimate some 20,000 books in all, none of which seems to relate to Petrarch, especially as most were acquired in 1820 from the library of Francesco Redi, a local poet, physician famed for his research into maggots in meat and, evidently, as a book collector. Redi died 323 years after Petrarch, by which time the maggots would have had their revenge. There are some coins in a glass case and a few paintings, 'some of which', says the brochure, 'date back to the seventeenth century'.

I accept that Petrarch was born in 1304, but doubt if it was in this house, which I am told was rebuilt in the sixteenth century, *on top of* a fourteenth-century house. The only evidence I can find in support is that the well outside the front door is known as Tarlati's Well – the one mentioned by Boccaccio in one of his *Decameron* tales. I leave, not knowing if my literary pilgrimage was achieved. 'Petrarch's House', much restored in recent years, is now the Accademia Petrarca, an international centre for literature, art and science.

20 *Petrarch's house, Arezzo*

In addition to its architectural heritage, Arezzo is a treasury of art, famed for its eclectic range of native artists of all kinds. The province's best-known artist from the Renaissance period is Piero della Francesca, who created the outstanding frescoes in the Church of San Francesco di Arezzo depicting the legend of the True Cross – a work that he began in 1452 and finished 24 years later. Recently restored, they are Arezzo's most precious treasure, and were seen as a background in the successful British film, *The English Patient*.

Frescoes are a peculiarly Tuscan art form, in which the artist paints into the plaster as it sets, creating an almost indelible image. Della Francesca was one of the great masters of the form, and his work can be found in many of the villages of the region. The English writer Aldous Huxley, in his essay on della Francesca's painting *The Resurrection*, in nearby Sansepolcro, described it as 'the greatest painting in the world'. Huxley's words saved the painting from destruction during the liberation of Italy in 1945. As the village was being lined up as a target by the Allied artillery, the name Sansepolcro reminded one junior officer of Huxley's essay. The officer told his commander of Huxley's words, and a Plan B was established. It is not known if the commander ever returned to Sansepolcro, but years later the former junior officer, by then living in Capetown, South Africa, recounted his story to an English travel writer, H. V. Morton, who retold it in his *A Traveller in Italy*. In the same book, Morton also writes movingly of another della Francesca portrait, the *Madonna del Parto – The Pregnant Madonna*:

> She is one of the most beautiful of Piero della Francesca's women. Like all of this artist's pictures, this lingers in the memory, and afterwards I was haunted by it and wanted to see it again, as I was to do on three occasions. Every time I returned to see the fresco, it refreshed my mind like a great poem one has committed to memory.

The painting is in the mortuary chapel of a country cemetery, and has become a shrine for expectant mothers, who come to ask the Madonna for a trouble-free delivery.

✧

In the mountains that slope down to the valley of the river Tiber on its way to Rome, a winding road leads to the village of Caprese, a small settlement 13 kilometres north-east of Arezzo, where, in Morton's words, 'upon the sixth of March in the year 1475, an unexplainable miracle occurred when a nice, commonplace couple brought a genius down to earth.' The village has since, for obvious reasons, changed its name. It is now Caprese Michelangelo.

The cloister-like colonnades at the upper end of Arezzo's Piazza Grande were built by the local artist and historian, Giorgio Vasari, who was born here five hundred years ago. As already mentioned, he built the building that now houses the Uffizi Gallery in Florence. He was attending a dinner in Rome in 1546 when Cardinal Farnese suggested that there should be 'a catalogue of artists and their works, listed in chronological order'. Vasari took up the challenge, and four years later published his *The Lives of the Most Excellent Painters, Sculptors and Architects*, first published in 1550. Vasari dedicated the book to its sponsor, the Grand Duke of Tuscany, Cosimo I de' Medici

The fact that Cosimo I was its sponsor might also explain why Vasari's book is an unashamed eulogy for Florence and its artists – in particular Giorgio Vasari. He greatly admired Giotto, a Florentine, but did not accord comparable status to the more talented Duccio di Buoninsegna, a Sienese artist – not entirely for parochial reasons, but possibly also because Vasari would have been less familiar with Sienese artists' work – his book dates some of Duccio's work some thirty years after the painter's death.

Vasari's *Lives* – as it is known – made Vasari the world's first art historian. It also made him famous, and he never again wanted for prestigious commissions. The book is still in print, but is much criticised by modern art historians for its idiosyncratic selections, its inaccuracies and Vasari's blatant self-promotion – he was the Max Clifford of Renaissance artists. Nevertheless, his influence in the art world was still strong enough in 1877 for the respected critic John Ruskin, in his *Mornings in Florence*, to write, 'My general directions to all young people going to Florence or Rome would be very short: "know your first volume of Vasari".' Vasari's house in the Via XX Settembre in Arezzo was not his place of birth, but he did buy it. His fresco paintings there have lasted almost five centuries and now form part of the unquestionably authentic Vasari Museum.

Artists, writers and musicians apart, however, Arezzo's greatest pride is in its medieval architecture, which survived the bombardments of the Second World War relatively unscathed. The city is so lovingly but tastefully preserved that it looks like a film set – and often is. It was the setting, not only for Anthony Minghella's *The English Patient*, which in 1997 took nine Oscars, including the award for best picture, but also for Roberto Benigni's Oscar-winning film about wartime resistance, *La Vita è Bella* (*Life is Beautiful*), and parts of Franco Zeffirelli's *Tea with Mussolini*.

Arezzo itself may not be everyone's cappuccino – the Italian-American writer Barbara Grizzuti-Harrison wrote 'I tried hard to like Arezzo,' and, just as equivocally, a jaded Aldous Huxley, called it 'a boring sort of town, almost self-consciously devoid of effusion or prettiness'. Had he forgotten his unqualified admiration for the city's most important artist, or was the author of *The Art of Seeing* having an ocularly challenged day?

✿ 8 ✿

SAN GIMIGNANO

City of Towers

The fantastic towers of San Gimignano dominated each bend of the road like some persistent mirage. (Edith Wharton, *Italian Backgrounds*)

Like many of its neighbouring towns, San Gimignano is built on top of a hill – villages perched on hilltops were easier to protect against aggressors, pirates and plagues. Like those of its neighbours, the museums of San Gimignano exhibit tombs and other relics of its Etruscan roots, and, like many central Tuscan towns, it owed its medieval prosperity to the Via Francigena, the ancient trade and pilgrim route between Rome and northern and western Europe. Thanks to its location on this route, San Gimignano became an important commercial centre, its early wealth deriving primarily from *lo zafferano*: saffron from native crocuses grown in the shadow of its towers was being exported to England as early as the thirteenth century. Well-heeled citizens built houses with towers, partly as status symbols and partly as watchtowers against the warring cities to the north and south, and sometimes rivalling neighbours, each trying to over-tower the other. In 1311, the town's rulers passed a law forbidding constructions higher than their own, the Torre del Podestà, which topped out at 54.25 metres, after which a family could flaunt its wealth only by the number of towers it owned – over which there was no restriction. Today only about one-fifth of San Gimignano's original towers remain, but there are enough to give an impression of how the city would have looked in its prime. Seen from a distance in profile, it must

21 The towers of San Gimignano

have resembled a recumbent St Sebastian, or, as D. H. Lawrence put it, 'like an angry porcupine'.

E. M. Forster set his novel *Where Angels Fear to Tread* in San Gimignano. In the book he calls it Monteriano, but Forster's descriptions leave the reader in no doubt:

> as they climbed higher the country opened out, and there appeared, high on a hill to the right, Monteriano. The hazy green of the olives rose up to its walls, and it seemed to float in isolation between trees and sky, like some fantastic ship city of a dream. Its colour was brown, and it revealed not a single house – nothing but the narrow circle of the walls, and behind them seventeen towers – all that was left of the fifty-two that had filled the city in her prime.

There are coach tours from Pisa to San Gimignano, but, as usual, public transport is more interesting. A train takes you to Empoli, another from there to the melodic-sounding Poggibonsi, from which a sardine tin disguised as a bus covers the last circuitous 20 minutes to San Gimignano. Despite Forster's description in *Where*

Angels Fear to Tread, San Gimignano has no railway station. The problem at Poggibonsi is that the allegedly half-hourly bus carries only 30 people, and because other trains keep bringing more travellers, there are at least 50 people waiting for it. When I get on the bus, the driver tells me that I should have bought a ticket for €1 at the nearby bar. Knowing that if I go back to the bar for a ticket I will lose my place in the queue and miss the bus, and possibly the one after it, I do the only thing possible: I look forlorn. Fortunately, the driver has a solution: he sells me a ticket for €3.

The Italian-American author Barbara Grizzuti-Harrison had obviously arrived by the same route: 'I had the sensation, for the first time in Tuscany, not of passing but of being in the countryside, part (not merely an observer) of a gorgeous (and calm) crazy quilt of silver-green olive trees and flowering peach and cherry trees; as the yellow-and-red bus wound its way through the intricate sensual folds of hills dignified by cypress trees.'

But San Gimignano is worth every centime. If Disney were to make a medieval Italy, this is how it would look: skyscrapers sprout in all directions. There used to be 76 towers at one time, but some have fallen or have had houses built around them. By the town's official count, 15 towers remain, but literary assessments vary: Grizzuti-Harrison claims that only 14 remain out of an original 72, 'surrounded, on the narrow city streets, by palazzi, and modest houses, all higgledy-piggledy, with projecting Tuscan roofs'. Archibald Lyall, in *The Companion Guide to Tuscany*, claims 15 towers survive out of 72; and, as we saw, E. M. Forster identifies 17, from an original 52. The English poet and author Laurie Lee, in San Gimignano in the summer of 1949, came up with yet another number. The city was, he said,

> a place that makes the hair stand on end . . . on a hill surrounded by wild oak woods, & creaking with medieval secrets, nothing can have changed here for 600 years. 13 great stone towers clashing their bells & fresh memories of Dante at every step. It is quiet & still in the spicy yellow sun, & people sit in groups as though

sleeping in a dream of the past. There is no tourist sense here at all
. . . Nothing has stirred me so much.

I did not attempt to verify the tower count: it was never possible
to see them all at the same time.

Grizzuti-Harrison stayed in a hotel in the middle of the town,
in the triangular Piazza della Cisterna, which takes its name from
the *cisterna* (well) built in 1237 that still stands in the square, where
its ropes have worn deep grooves in the granite wall. Around the
piazza, medieval palaces lean against each other, some of them now
hotels: the palazzo Razzi with mullioned windows, the thirteenth-
century Salvestrini House, the Tortoli-Treccani Palace and the Lupi
Palace, with its strangely named Tower of the Devil.

In the north-western corner of the triangle, slightly hidden
from view, is the Duomo, with its two entrances: women to the
left and men to the right. In its Romanesque interior, an extra
fee admits you to the Chapel of Santa Fina, dedicated to the
city's second favourite saint, after San Gimignano himself. There
are many differing legends about the martyrdom of Santa Fina,
but most agree – and the Ghirlandaio fresco on the chapel wall,
painted in 1475 and picturing the painter himself, confirms – that
she died through fasting. She is said to have decided, as a child
of 10, to refuse food and drink, as penance for having taken an
apple from a boy, and she died five years later, severely emaciated.
The remains of Santa Fina lie in the altar of the chapel built in her
name, in a very small gilded casket.

While the factual reasons for Santa Fina's draconian diet are a
matter of debate among theologians, the fictional ones have no such
constraints: E. M. Forster, in *Where Angels Fear to Tread*, renamed
her Santa Deodata.

So holy was she that all her life she lay upon her back in the house
of her mother, refusing to eat, refusing to play, refusing to work.
The devil, envious of such sanctity, tempted her in various ways.
He dangled grapes above her, he showed her fascinating toys, he

pushed soft pillows beneath her aching head. When all proved vain he tripped up the mother and flung her downstairs before her very eyes. But so holy was the saint that she never picked her mother up, but lay upon her back through all, and thus assured her throne in Paradise. She was only fifteen when she died, which shows how much is within the reach of any schoolgirl.

Opposite the Duomo, on the other side of the piazza, is the Palazzo Communale, whose tower, the Torre del Podestà, effectively outlawed tower envy. Eleven years earlier, in 1300, in a room on its first floor, the council was addressed by a member of the Florentine priori, who urged them to join Florence in the Tuscan League. He never returned to Florence, and two years later was exiled for life. His name was Dante Alighieri.

22 *Piazza della Cisterna, San Gimignano*

The Italian film director Franco Zeffirelli set much of his autobiographical film *Tea with Mussolini* in San Gimignano. It is the story of a group of middle-aged expatriate women in 1930s Florence – played by indomitable English actresses of the Judi Dench/Joan Plowright school, with Americans Lily Tomlin and Cher added for American audiences – who complain to Mussolini about the violent behaviour of his followers in storming their favourite English tea rooms. Refusing to leave Florence despite pressure from the Blackshirts, the women are arrested and interned as enemy aliens in San Gimignano, where they take under their capacious wings a young boy, Luca (the youthful persona of Zeffirelli), whose mother has died and whose father has left home. The local church has the obligatory *trecento* frescoes that will be destroyed by the philistine *Fascisti* if someone doesn't stand up to them. The redoubtable Anglo-American women are not intimidated, so all ends well: the lad goes off to join the Resistance and the frescoes are saved for posterity. The film's scenario, incidentally, was written by another expatriate British writer in Tuscany, John Mortimer, creator of the popular television series *Rumpole of the Bailey*.

Visits to San Gimignano are best made out of season, or should include an overnight stay, or both: for not only is the town barely large enough to hold its own population and its vacationers, but it is also a comfortable day's outing from Florence and Siena, so it can be overwhelmed with day trippers.

Leaving through the gate in the massive outer wall at the southern end of the town feels as if you are leaving a sanctuary, there's a sense of exile reminiscent of Masaccio's fresco of Adam and Eve's expulsion from Paradise. The American author Edith Wharton may have known the sensation, as she described in her *Italian Backgrounds*:

> As we dashed out under the gateway of San Gimignano we felt the thrill of explorers sighting a new continent. It seemed, in fact, an unknown world which lay beneath us in the early light. The hills, so definitely etched at midday, at sunset so softly modelled,

had melted into a silver sea of which the farthest waves were indistinguishably merged in billows of luminous mist. Only the near foreground retained its precision of outline, and that too had assumed an air of unreality. Fields, hedges and cypresses were tipped with an aureate brightness which recalled the golden ripples running over the grass in the foreground of Botticelli's 'Birth of Venus.' The sunshine had the density of gold-leaf: we seemed to be driving through the landscape of a missal.

She wrote it a century ago, but nothing much has changed: apart from the antiquarians, the souvenir stalls and *gelaterie*. As I leave, I notice a familiar name on a plaque on the outside wall, and dig out my camera. The sign commemorates the visit, in May 1507, of the Secretary of the Florentine Republic, Niccolò Machiavelli.

Ten kilometres away, I turn back for another photograph. The towers of San Gimignano glow like funnels in the fading sun, confirming Forster's description: it is indeed 'some fantastic ship city of a dream'. It is no surprise that Zeffirelli chose these photogenic towers as his backdrop.

✌ 9 ✌

VOLTERRA

The Etruscan City

It was a city full of dread – a city of bitterness, outraged and very old.
(Edward Hutton, *Siena and Southern Tuscany*)

Volterra's history goes back for almost a millennium. It owed its political strength to its aura of impregnability, and in medieval times it repelled many attacks and sieges, but, once overcome by the Florentines in 1361, it was a hairless Samson, weak and vulnerable. Today it is a mysterious ruin – an aspect that must have encouraged the English writer D. H. Lawrence to go there. He concluded that 'no doubt Volterra was a city long before the Etruscans penetrated into it, and probably it never changed character profoundly. To the end, the Volterrans burned their dead: there are practically no long sarcophagi of *lucomones* [high priests].'

In his *Essays on Etruscan Places*, Lawrence wrote:

Volterra is the most northerly of the great Etruscan cities of the west. It lies back some thirty miles from the sea, on a towering great bluff of rock that gets all the winds and sees all the world, looking out down the valley of the Cecina to the sea, south over vale and high land to the tips of Elba, north to the imminent mountains of Carrara, inward over the wide hills of the Pre-Apennines, to the heart of Tuscany. Strange, dark old Etruscan heads of the city gate, even now they are featureless they have a peculiar, out-reaching life of their own. They were city deities of some sort.

Volterra is in western Tuscany, and although not far from the sea, it could never be called seaside. The following words by the English travel writer Edward Hutton in his book *Siena and Southern Tuscany* reveal his view of its touristic potential: 'No traveller can, I think, approach this outraged stronghold of old time without a certain apprehension and anxiety.'

Apprehension and anxiety are writers' most common first impressions here. Hutton, who walked there from San Gimignano, a distance of 20 kilometres, was intimidated even before he arrived.

> On either side of the way vast cliffs rose over immense crevasses seamed and tortured into shapes of ruined cities. Yonder a dreadful tower set with broken turrets tottered on the edge of sheer nothing: here a tremendous gate led into darkness; there a breached wall yawned over an abyss. If there be such a thing as traveller's fear, it is here you will meet it. As for me, I was horribly afraid, nor would any prayer I knew bring my soul back into my keeping.

Hutton's sense of foreboding was shared by Archibald Lyall in *The Companion Guide to Tuscany* as he approached 'gaunt Volterra'; even the intrepid Henry James, whose knowledge of Tuscany after a 40-year association could be called encyclopedic, seems not to have dared to venture there. Even in the world of fiction, terror-free first-timers in Volterra are rare: Bella Swan, the heroine of Stephenie Meyer's *New Moon*, although engaged to be married to Edward, a vampire, and unfazed by intimate association with demons, was conscious of 'a new kind of fear' at the sight of Volterra. 'As I stared at the ancient sienna walls and towers crowning the peak of the steep hill, I felt another, more selfish kind of dread thrill through me. I supposed the city was very beautiful. It absolutely terrified me.'

Volterra has retained its unique character thanks to its inaccessibility. Unless you are on the 'Bella and Edward' tour, Volterra is not on the average tourist itinerary. A bus from Florence or Siena can get you to Colle, 25 kilometres east of the town, from where a bus goes to Volterra, but only twice daily. In the end I took a train to coastal Cecina, at the mouth of the Cecina River, where Ali, the local taxi driver, agreed to take me to Volterra for a mere €100. When I demurred, the resourceful Ali rustled up a few more passengers to share the cost. Our approach, far from being fearful, was a pleasant drive between small vineyards and vast acres of sunflowers, gazing cyclopically in the same direction.

The French author Stendhal came to Volterra in May 1819, arriving by sea from Genoa. His main fear was of another rejection from the Countess Mathilde Dembowska, with whom he had fallen in love the previous year – 'the greatest event of my life' – but his persistence went unappreciated. Although she had told him not to bother her again, he turned up in Volterra in disguise. Yet again, he was, as he put it 'mal reçu', and left immediately for Florence. His rejection, like Petrarch's five centuries earlier, was to prove inspirational, and resulted in his philosophical discourse, *On Love.*

No less ominous was the visit of Bella Swan, the only human protagonist in *New Moon,* whose quest in Volterra is to release her vampire lover, Edward, from a suicide pact rashly sworn while they watched *Romeo and Juliet* together. Edward promised her that, should he ever learn that she had killed herself, he would, like Romeo, do the same. Unfortunately, someone who is evidently not the couple's best friend tells Edward that Bella has jumped off a cliff, and without waiting to check the facts, he rushes off to Volterra. The standard suicide procedure for fanged fiancés, according to author Meyer, is to go to Volterra and annoy the Volturi – the local 3,000-year-old coven – who are always pleased to assist. The distraught Bella, with the help of a friendly witch, steals a yellow Porsche Turbo and races after him, intent on proving that she has not topped herself. It is essential that this be done in person, and in front of the Palazzo dei Priori before the clock finishes striking twelve noon. Swan's way to achieve this is to fight her way through the crowded town and, to no one's surprise, reach Edward just on the stroke of twelve, so all is well. Why she could not just have telephoned is not explained.

During the summer months, the local Volterra Tourist Office runs a three-day package called *Sulle tracce di Edward e Bella* – On the Trail of Edward and Bella – which includes a pizza in a palazzo preceded by 'a blood red aperitif' and followed by a visit to a shop selling alabaster souvenirs.

D. H. Lawrence visited Volterra three times in the 1920s. He had been plotting his trip since he first encountered Etruscan relics at Fiesole at least four years earlier. He had long been interested in Etruscan culture and history, and in the lifestyle that disappeared with them when they were absorbed into Roman civilisation. He had written to his friend, Richard Aldington, in April 1926, explaining his interest in the Etruscan civilisation: 'the Etruscan things appeal *very much* to my imagination. They are so curiously natural – somebody said bourgeois, but that's a lie, considering all the phallic monuments,' and had promised his publisher a book on the subject. He died in 1930, leaving his collection of essays unfinished, and they were published in 1992 as *Sketches of Etruscan Places*. The book's editor, Simonetta de Filippis, professor of English literature at the University of Naples, says in her introduction, 'For Lawrence, the Etruscans were the keepers of the old, great secret of life, and when finally he came to write the book, they were to symbolise naturalness, spontaneity and simplicity – aspects of the positive civilisation which was dramatically antithetical to the modern, mechanical and corrupted world.'

Lawrence had already discovered the alabaster shops:

Everybody knows Volterra marble – so called – nowadays, because of the translucent bowls of it which hang under electric lights, as shades, in half the hotels of the world. It is nearly as transparent as alum, and nearly as soft. They peel it down as if it were soap and tint it pink or amber or blue, and turn it into all those things one does not want: tinted alabaster lampshades, light-bowls, statues, tinted or untinted, vases, bowls with doves on the rim, or vine-leaves, and similar curios.

An imposing building as you leave Volterra is the town gaol, formerly a castle. It left a lasting impression on Lawrence and his American friend:

> We walk up the hill and out of the Florence Gate, into the shelter under the walls of the huge medieval castle which is now a state prison. There is a promenade below the ponderous walls, and a scrap of sun, and shelter from the biting wind. A few citizens are promenading even now. And beyond, the bare green country rises up in waves and sharp points, but it is like looking at the choppy sea from the prow of a tall ship; here in Volterra we ride above all.

Two of the prisoners had escaped: 'Silently and secretly', wrote Lawrence, although he is unlikely to have been present at the time, 'they made effigies of themselves out of the huge loaves of hard bread the prisoners get. They laid them in bed so that when the warder's light flashed on them they would seem to be sleeping; the men escaped, and the governor was kicked out.' Lawrence thought this 'curious. He should have been rewarded for having such clever children, sculptors in bread.'

Other than Lawrence, few expatriate writers have shown more than passing interest in the town. The American Beat poet Lawrence Ferlinghetti, born in New York of Italian parents and brought up in France, could admire only Volterra's 'red tile roofs and lush green vineyards'.

A young sergeant in the US Army named William Zinsser – later to become professor of English at the University of Princeton and author of bestselling works on language, in particular *On Writing Well* – arrived at a US Army base near Livorno in 1945 to find the war over and nothing to do – 'I remember that we played a lot of baseball,' he wrote – and hit upon the idea of borrowing a company jeep for a day.

> The gravel road left the coast and climbed across a landscape of hills and farms and brought us to Volterra, an old Etruscan town,

hunched like a fortress on a hilltop. It was famous for its alabaster, and with the fervour of all tourists coming upon a local specialty of unsuspected beauty, we bought alabaster cigarette boxes and ashtrays for our unsuspecting families back home. The ancient city held us with its power, and it was mid-day before we pushed on.

The final comment is ironic only if you know that he was unlikely to have been able to reach Volterra before 11 a.m.

❧ 10 ❧

SIENA

The Medieval City

Announcing itself to us from a distance, it looked both proud and playful, arrayed across three hills and sprawling down the sides.
(William Zinsser, *Siena Revisited*)

Despite Siena's long civic rivalry with Florence, it was a twentieth-century Florentine poet, Mario Luzi, who called Siena 'simultaneously both reality and a dream'. Certainly one's first sight of Siena, astride its hilltops and surrounded by green, undulating countryside, is a chimerical one, a view that has inspired authors for centuries. My own first sight of the city, its terracotta walls and rooftops ablaze in the setting sun, took me back to my childhood, and a box of paints, one of whose tiny rectangles was labelled 'Burnt Sienna'. I had seen that colour again more recently, in the Italian Rooms at the National Gallery in London – in a work by Duccio di Buoninsegna, the fourteenth-century Sienese painter.

While not everyone might agree – certainly not the Florentines – with Siena's claim to be Tuscany's most beautiful city, it certainly comes close: and there is no doubt at all that it is the best-preserved medieval one, not only in Tuscany, but in Europe. Charles Dickens called it 'a bit like Venice without the water'. It is better to arrive in Siena, not by rail, but by bus, especially on a hot day, because the former involves a climb, the latter a descent – in both altitude and time. Sheltered behind its ancient city walls, traffic-free and devoid of television antennae, medieval Siena is a maze of narrow lanes and arched, cobbled and stepped alleys, which the Portuguese author

23 *The Palazzo Pubblico, Siena*

José Saramago called 'Timeless dwellings where I would love to live one day with a window of my own overlooking the clay tiles and green shutters'. As I walked down these lanes each turning revealed a new surprise – a fountained piazza, a flowery terrace or Renaissance palazzo (for beginners, the American author Sinclair Lewis, in his *World So Wide,* defined a palazzo: 'a large house, usually of stone, built a few hundred years ago for a very rich and very noble family who became rich and noble by conducting a war, with a large cut on the pillage, or by lending money to popes and kings and dukes who conducted wars').

The best was yet to come: those winding lanes converged on the vast Piazza del Campo, the political and emotional heart of Siena. The Campo is a vast area in the 'D' shape of a Greek amphitheatre – or an outsize baseball park – paved with russet bricks and divided, fan-like, into nine segments. The pitcher's mound is replaced by a shimmering fountain, the Fonte Gaia, while, on its southern side, behind the batter, soars the impressive Piazza della Signoria, completed in 1344, one of the oldest buildings in Italy to have maintained its original governmental function, with its graceful, crenellated, 102-metre-high Tower of Mangia, whose shadow measures the time of day around the Campo like a sundial. 'It was', wrote William Zinsser, arriving as one of a group of sightseeing GIs at the end of the Second World War, 'the most beautiful square I had ever seen, partly because it wasn't square; it was shaped like an opened fan. Anchoring the Campo was the handsome Palazzo Pubblico, or city hall, which had a bell tower so slender and audacious, so much taller than anyone would expect that it set a tone of high civic enjoyment.' Zinsser and his colleagues were among the first Allied soldiers to enter the city after the war, to hugs and kisses and cries of 'Viva America', which they enjoyed despite feeling like imposters; as Zinsser put it, 'none of us had seen any combat – and we all had German names.'

The prolific American writer Henry James visited Siena in the 1870s, and in his *Italian Hours* describes the Campo as 'a Piazza being built on the side of a hill – or rather, as I believe science affirms, in the cup of a volcanic crater – the vast pavement converges downwards in slanting radiations of stone, the spokes of a great wheel, to a point directly before the Palazzo, which may mark the hub,' and the tower:

> from bracketed base to grey-capped summit against the sky, there grows a tall slim tower which soars and soars till it has given notice of the city's greatness over the blue mountains that mark the horizon. It rises as slender and straight as a pennoned lance planted on the steel-shod toe of a mounted knight, and keeps all to itself in the blue air, far above the changing fashions of the market, the proud consciousness or rare arrogance once built into it.

James set his novel *Confidence* in the city, which he called 'a flawless gift of the Middle Ages to the modern imagination', and described the Campo as a bow, 'in which the high wide face of the Palazzo Pubblico forms the cord and everything else the arc'. The book's hero, Bernard Longueville, would take a walk after breakfast 'in the great square of Siena – the vast piazza, shaped like a horse-shoe, where the market is held beneath the windows of that crenellated palace from whose overhanging cornice a tall, straight tower springs up with a movement as light as that of a single plume in the bonnet of a captain'. Only a pedant would point out that the market is in fact *behind* the Palazzo Pubblico and not visible from the Campo.

Like me, James had travelled from Florence, Siena's neighbour 65 kilometres to the north: 'Florence being oppressively hot and delivered over to the mosquitoes, the occasion seemed to favour that visit to Siena which I had more than once planned and missed.' The short journey draws inevitable comparisons between the two. The rivalry between the two cities is legendary, and has been violent – particularly during the long-running thirteenth- and fourteenth-century religious battles, in which Florence was Guelph and Siena Ghibelline. When their two armies met at the Battle of Montaperti in 1260, more than ten thousand Florentine soldiers were killed, and Siena became the ruling city, but only temporarily. The issue was finally settled three centuries later, in 1559, when Siena lost its independence and became a satellite of its ancient rival. Today their differences are settled on the soccer pitch.

Siena is smaller and friendlier than its neighbour, and, with the exception of its cathedral, its vista of reddish-gold terracotta is a gentle contrast to the variegated Renaissance marble of Florence. The city is built on the tops of three hills and surrounded by the vineyards of Chianti and a typically Tuscan landscape of gently rolling green hills dotted with other, smaller, hill towns and punctuated with elegant cypresses like inky exclamation marks. Virginia Woolf called it 'the loveliest of all landscapes'. It was on Siena's crenellated battlements that, in 1908, the art critic and historian Clive Bell swore undying love to Virginia Stephen – as she was then. She rejected him, on the not unreasonable grounds that he had only recently married her sister Vanessa. He did not take it well at the time, but 27 years later, when Virginia was in Siena with her husband, Leonard Woolf, she sent Bell a picture postcard of the same ramparts, with the words: 'It was on the spot now marked with a cross that Clive Bell quarrelled with his sister-in-law in September 1908. I dropped a tear here today under the orange blossom.'

An earlier literary expatriate in Siena was the French philosopher Montaigne, taking a break from his quest for relief from his agonising kidney stones. On his journey from Florence in 1581 his *Journal de Voyage* is strong on fact but weak on atmosphere: 'Siena – 32 *milles*, four changes of horses – is a unique city, stuck on top of a hill, the sides of which are covered with sloping streets. It is one of the most beautiful cities in Italy, not comparable in size with Florence, but of evident antiquity. There is an abundance of fountains, most of which syphon off into private systems.' Like other travellers, he compared it with his previous stopping-place:

> the cathedral compares favourably with that of Florence, and, unlike the usual construction material of brick, it is panelled, both inside and out, almost entirely in marble slabs, some the thickness of a foot. The most beautiful aspect of the city is a huge round

piazza, every segment of which points towards the palace, opposite which is a large fountain. A number of streets open into this piazza, some of them three or four hundred years old. Most of the women wear hats, which, like men, they remove as a gesture of respect.

A Scottish arrival, two centuries after Montaigne, was James Boswell, son and heir of a wealthy Scottish laird, Lord Auchinleck, and the writer who, with his *The Life of Dr. Samuel Johnson,* was to pioneer the craft of biography. A dedicated celebrity hunter, Boswell had tried unsuccessfully to buttonhole Frederick the Great in Potsdam, but managed to track down the French writer Voltaire at Ferney in Switzerland, and, having introduced himself by letter as a 'person of singular merit', the Swiss philosopher Jean-Jacques Rousseau, whom he appointed his reluctant pen-pal and confessor.

Once in Italy, Boswell's main cultural objective became the mollification of his voracious sexual appetite and recording these exploits in meticulous detail in his journals and correspondence. He arrived in Turin in January 1765, then made his way to Rome, where, after two months he was writing, 'At Rome I ran about among the prostitutes.' By April he was describing his first treatment for venereal disease.

He reached Tuscany in early August, but stayed in Florence for only two weeks – 'which I did not find very agreeable'. He had a recurrence there of what he liked to call 'the wounds of my Roman wars', and was anxious to move on, because 'the Florentines (especially the Florentine women) are very proud and very mercenary.' It was a view he shared with Stendhal, who passed through Florence half a century later and 'went alone for fun to see the women who let themselves be seen by anyone who wants', but found that their 'contemptible and wretched' lodgings 'do not approach in any way those of the Roman or Venetian prostitutes; nor do they themselves, in beauty or grace or dignity'.

An early Grand Tourist at the age of 25, Boswell's visit to Siena was not so much a study of Sienese art and architecture as a research of its seduction opportunities: 'I have been so busy with women that I felt no curiosity about inanimate objects,' he told Rousseau. Boswell found the Sienese much more to his liking: 'They have a simplicity, an openness, a gaiety which you cannot imagine.' He wrote to Rousseau: 'I was in a provincial city in the heart of beautiful Tuscany; a city completely at peace, where not a single soldier was to be seen.' There is nothing in Boswell's letters or memoirs about Sienese art, architecture or medieval charm: his last journal entry before leaving Florence is 'get condoms for Siena'. He boasted to Rousseau, 'Your Scot was very attentive to the ladies in Siena. I found that people lived there in a completely natural fashion, making love as their inclinations suggested. It was the custom of the society in which I lived. I yielded to the custom.'

Sienese women, it seems, were not only submissive, but gullible. 'I was wicked enough to wait at the same time on a very amiable little woman to whom I made declarations of the most sincere passion, as can be easily done when one feels only a slight inclination,' he wrote.

> I fancied that she had no heart, and as I believed everything fair in the war of gallantry, I lied to her certainly no fewer than a hundred times a day. Behold me, then, very busy indeed, with two affairs going at the same time. It required an unparalleled dexterity, and I had it. Then nothing was difficult for me. I drifted pleasantly between my two loves, and my valet de place was despatched . . . to carry a letter for Signora A. in his right-hand pocket and a letter for Signora B. in his left.

Their husbands, it seems, were no less compliant: 'The times, Sir, are much changed in Italy,' Boswell told Rousseau, 'no longer does one have to fear the stiletto of a jealous husband.'

He was moderately concerned at having to leave Siena: his Signora A – Porzia Sansedoni – was grief-stricken: 'Her sighs pierced my heart.' But he was under pressure from his father to return; Lord Auchinleck was beginning to tire of his son's repeated excuses and requests for money, and did not yet know that his son also planned to visit Corsica on his way home.

Another Scottish author in Siena in the same year was less enthusiastic about it than the much younger Boswell. Tobias Smollett passed through with his wife on their way from their home in Nice to Rome. One has to wonder if he spent much time in Siena: for such an observant traveller, his comments in his *Travels through France and Italy,* are untypically brief and non-committal:

> of Siena I can say nothing from my own observation, but that we were indifferently lodged in a house that stunk like a privy, and fared wretchedly at supper. The city is large and well built: the inhabitants pique themselves upon their politeness, and the purity of their dialect. The mosaic pavement of their Duomo, or cathedral, has been much admired.

For Smollett to have dismissed Siena's Duomo in so few words, one can only assume that, like both Goethe and Nathaniel Hawthorne at this point in their journeys, he was seduced by the siren call of Rome.

Smollett was right to mention the cathedral floor, if only briefly and by proxy, for it is deservedly 'much admired'. It is made up of huge marble rectangles inlaid with decorations in graphite and marquetry, and was built between the fourteenth and sixteenth centuries. Together with the Gothic ceiling and the variously shaped marble pillars, it is part of a harmonised interior which puts that of even Florence's Duomo to shame, but for me an unforgettable feature of Siena's Duomo, like that of Pisa, is its sculptured pulpit: with its bas-relief representations of biblical scenes, the liberal arts, and what Paul Johnson, in *The Renaissance,* calls, 'faint echoes of classical Greece'. The octagonal pulpit was an all-Pisan affair: Nicola Pisano, who had already sculpted the pulpit for the Duomo in Pisa, was assisted by his equally – some critics say more – talented son, Giovanni, in whose hands, wrote the English art historian and author Robert Langton Douglas, 'marble becomes as ductile and pliable as molten glass'. Giovanni Pisano's work had a strong influence on that of the twentieth-century English sculptor and Tuscany resident Henry Moore, who said of Giovanni Pisano that he 'used the human body to express his deep philosophical understanding of human nature, human tragedy'. Pisano senior had studied ancient sarcophagi in Rome as a youth – probably the origin of those 'faint echoes of classical Greece'.

Giovanni completed the work late in the thirteenth century, and went on to take charge of the entire completion of the Duomo, including its magnificent façade. The writer and critic John Ruskin claimed that the images in the Pisanos' work had Etruscan roots: 'the same black eyes, the same sharp-ridged noses', supporting the generally held belief – since supported by DNA tests – that present-day Tuscans are descended from early Etruscans, who are believed to have migrated from the Aegeo-Asian area during or after the twelfth century BC.

In October 1858, Nathaniel Hawthorne stayed in Siena on his way to Rome and home. On the night before he and his family left their mansion in Florence, as Hawthorne sat in his tower smoking a cigar and listening to the church bells, he wrote, 'I am not loath to go away; – impatient rather; for, taking no root, I soon weary of any soil that I may be temporarily deposited in' – and to prove his point, stayed only one week in Siena and left no record of his visit. He was coming to the end of his summer in Tuscany, feeling homesick and thinking of New England.

Ernest Hemingway's visits to Tuscany were somewhat peripatetic: his only recorded sojourn in Siena was spent in bed and merits a brief mention here only because in 1923 he and his first wife, Hadley, and Ezra Pound and his English wife, Dorothy, all keen walkers, decided to walk to Siena, by way of Pisa, from Pound's home in Rapallo on the Italian Riviera, enjoying leisurely picnic lunches on the way. That this is a distance of over 250 kilometres could explain why, having seen the Pounds onto their train back to Rapallo, Hemingway had to spend the next few days in bed, resting the knee allegedly injured in the First World War. His next Tuscany tour, in 1927, was made by car.

This group were not the only writers to arrive in Siena on foot. Valerie Grove, the biographer of English author Laurie Lee, recalls in *Laurie Lee: The Well-Loved Stranger*, that in 1949, when Lee's wife-to-be, Kathy, left him in Florence while she went to visit a friend in Siena, he decided 'in a moment of bravado' to follow her on foot through the Chianti country. Lee himself wrote, 'The heat was terrific & I was carrying about 30 kilos on my back. But I did the 70-odd kilometres in two days and terrorized the local peasants on the way with my wild blond looks & Nordic tongue. They took me for a German.' He had watched the sun set on the Arno and slept in a monastery in Fiesole, and was 'stuffed with impressions like a jar of olives'.

Albert Camus, a contemporary of Hemingway and fellow Nobel Literature prize-winner three years after him, saw Siena in his youth and much later was to write in his journal:

> most of all I'd like to go back and hike down the road from Monte San Savino to Siena and pass through that countryside's vineyards and olive groves which I can still smell. I want to walk over those bluish hills of *tufa* that led away as far as the eye can see and finally to make out Siena on the horizon at sunset with its towers like some perfect Constantinople. I want to arrive at night, penniless and alone, sleep next to some wellspring and be the first to enter the Piazza del Campo in the morning. That palm-frond shape seems like a hand offering up the highest achievement of humanity after ancient Greece.

William Zinsser, arriving from San Gimignano in 1945, wrote 'If San Gimignano was the perfect miniature, Siena was the master painting. Bestriding the city from its highest ridge was an immense white cathedral.' Almost half a century later, in 1992, when Zinsser, by then a respected author and academic, was planning how he might spend his seventieth birthday, his location of choice was Siena: he wanted, he said, 'to celebrate the day by going back to the place where I spent the most celebratory day of my life: to make a connection with its emotions – to borrow its essential joy.'

Siena is famed for the Palio, the annual horse races around the Piazza del Campo that have taken place on 2 July and 16 August every year since the seventeenth century. The word derives from the winner's prize of a *pallium* – a banner made of precious cloth. It is more a medieval pageant than a horse race, and parochial rivalries are intense. William Zinsser called it 'a ritual acting out of an arcane system of municipal governance'. The English historian, John Julius Norwich, toured Tuscany with his parents in the 1930s. 'Siena', he wrote in *The Italian World*,

> was a *coup de foudre* – love at first sight – where, on a memorable blazing afternoon, from a high window above a restaurant, we watched the Palio. To this day it is the only horse-race I have ever witnessed, and I am content that it should remain so: any other would be an anti-climax. And yet, strangely enough, my clearest memory from those days in Siena is of something else: for it was there, for the first time in my seventeen years (for I was an unprecocious child), standing in front of Simone Martini's glorious fresco of Guidoriccio da Fogliano on his way to battle, that Italian painting suddenly came to life.

It was a contemporary of Martini, Duccio di Buoninsegna, who is recognised today as having founded the Sienese school of painting. Duccio's artistic genius has taken many centuries to achieve recognition. His special talent was in working within the constraints of traditionally minded sponsors while incorporating the new Byzantine influences deriving from the burgeoning trade between northern Italy and the eastern Mediterranean.

His masterpiece, the *Maestá – Madonna in Majesty –* was commissioned in 1308 as an altarpiece for the Duomo of Siena. It was indeed majestic: 4.5 metres high, 4.8 metres long, and painted on both sides of a block of poplar 17 centimetres thick. Its 34 illustrations depicted scenes from the life of Jesus. Because most of its viewers would have been illiterate, it was meant to be walked around and 'read', like a strip cartoon.

The work took Duccio and his assistants almost three years, and the day the completed *Maestá* was finally installed – 9 June 1311 – was a public holiday. Church bells rang and the shops closed as the incredible painting was borne in procession through the streets of Siena, followed by church and civic dignitaries, musicians and citizens, to its place of honour over the high altar in Siena's Duomo.

Tragically, in 1771, almost five centuries later – either to increase its visibility or to produce some revenue – the *Maestá* was sawn vertically along its entire thickness, separating front from back, and cut up like vast jigsaw puzzle. The result of this authorised vandalism is that, although most of the segments remained in Siena, many are scattered in galleries around the world and five have been lost completely.

That Duccio's reputation has long lain in the shadow of that of Giotto has much to do with the historic rivalry between the two cities, and Duccio's treatment by the Florentine literati of the day. With Giotto's reputation trumpeted by Florentine writers of the stature of his friend Dante, Vasari and others, Duccio would always be an outsider from a PR point of view. As late as 1901, John Ruskin would open his *Mornings in Florence* with the words, 'If there be one artist, more than any other, whose work it is desirable that you should see in Florence . . . it is Giotto.'

Siena has, like its football team, tended to be overshadowed by its wealthier and more enterprising neighbour. Perhaps the last word on this rivalry should come, not from a Sienese, but from the Nobel Prize-winning Portuguese novelist, José Saramago. 'I look at the old palaces of Siena,' he wrote, 'the ancient houses where I want one day to live, and try vainly to decipher wherein lies the secret that Siena whispers and that I will continue to hear until the end of my life.' His wish was not granted: he died in 2010, his eighty-eighth year, not in Siena, where he never lived, but in Las Palmas, in the Canary Islands, where he had moved in protest at Portuguese political censorship.

≈ 11 ≈

COAST AND COUNTRY

The July sun enclosed in a ring of fire the ilex grove of a villa in the hills near Siena.   (Edith Wharton, *The Custom of the Country*)

This chapter is devoted to the writers who spurned the Renaissance glories of urban Tuscany to find their retreats on its coasts or countryside. Some, like Boccaccio, were indigenous rural Tuscans; some came there by choice, or on the recommendation of others; and some – the majority, in fact – came by chance, and stayed. Their retreats of choice are too remote to appear on maps: they are mostly found in southern and eastern provinces: Siena, Arezzo and Massa. One of the favourite areas is the Val di Chiana, that fertile stretch of the lower Appenines in south-eastern Tuscany around and to the south of Arezzo. The Val di Chiana continues to inspire artists today as it did its native genius, Michelangelo, five centuries ago. The Scottish writer, Muriel Spark, author of *The Prime of Miss Jean Brodie*, came to visit a friend who was restoring for residence a long-neglected church on a remote hillside near Civitella, and remained for the last 30 years of her life.

The area south and west of Siena; known to Britons – unless they are residents – as Chiantishire, has had a magnetic attraction for cloistering Anglo-Saxons, while the coastal provinces, tainted by ports and seaside resorts, have tended to attract the more gregarious: the literary Saint Jeromes preferred to ruminate in the coastal Apennines, the Garfagnana and the islands.

Santa Maddalena, Donnini

Romance and poetry, ivy, lichens, and wall-flowers need ruin to
make them grow.   (Nathaniel Hawthorne, *The Marble Faun*)

Many city-based writers strive to escape from their day-to-day existence to concentrate on their work, only to find that other distractions – artistic, cultural or social – place demands on their time. Yet the answer – the writers' retreat – is, almost by definition, hard to find: and, when found, tends to have limited access to research needs, such as libraries and computer facilities. It was a compromise that challenged the Baronessa Beatrice Monti della Corte von Rezzori. She set out to solve it at her converted fifteenth-century stone farmhouse, Santa Maddalena, hidden in wooded hills near the village of Donnini, about 25 kilometres east of Florence. A feature of the property is a medieval tower on a promontory at the end of the garden, overlooking the valley of the Arno. It was built as a signalling tower in the days of the violent battles between Ghibbelines and Guelphs. Following the death of her husband, the author Gregor von Rezzori, the Baronessa restored the tower structurally and internally, renamed it 'The Writers' Tower', and invited her first 'guinea-pig' hermits, Anita and Kiran Desai. 'It was good for them,' she said in an interview with the *New York Times*, 'so we continued.'

The next invitee was the English novelist and travel writer, Bruce Chatwin, author of *Song Lines*. In his gap-year days in France, he had visited the tower in the Périgord to which the sixteenth-century French philosopher Montaigne retired to spend his last years in writing his *Essays*. Chatwin nurtured a fantasy of retiring to just such a place: remote, ivy-clad and ancient. Chatwin called himself a 'restless' writer, of the kind who 'are paralyzed by home'; for whom 'home is synonymous with writer's block', and who believe naively that all would be well if they were somewhere else. His dream came true when he was invited to the 'Tower' in deepest Tuscany. Accustomed, as a former travel writer, to remote places – his first bestseller was *In Patagonia* – he found the tower at Donnini a perfect retreat, and would come and work there for months at a time. Much of his novel *On the Black Hill*, which is set in the Welsh Borders, was written, not in the Brecon Beacons but in Tuscany. He also wrote of the tower and its influence in his *Anatomy of Restlessness* in 1987:

> Whenever I have been in residence, the place becomes a sea of books and papers and unmade beds and clothes thrown this way and that. But the Tower is a place where I have always worked, clearheadedly and well, in winter and summer, by day or night – and the places you work well in are the places you love the most.

Since those early days, many novelists, poets, playwrights and scenarists have worked in the 'Tower': Zadie Smith, author of *White Teeth*, winner of the Whitbread Award for best first novel; Michael Ondaatje (*Anil's Ghost* and the Tuscany-based *The English Patient*); and Irish novelist and biographer, Colm Tóibín (*The Story of the Night*), as well as an assortment of poets and non-fiction authors.

Chatwin's later wanderings took him, not through restlessness but on medical advice, to a fifteenth-century château in the mountain village of Seillans, in French Provence. Despite having tested HIV-positive at least four years earlier, he staunchly refused AIDS-related treatment, blaming his illness on having eaten a thousand-year-old egg in China. It was his penultimate piece of fiction: he wrote his novel *Utz*, published in 1988, on the château's vast south-facing terrace, but it was his last retreat; he died the following year in the public hospital in Nice.

The Val de Chiana

*Our window . . . opens onto an expansive view over the ancient roofs of
Cortona, down to the dark expanse of the Val de Chiana.*

(Frances Mayes, *Under the Tuscan Sun*)

The Val de Chiana runs roughly southwards from the river Arno
at Arezzo to Lake Trasimeno and its neighbouring Lake Chiusi.
While it is known to have been an area of Etruscan settlement, little
is known of its history in the first millennium AD. The valley follows
the border with Umbria so closely that it is often difficult to know
in which region one is. While its historical towns are beautiful, and
can be useful for orientation and sustenance, it is its bucolic charm
that attracts the meditative writer.

Frances Mayes was born in Fitzgerald, Georgia, USA in 1940,
and is now professor of English and creative writing at San Francisco State University. Her Tuscany-based travel and recipe books,
articles, website, lectures and films on all matters Tuscan have made
her almost a tycoon of Tuscan travel. She and her husband Ed came
across a neglected 200-year-old house in the countryside outside
Cortona, 29 kilometres south of Arezzo, in 1990 and spent the
next few years renovating it. Her book about the experience, *Under
the Tuscan Sun* – following in the footsteps of Peter Mayle's block-
busting *A Year in Provence*, published the previous year – sold over
a million copies and was made into a film. Success for both authors
was something of a poisoned chalice: as Mayle had already discovered, literary fame can seriously impair your private life. When he
encountered a tsunami of curious tourists in his swimming pool, he
decided it was time to decamp, and although he is still in Provence,
his address is known only to close friends. Frances Mayes paid a
similar price following the success of her 'Tuscany' books. As the
anthologist Alice Leccese Powers explains in her *Tuscany in Mind*,
'thousands of tourists have made the pilgrimage to Cortona; in
high season thirty or forty may be standing outside of [her home]
Bramasole, hoping to catch a glimpse of the author.' Unlike Mayle,

Mayes did not leave her home: it is now on an advertised tour route and, twenty years after discovering it, she is still 'wild about the place. . . . Here's where I discovered writing memoirs, where my cooking totally changed, where I made new lifelong friends and had the joy of welcoming many old friends.'

Henry James walked the hills of Cortona in his *The Art of Travel*. He 'strolled forth under the scorching sun and made the outer circuit of the wall. There I found tremendous uncemented blocks; they glared and twinkled in the powerful light, and I had to put on a blue eyeglass in order to throw into its proper perspective the vague Etruscan past . . .'

The expatriate Scottish novelist, Muriel Spark was a long-term resident of the Val de Chiana. She was born in Edinburgh in 1918, and her first attempt at fiction was for a short-story competition in the *Observer* in 1951, which she won. The story was read by the novelist Graham Greene, who encouraged – and financed – her to write a novel. At the same time, Greene was helping to launch the career of another budding novelist, Vladimir Nabokov. Spark's first book, *The Comforters*, published in 1957, was favourably reviewed, and she went on to write 23 more. After living in Africa, London, New York and Rome, in 1979 she finally settled in a converted presbytery in San Giovanni, a village near Civitella, about 15 kilometres west of Arezzo, with the sculptor Penelope Jardine, whom she had first met at a hairdresser's in Rome in 1968. She remained there, except for brief but frequent trips abroad, until her death in 2006. Early in her stay in Tuscany – in what her biographer Martin Stannard calls her 'well-regulated' period – she wrote a travel article, 'Side Roads of Tuscany', of which Stannard wrote,

If *My Rome* was a portrait of the metropolitan artist, *Side Roads* presents the bucolic, rooted Muriel, depressed by the English voices of tourists. She avoids the poshocracy of Chiantishire, seeks the timeless: the resignation of the local people, the masterpiece murals in obscure churches, the peasant faces ghosting those of

Renaissance painting. 'It was by chance, not choice, that I came to Tuscany five years ago', she wrote, and it was by chance, not choice, that she had happened upon a capacity for love in herself.

Hunter Davies, the English author and journalist, in writing his 1966 memoir, *Grand Tour*, braved the autostrada to seek out the couple in their firmly shuttered hide-out, 'four kilometres down a dirt track' near Civitella. It was a less than fruitful interview: he was allocated one hour, with the more interesting subjects – personal, biographical and sentimental – banned, and Spark later rang his hotel to censor the article further.

In 'Side Roads of Tuscany', Spark describes her fascination with the people of Tuscany as much as its beauty spots:

> It isn't necessarily the great and famous beauty spots we fall in love with. As with people, so with places: Love is unforeseen, and we can all find ourselves affectionately attached to the minor and the less obvious. I notice the light and shade on buildings grouped on a hilltop, the rich skin colours and the shapes of the people around me. I love to watch people, to sit in a *trattoria* listening in to their talk, imagining the rest.

The love was not always reciprocal: her early publisher, Peter Owen, said in an interview for the *Sunday Times* that when she became successful, she became 'too big for her boots – the *grande dame*'.

Dame Muriel left all her assets and royalties to Jardine, and cut her estranged 68-year-old son out of her substantial estate. All she left him was a bitter letter that was sent to his solicitor following her death, telling him why. Martin Stannard, in *Muriel Spark: The Biography*, called her 'a cuckoo perching in others' nests', and to complete the ornithological metaphor, she left Robin behind in hers when he was 6 years old. Among her many literary honours, Muriel Spark became Dame Commander of the Order of the British Empire in 1993 in recognition of her services to literature. In 2006, aware that her cancer was terminal, she began to make plans for her demise. She wished to die in her adopted village of San Giovanni, and, although claiming Jewish and Anglican parentage, wanted Roman Catholic rites. She wished to be buried locally, dressed, not in the traditional Italian ornate manner but in a simple shroud. In fact, only the Roman Catholic rites took place: she died, aged 88, in hospital in Florence and was buried in Saint Andrea of the Apostle Churchyard in Oliveto.

Montepulciano

However one comes to the lofty city of Montepulciano the way is beautiful. The whole valley of the Chiana is spread out like some gracious fairyland.   (Edward Hutton, *Siena and Southern Tuscany*)

Dame Muriel was not the only Dame Commander of the Order of the British Empire who lived in the Val de Chiana. In 1924, the Anglo-Irish writer, Iris Origo, daughter of Lady Sybil Cutting, and her new husband, Antonio Origo, son of Marquese Clemente Origo, acquired the centuries-old neglected Tuscan estate of La Foce, in Chianciano Terme, near Montepulciano, 25 kilometres south-west of Cortona and roughly midway between Florence and Rome. The property was known as an important settlement from Etruscan times, on which burial-places dating from the seventh century BC to the second century AD have been excavated. Iris described it as 'a lunar landscape, pale and inhuman', and was to spend much of the rest of her life restoring and improving it. The estate of La Foce had been carefully selected by the Origos because it was a barren region that could be improved only by a planned programme of intensive cultivation. The new owners set about restoring it to life. They also inherited from Iris's mother her apartment in Rome and the villa Gli Scafari at Lerici.

Edward Hutton wrote, describing his entry to Montepulciano: '. . . one is struck at once by the splendour of her walls and gates, and once within the city, the palaces of Antonio da Sangallo astonish one by their splendour.' Because of its fortress-like position, Montepulciano was a bone of contention over which the states of Siena and Florence quarrelled for centuries. On the map, the town looks narrowly pear-shaped: it clings to a 3-kilometre-long ridge in south-eastern Tuscany close to the border with Umbria. The main entrance to the town is the double-arched Porta di Prato, from which the main street follows the twists and turns of the crest, first as the Viale Sangallo, named after the principal architect of the town, and then, as the Via di Gracciano nel Corso, winds southwards, flanked by sixteenth-century palaces, to the aptly named Piazza Grande, where stand the Duomo, the fourteenth-century Palazzo Comunale and more palaces. Walking the length of the street, one could well imagine oneself in the sixteenth century – were it not for the countless antique shops and cheek-by-jowl *gelaterie*, each offering 20 flavours of ice cream.

In the Second World War, the Origos, although formerly enthusiastic supporters of Mussolini's Fascists, made La Foce into a home for refugee children, and, after the surrender of Italy in 1943, made it a 'safe house' for the shelter and assistance of escaped Allied prisoners, in recognition of which Iris was appointed Dame Commander of the British Empire in 1977, becoming Dame Iris Margaret Origo, Marchesa of Val d'Orcia, DBE. Iris's first successful book, *War in the Val D'Orcia*, published in 1947, was her account of life at La Foce throughout the war. She died there in 1988, aged 86.

Today, La Foce is an upmarket holiday hotel. The surrounding farmhouses that dot the south-facing hillside overlooking the Val d'Orcia have been refurbished to a high level of luxury and are available for rental. In its formal gardens, still immaculately maintained by three full-time gardeners, is a small funerary chapel, beside which, enclosed by a wall of cypresses, is the cemetery in which Iris Origo lies buried beside her husband Antonio.

An occasional neighbour of the Origos was the barrister, Queen's Counsel, novelist, playwright and scenarist, Sir John Mortimer. As a QC he had been a defence advocate in the litigation against the publication of *Lady Chatterley's Lover.* Already famous as the creator of the book and television character *Rumpole of the Bailey* (a dedicated defence barrister at London's Central Criminal Court), Mortimer was a true Tuscanophile: a summer resident of the Chianti for two decades before his death in 2009 and scenarist of the Franco Zeffirelli film, *Tea with Mussolini.* He was also a novelist, and author of the Tuscany-based novel, *Summer's Lease* – whose clever title is taken from a line of a Shakespeare sonnet: 'And summer's lease hath all too short a date'. The novel tells of the bizarre adventures of an English family who rent a villa in the Sienese countryside for a summer holiday. Mortimer was a prodigious imbiber of the local product, claiming that *Summer's Lease* was conceived in Dante's Bar in Radda, 30 kilometres from Siena. A vigorous defender of leftist causes and friend of former Labour leader Neil Kinnock, Mortimer was once accused of being a champagne socialist. His response was, 'No, more a Bollinger Bolshevik'.

Apart from its touristic attractions, the main industry of Montepulciano is the wine that bears its name. During the summer months, the town celebrates I Mercoledì del Nobile – the Wednesday of the Wine – a marathon wine-tasting in which those with the stamina may test the past vintage by visiting the town's seven cellars and nine wine-shops. The commune's 42 *vitivinicole* – wine producers – also offer tastings by appointment.

Wines have been produced in the region since the Etruscans domesticated the Sangiovese grape more than three thousand years ago, its name deriving from *sanguis Jovis* – the blood of Jove. Writers have sung the praises of the local wines for centuries. In the Gothic Duomo of Arezzo, 60 kilometres from here, there is a monument celebrating the life of the seventeenth-century local poet and physician, Francesco Redi, one of whose works, 'Bacchus in Tuscany', eulogises the local wines. The English poet Leigh Hunt translated it as:

> Give ear and give faith to the edict divine:
> Montepulciano's the king of all wine.

In 1765, the Scottish biographer James Boswell had boasted, 'I regaled myself with the excellent Montepulciano,' and two centuries on, the novelist Saul Bellow, as he tells in his essay 'Winter in Tuscany', made a visit to a *fattoria* in nearby Montalcino to seek out its famous Tuscan wine, the lusty Brunello, the great oak vats of which seemed to resemble the engines of 747 jets. Unlike other Chiantis, the Brunello is made exclusively from Sangiovese grapes. 'The almost sacred bottles are dimly, somewhat reverentially, lighted,' he wrote. 'You feel called upon to pay your respects to this rare Brunello di Montalcino.' More recently, the versatility of Chianti as an enhancement to a variety of meats was endorsed by Hannibal Lecter in Thomas Harris's novel, *The Silence of the Lambs*.

Montegufoni

In the Florentine light, of an evening especially, though so bare except in its essentials, it seemed to offer the whole of Italy.

(Osbert Sitwell, *Great Morning*)

In the summer of 1909, Sir George Reresby Sitwell, the eccentric writer and twice Conservative MP for Scarborough, was driving in remote Chianti countryside between Florence and Siena when his 'motor car' broke down in the shadow of an even more ancient and dilapidated *castello* that had what he called 'an air of forlorn grandeur'. He fell in love with the castle and purchased half of it on the spot, in the name of his elder son, the future novelist Osbert Sitwell, for £2,200, intending to restore it to its former glory. 'The other half belongs to the village usurer,' he told Osbert. The original Castello di Montegufoni, parts of which remain, was built in the eleventh century, but its more 'recent' elements dated only from the thirteenth. In the eighteenth century, the British Minister to Tuscany, Horace Mann, wrote to his friend Horace Walpole about 'the bad taste of the Florentine villas', citing Montegufoni as a prime example. It is a pity that Mann did not live another 200 years to be able to see it after Sir George had finished restoring the castle and its gardens.

When Sir George acquired the castle in 1909, it housed 158 people, whom he relocated, and he moved there in 1925, with the nucleus of the extraordinary literary dynasty that would become the Sitwells: his wife Ida and three children whose names were as memorable as his own: the novelist and poet Osbert (Francis Osbert Sacheverell), his art critic brother Sacheverell, and their sister, the poet Edith Louisa, whom a geographically challenged Sir Harold Acton once described as, 'the purest English poet since Yeats'. Sir George and Osbert also set about developing the castle's Chianti production – judged by the same Sir Harold to be the purest in Tuscany – although very little of it got any farther than the family table. A visitor in 1926, D. H. Lawrence, was impressed, both by the number of beds – 'Sir G. collects beds . . . room after room and nothing but bed after bed' – and by the fact that they were not there for people to sleep in, but as precious antiques.

At the beginning of the Second World War, the Italian government decided that the Castello di Montegufoni offered a secure sanctuary behind which to shelter the most priceless exhibits of the art galleries of Florence, and deposited a curator and more than two hundred works of art within its sturdy walls, not anticipating that, after Italy's surrender in 1943, the curator would be expelled and the castle requisitioned to house invading German troops. Blissfully unaware of the treasures that the government had entrusted to them, the new residents ignored Botticelli's *Primavera*, Giotto's *Madonna*, Cimabue's *Prophets* and the several Uccellos, and selected the four-centuries-old *Adoration of the Magi*, by Ghirlandaio as their dinner table – not for its early Renaissance charm, but because it was circular. It was not until the liberation of the castle by Allied forces in 1945, accompanied by the British novelist Eric Linklater – by then working in military public relations – and the BBC war correspondent Wynford Vaughan Thomas, a cultured Welshman, that the trove was discovered and its gems restored and returned, wine- and food-stain free, to their rightful homes in the appropriate Florentine museums. Linklater records the event in his autobiographical *Fanfare for a Tin Hat*.

Sir George had been determined to remain in the castle for as long as the war lasted, and spurned the general exodus from Tuscany so movingly described by his son Osbert in his autobiography, *Tales My Father Taught Me*: 'The trains to the frontier were crowded with English invalids, who had spent whole decades in Italy and were now obliged to abandon the homes they loved, and the people they liked . . . Few English remained – few even for Florence, for centuries their chosen city. But my father stayed on, in his castle.' Fortunately for the patriarch, he was persuaded in 1942, at the age of 80, to move to Switzerland, where he died in the following year.

The Sitwells returned to Montegufoni at the end of the war with Osbert in charge, and he remained there, in a life of what biographer Michael Holroyd called 'disarming uselessness' until his own death from Parkinson's disease in 1969 at the age of 76. The Castello di Montegufoni is now a 58-bedroom holiday complex, renting apartments and villas – and guests are permitted to sleep in the beds.

Fosdinovo

The only illumination was provided by several small, home-made brass lamps, fuelled with olive oil that looked as if they might have been looted from an Etruscan tomb.

(Eric Newby, *A Merry Dance Around the World*)

In the Second World War, after the British Eighth Army had forced the Germans and Italians from the western desert, the German troops occupied the whole of Italy in order to protect what Winston Churchill had called 'the soft under-belly of the Axis'. His intention was to create action in Italy to divert attention from the preparations for the Allied attack in Northern France, but, although successful, the ploy placed greater pressure on the Allied forces preparing to invade Italy. In the early stages of the British invasion, the veteran travel writer Eric Newby was a young soldier attached to the SBS – Special Boat Section – whose function was to land troops from submarines or small boats onto enemy coasts to carry out acts of sabotage. Newby was taken prisoner by the Germans off the west coast of Sicily, and finished up, after a number of transfers and marches, as an injured prisoner confined in a prison hospital – a former Catholic orphanage – in Fontanellato, in the Po Valley. Warned by local people that the Germans were beginning to ship British prisoners to prison camps in Germany, he decided to try to escape, and, having fallen in love with Wanda, the daughter of the family that helped him to escape, he set off into the mountains, promising Wanda that he would return after the war. After more than year on the run, Newby was recaptured in 1944 and sent to a prison camp in Czechoslovakia, where he was released by American troops in April 1945. He wrote of the episode in a memoir, *Love and War in the Apennines*, published in 1971, which he dedicated to 'To all those Italians who helped me, and thousands like me, at the risk of their lives'. Fosdinovo is now home to the Museum and Documentation Centre of the Italian Resistance Movement.

After the war, Newby returned to find Wanda, and in the spring of 1946 the couple were married in the Bardi Chapel of Florence's Santa Croce. After a brief and what he called an 'inconspicuous' career in the rag trade, Newby became a successful travel writer and he and Wanda decided to make their home in rural Tuscany. In 1966 they found the stereotypical dilapidated farmhouse, I Castagni (The Chestnuts), near Fosdinovo, in the north-west corner of Tuscany, a few kilometres from the Gulf of La Spezia. Newby describes it in *A Merry Dance Around the World*:

it was a small, two-storey farmhouse, built of stone partially rendered with a cement that over the years had turned a creamy colour in some places and in others a lichenous green. The overall effect was of a building on the verge of becoming a ruin. Every bit of wood was riddled with worm-holes. . . . I felt that one of us would only have to emit one really hefty sneeze to bring the whole lot down around our ears.

On one wall of the ruin was a print of the church in Fontanellato, the village in which they had met when Newby was a prisoner 23 years earlier. In true Tuscan tradition, they fell in love with the ruin on sight, and it was to be their home and refuge for the next 25 years. Eric Newby died in October 2006 at the age of 86.

The Garfagnana

It has a splendid name – like the clashing of cymbals. Garfagnana!
(Hilaire Belloc, *The Path to Rome*)

In north-western Tuscany, a mountain range rising in places to 2,000 metres forms the border with the province of Liguria. It is now part of a huge national park of mountains and lakes known as the Garfagnana. It was through this area, along the famous Via Francigena, that the early pilgrims made their way to Rome, and it was the route chosen by a twentieth-century pilgrim, Anglo-French writer Hilaire Belloc. Born in 1870 in St-Cloud, near Paris, to a French father and an English mother, he had been brought up in England, but after leaving school moved to France and was conscripted into the French army in 1891 and posted to a barracks in Toul, in Alsace-Lorraine, in north-eastern France. On demobilisation, he became a prolific poet and well-known historian, and, 10 years later, finding himself again in Toul, he decided, as a devout Roman Catholic, to make his own peregrination to Rome – on foot. His account of the journey, *The Path to Rome*, published in 1902, is a light-hearted jaunt through France, Switzerland and Italy, describing his encounters along the way: a sort of one-man *Canterbury Tale*. The book seldom reaches the level of his poetry, but was popular in its day and is still in print.

The pace of Belloc's journey, like that of other writer-pilgrims such as Goethe, Evelyn Waugh and Nathaniel Hawthorne, increases as the writer approaches his Christian goal: so much so that in the last part of the trek, the pilgrim resorts to public transport, travelling by train from Florence to Siena, which, apart from missing places such as San Gimignano, does not seem in keeping with pilgrim tradition. Crossing the Tuscan border at the village of Sillano, a few kilometres north of Bagni di Lucca, Belloc descended beside the River Serchio:

> The hither side of that bank, I say, had been denuded of its trees . . . Now, at the summit, the highest part was a line of cool forest, and the late afternoon mingled with the sanctity of trees. A genial dampness pervaded the earth beneath; grasses grew, and there were living creatures in the shade. Nor was this tenanted wood all the welcome I received on my entry into Tuscany. Already I heard the noise of falling waters upon every side, where the Serchio sprang from twenty sources on the southern slope.

As he crosses the Serchio River, his journal has a triumphant tone:

> the Appennines [sic] were conquered, the last great range was passed, and there stood no barrier between this high crest and Rome. A glade opened, and, the trees no longer hiding it, I looked down the vale, which was the gate of Tuscany. There – high, jagged, rapt into the sky – stood such a group of mountains as men dream of in good dreams, or see in the works of painters when old age permits their revelation. It was as though these high walls of Carrara, the western boundary of the valley, had been shaped expressly for man, in order to exalt him with unexpected and fantastic shapes, and to expand his dull life with a permanent surprise.

Ninety years later, another English author set off, armed with Belloc's journal, to retrace his pilgrimage. Peter Francis Browne also entered Tuscany at the village of Sillano and followed the Serchio River through the Garfagnana to Castelnuovo and Lucca. Browne's memoir of his walk, *Rambling on the Road to Rome*, chronicles his walk south through Tuscany. On leaving Sillano, he was surprised to see what he thought were snow-covered mountains. 'But it was not snow. It was pure white marble. As I watched the skyline a succession of serrated rocky peaks emerged to form a truly alpine range rising from the green forests of the Garfagnana – as the Serchio valley is called.' This sudden change of colour from green to white, where vegetation has been removed to render the marble more accessible, often gives the impression of snow-capped mountains, whether one is walking to Rome or, as I was, sitting in a train 20 kilometres away at Marina di Carrara on the main coastal railway line. The illusion is reinforced by the clarity of the mountain air, or as Leigh Hunt explained it: 'The mountains in which you fancy you see the marble veins (for it is from these that the marble of Carrara comes) tower away beautifully at the further end, and owing to the clear atmosphere, seem to be much nearer than they are.'

24 *Marble quarries at Carrara*

Browne had reached the Carrara mountains, to which, for two millennia, architects and sculptors – from pre-Christian Romans to the likes of the Tuscan Michelangelo, Venetian Canova and the Yorkshireman Sir Henry Moore – have come to select their raw material. Moore actually lived in the beach resort of Forte dei Marmi (Marble Fortress), a few kilometres farther south, within sight of these mountains, to be near enough to know them and select the marble of his choice for each individual project.

Here Charles Dickens was entranced: 'Carrara, shut in by great hills, is very picturesque and bold. Few tourists stay there; and the people are nearly all connected, in one way or other, with the working of marble. There are also villages among the caves, where the workmen live.' Dickens wrote in *Pictures from Italy*,

> Some of these caves were opened by the ancient Romans, and remain as they left them to this hour. Many others are being worked at this moment . . . marble enough for more ages than have passed since the place was resorted to, lies hidden everywhere; patiently awaiting its time of discovery. Standing in one of the many studii of Carrara, that afternoon – for it is a great workshop, full of beautifully-finished copies in marble, of almost every figure, group, and bust, we know – it seemed, at first, so strange to me that those exquisite shapes, replete with grace, and thought, and delicate repose, should grow out of all this toil, and sweat, and torture!

Dickens extended his journey to see more of Carrara. John Ruskin wished he could do the same, finding the mountain scenery 'so exquisite about Carrara that I saw at once if I began stopping at all, I might stop all May.' I was fortunate enough to be able to make a second visit.

The railway lines around Carrara are lined for miles on both sides with stacks of marble waiting to be loaded onto trains, to be shipped around the world to enhance palaces, hotels and apartment buildings in New York, Paris or Monaco. Even in the railway stations – Marina di Carrara, Massa, Apuana and Forte dei Marmi – the walls, pillars and stairways are faced in marble. Its ubiquitous presence was the obvious answer to the question that so troubled Mark Twain: 'I can not understand how a bankrupt government can have such palatial railroad depots.'

Another resident of Forte dei Marmi in the late 1920s was the novelist Aldous Huxley. He and his Belgian wife Maria were good friends of D. H. and Frieda Lawrence, and the couples visited each other in Florence and Forte dei Marmi. At the time, Lawrence was on his third and final draft of *Lady Chatterley's Lover* and Huxley finishing *Point Counter Point*. They were still close, but more a trio plus Frieda than a quartet: as Huxley put it: 'being with her makes me believe that Buddha was right when he numbered stupidity among the deadly sins'. By the end of the decade both couples had left Italy for coastal Provence.

Elba

If this is a prison, throw away the key.

(Paul Mansfield, *Observer*, 2005)

Elba is the largest of the group of islands that is the Tuscan archipelago: it is a tiny strip of land, 25 kilometres long by 10 wide that is best remembered as part of a well-known palindrome. The island lies between the north of Corsica and the coast of Tuscany; its capital is Portoferraio – the port of iron, referring to its main export – and its most famous resident was Napoleon Bonaparte, who was sent there as a prisoner in May 1814 following his disastrous attempt to invade Russia and his defeat by combined European armies at Leipzig. He arrived on the Royal Navy frigate *Undaunted* with his immense library, his pictures and porcelain, his 600-strong Imperial Guard and his army of doctors, engineers, butlers, cooks, sommeliers, valets, grooms, masons, gardeners, artists, historians and personal staff. It turned out to be an excess of baggage in view of the fact that he stayed for only nine months. The following March, while his jailer, Colonel Campbell, was on the mainland visiting his girlfriend, Napoleon sailed away with his troops, and they paddled ashore the next day on the beach at Golfe Juan, on what is now known as the French Riviera. Napoleon marched through the mountains, recruiting on the way, and took an eager Paris by storm, but one hundred days later, defeated by the European forces at Waterloo, he was given more secure accommodation on the remote island of St Helena.

Napoleon was followed to Elba 133 years later by a Welsh poet, Dylan Thomas, who had left the Florence suburb of Scandicci and sailed from the mainland port of Piombino with his wife, Caitlin, and their children, but without soldiers, personal staff or naval escort. An hour later they arrived at Rio Marina, a port and mining town at the eastern end of the island. I arrived by ferry from Bastia, Corsica some fifty years later. There were many traces of Napoleon: his hilltop residence, the Villa San Martino, a few kilometres inland from Portoferraio, remained just as he had left it, except that the bed had been made, but I found no trace of Thomas's passing.

It was at Rio Marina that the Thomas family finally found their Tuscan paradise, as their letters to friends and family at home showed: Caitlin and the children spent most of the time in the sea, while, after an unproductive time in Florence, Thomas, still 'bumpy with mosquito bites', started to write again. 'Lucky Napoleon!' wrote Dylan Thomas.

This is the most beautiful island; and Rio Marina the strangest town on it: only fishermen and miners live here: few tourists: no foreigners. Extremely tough. Notices 'Fighting Prohibited' in all bars . . . And the green and blue transparent yachted winkled and pickling sea. We are rarely out of it, except to drink, ride, write, quarrel, cave and café crawl, read, smoke, brood, bask in the lavatory, over the parroty fruit market. There is no winter on Elba; cognac is threepence a large glass; the children have web feet; the women taste of salt.

Before leaving Florence, Thomas had written to friends that he wanted to write a radio play, and there are many indications that his writings on Elba paved the way for his most successful work: what he called his 'play for voices', *Under Milk Wood*. Many Thomas scholars, both British and Italian, feel that in Rio Marina, with its steep streets, harbour and quarries, Thomas found an affinity with coastal South Wales, his drinking mates in Lougharne, and the fictional fishing village, Llareggub – 'Bugger all' backwards – that is the setting for *Under Milk Wood*. He also found, as a Welshman, a natural kinship with the local miners and fisherman, and some of the language of his writings from Elba – expressions like 'crowblack' and 'webfooted waterboys' – would later reappear as the 'webfoot cocklewomen' in the 'starless and bible-black' town of Llareggub in *Under Milk Wood*.

The Society of Authors, who had partly financed Thomas's travelling scholarship to Italy, must have been pleased with the result: his 'play for voices' was performed in New York, with Thomas as narrator, shortly before his death in 1953. Since then it has become a stage play and a film directed by Andrew Sinclair, and been translated into many languages. Thomas wrote to his wife from New York in May 1953, 'I've finished that infernally eternally unfinished "Play" & have done it in New York with actors.'

One of Thomas's best-known poems was the angry villanelle he wrote for his dying father, 'Do Not Go Gentle into that Good Night'. The son Dylan's departure for the good night was anything but gentle: Constantine Fitzgibbon's biography, *The Life of Dylan Thomas*, records that he arrived in New York's Chelsea Hotel at 2 a.m. on the morning of 4 November after the last performance of *Under Milk Wood*, claiming 'I've had eighteen straight whiskies, I think that's a record.' He did not go angrily; he went into a coma and died in hospital five days later. His body was brought back to Wales and buried near his home in Lougharne. A few weeks later, Caitlin left for Elba.

Certaldo

Certaldo has much curious beauty of her own . . . besides the grave of that great and heroic man, who has entranced the whole world with his stories.   (Edward Hutton, *Siena and Southern Tuscany*)

Not many of the writers in this book have their names in *The Oxford English Dictionary*. One whose name does appear in it is the eighteenth-century expatriate Englishman, Horace Walpole. The word he coined was 'serendipity', based on his Persian fairy tale, *The Three Princes of Serendip*, and it has come to mean a chance discovery when seeking something unrelated. It was through serendipity that I came across Certaldo. I had not been able to find it before; it wasn't in the Michelin guidebook or on my maps. Then one day, I was looking out of the window of a train that thought – as I did – that it was taking me to Poggibonsi when I saw the sign: Certaldo. Fortunately, the train stopped and I clambered out. Poggibonsi would have to wait.

Certaldo was the family home of the Boccaccio family, in which their son Giovanni was born. A contrary view, supported by no less an authority than his friend Petrarch, was that he was born in Paris as the result of an extra-marital affair of his father with an unknown woman. Boccaccio was one of the distinguished trio of fourteenth-century Florentine poets and is often mentioned in the same breath as Dante and Petrarch.

Boccaccio's best-known work, the *Decameron*, was inspired by the onset of the plague in 1348. In order to avoid infection, a group of 10 ladies and gentlemen retreat to a country house just outside Florence, and decide to pass the time by taking turns in telling each other stories of varying degrees of impropriety and bawdiness. The original book, the handwritten version of which appeared around 1370, and the first printed edition about a hundred years later, purported to be a collection of 100 of the stories.

Boccaccio spent most of his working life in Naples and Florence, but he returned to Certaldo permanently in 1372 and was there in

1373 when Geoffrey Chaucer visited Florence, but it is believed that Boccaccio was too ill for them to meet. He died in his natal home in Certaldo in 1375, supposedly as a lingering result of the plague which had inspired his greatest work.

Certaldo is a split-level town, the lower part of which was built in the nineteenth century around the railway. Looking around the lower town, there seems to be nothing older than a century or two – not even the giant statue of a man in a cowled cloak standing high on a pedestal in the vast Piazza Boccaccio, bearing the inscription: Giovanni Boccaccio (1313–1375). But high on the hill behind it is Certaldo Alto, an old hill town whose roots go back to the Etruscans, but whose visible construction is mainly medieval. Like most ancient central Tuscan towns, it prospered in the commercial trade along the Via Francigena.

Stepping from the funicular cable car that takes you up to the old town is to step literally into another era. Buildings and roadways are constructed in narrow red bricks, the pavement in herringbone

25 *San Gimignano, from Certaldo*

pattern, like well-preserved Roman remains. A main street – the Via Boccaccio, of course – divides the town down the middle, rising up to the twelfth-century Palazzo Pretorio. The town's tallest building, it has been a garrison and a prison, but one hopes its present function is neither of these, for when I visited it was serving as a wedding venue.

About halfway up the street is the Casa Boccaccio, the family home in which, reportedly, Giovanni was born. The house was almost destroyed during the Second World War in strategic bombing by American B-26s between November 1943 and May 1944, but the house has been faithfully restored and looks as good as old. It is now a museum featuring Boccaccio's life and works, a library containing more than 3,500 of his books, and a fresco of the great poet by Pietro Benvenuti. The view from its roof terrace is a 360-degree panorama of typical Tuscan countryside, with views of vineyards and olive groves. But there is one final surprise: there, eight miles to the south-west across an expanse of more vines and cypresses, stands a serendipitous cluster of towers that could only be San Gimignano.

❧ 12 ❧

EPILOGUE

He who hath lived in this country can enjoy no distant one. He breathes here another air; he lives more life.

(Walter Savage Landor, *Imaginary Conversations*)

In researching the writers of Tuscany, I have travelled its length and breadth in their footsteps: in the process, not only discovering writers who were strangers to me, but, through them, being introduced to unknown regions of Tuscany. But the most fascinating aspect of the journey has been the opportunity to observe writers as they developed through their experience of this fabled region: to watch new writers such as 'Kinta' Beevor, Frances Trollope, Iris Origo and others as they find their literary voices; to follow a brash young Mark Twain as he changes from bored hack to committed Europhile intent on spending the rest of his writing life in Tuscany; to watch the 21-year-old John Ruskin progress from telling visitors to 'Know your Vasari' to enjoying the same author's 'brightly blundering' mistakes; to hear the words of Henry James as they mellow and Anglicise through four decades of Tuscan awareness; to learn, like Kipling, *Something of Myself*, and to observe that, through all these changes – through war, invasion, pestilence and plague; Garibaldi, Mussolini and Berlusconi – Tuscany itself remains stubbornly unchanged.

It has been an enthralling quest, but an incomplete one, leaving so much more to be discovered. One of the book's most quoted writers, Henry James, wrote 'Never say you know the last word about any human heart.' Just as there is no such thing as a definitive biography, there will never be a definitive guidebook. 'Books read us', wrote Virginia Woolf, 'because they change (like people) as we read them, and change us as we read.' My wish for the readers of this book is for many more discoveries – literary and topographic. May they, in looking at Tuscany through the eyes of its centuries of writers – expatriate and indigenous – better know the writers, Tuscany and themselves; just as I did.

As I reach my last writer – who was also my first – I sense, on an infinitely smaller scale, the mixture of sadness and immense relief as, just before midnight on a summer evening in 1787, in a small summer-house in his garden in Lausanne, he lay down his pen at the end of his monumental 23-year, six-volume task: *The History of the Decline and Fall of the Roman Empire:*

> After laying down my pen, I took several turns in a *berceau,* [arbour] or covered walk of acacias, which commands a prospect of the country, the lake, and the mountains. The air was temperate, the sky was serene, the silver orb of the moon was reflected from the waters, and all nature was silent. I will not dissemble the first emotions of joy on the recovery of my freedom, and, perhaps, the establishment of my fame. But my pride was soon humbled, and a sober melancholy was spread over my mind, by the idea that I had taken an everlasting leave of an old and agreeable companion.

Author Profiles

Richard Aldington (1892–1962)
English poet, novelist, critic and biographer. His best-known works include the novels *Death of a Hero* and its sequel *All Men Are Enemies*; his book of poems *A Dream in the Luxembourg*; and biographies of Voltaire, Robert Louis Stevenson, the British soldier T. E. Lawrence and the author D. H. Lawrence (*Portrait of a Genius, but*). He stayed with D. H. and Frieda Lawrence in Florence in 1926 and two years later was their host in Provence.

Hans Christian Andersen (1805–75)
Danish writer, son of a cobbler, who trained as an actor but achieved international recognition as a master of the fairy tale. He also wrote plays, novels, poems, travel books and autobiographies. His fairy tales, such as *The Little Mermaid* and *The Emperor's New Clothes*, are among the most frequently translated works in literary history. In Florence in 1861, he met Elizabeth Barrett Browning, whose last poem, 'The North and the South' was written as a tribute to Andersen.

Matthew Arnold (1822–88)
English poet and critic, son of the educator and scholar Thomas Arnold, headmaster of Rugby School. Matthew Arnold wrote the bulk of his most famous critical works, *Essays in Criticism* and *Culture and Anarchy* during his time as professor of poetry at Oxford. He was also a governmental Inspector of Schools for 35 years, a job that required him to travel extensively in Britain and continental Europe. Florence became one of his favourite cities for pursuing his research.

Saul Bellow (1915–2005)
Novelist, born of Russian-Jewish parents in Quebec, Canada but brought up in Chicago, the setting for a number of his works, including *The Victim* and *The Adventures of Augie March*, many of which dealt with Jewish-

American and academic themes. After the Second World War Bellow joined the University of Minnesota English Department and spent a year in France and Italy. He was awarded the Nobel Prize for Literature in 1976 and toured Tuscany in the 1990s and wrote 'Winter in Tuscany', which appeared in his non-fiction collection, *It All Adds Up*.

Arnold Bennett (1867–1931)

English novelist, playwright, critic and essayist. In 1889 he went to London, where he worked as a solicitor's clerk, but soon gained a footing writing popular fiction and editing a women's magazine. After his first novel *A Man from the North*, he became a professional writer and is best known for his novels of the 'Five Towns' (the Potteries) in his native Staffordshire. He visited Florence in 1912, staying at the Pensione White on the Lungarno.

Giovanni Boccaccio (1313–75)

Italian writer and humanist. Believed to have been born in Certaldo, he was educated in Naples, where he began writing. His relationship with the King of Naples's illegitimate daughter brought him into contact with the Neapolitan court and he returned to Florence in 1340, witnessing the worst effects of the Black Death, the inspiration for his major work, the *Decameron*. He rose to an important position in the Florentine government, became a close friend of his contemporary writer, Petrarch, and delivered public lectures on the works of Dante as well as writing his biography. In 1373 he retired to the family home in Certaldo, near Florence, where he died two years later, surviving Petrarch by only a year.

James Boswell (1740–95)

Scottish diarist who in later life became famous for his biography of Samuel Johnson. He met Johnson in 1763 and, despite the 30-year age gap, began a life-long friendship. He visited Pisa, Florence and Siena in 1765 at the age of 25 and returned to England via Livorno and Corsica, the inspiration for his *An Account of Corsica*.

Rupert Brooke (1887–1915)

English poet whose early poems included 'The Old Vicarage, Grantchester', which celebrated his love of the countryside. He became a national hero with his wartime sonnets, which appealed to the idealism at the start of the First World War. He joined the Royal Navy but died of septicaemia in Greece on his way to Gallipoli. He is best remembered for 'The Soldier' ('If

I should die, think only this of me'). He visited Florence and Siena in 1908 and 1912.

Elizabeth Barrett Browning (1806–61)

English poet. Her *Sonnets from the Portuguese* is considered to be her best work. She came to Florence in 1847 with her husband Robert Browning, and lived for most of that time in the Casa Guidi in the Oltrarno, where she expressed her support for the struggle for the independence and unification of Italy with *Casa Guidi Windows* and 'The Dance'. She died in Florence and is buried in the English Cemetery there.

Robert Browning (1812–89)

English poet who, after arriving in Florence with his wife Elizabeth, wrote his collection of poems *Men and Women*, which he dedicated to her. After her death in 1861 he left Florence with their son Pen, never to return. Back in London, he published Elizabeth's collected poems, which he dedicated to the city of Florence, and the acclaimed *The Ring and the Book*, and spent much of the rest of his life in Venice, where he died 28 years later.

Lord Byron, George Gordon Byron (1788–1824)

British poet and a leading figure in Romanticism who also gained notoriety for financial and sexual excesses and self-imposed exile from England. He took the Grand Tour in the Mediterranean between 1809 and 1811, had early literary success with *Childe Harold's Pilgrimage* in 1812, and finally left England in 1816 after a scandal over an alleged incestuous affair. In Venice he met the newly married Count and Countess Guiccioli, with whom he stayed in Ravenna before eloping with the Countess. They stayed first at the Palazzo Lanfranchi in Pisa, where he wrote parts of *Don Juan*. In July 1822, shortly after Shelley's death and cremation in Viareggio, he left for Greece, where he died in Missolonghi in April 1824.

Albert Camus (1913–60)

Algerian-born novelist, essayist and playwright. He lived his early years in poverty in Dréan in French Algeria, where a teacher encouraged his writing and helped him to enter the Lycée of Algiers. In 1930 the first of several severe attacks of tuberculosis put an end to his career in football, and in 1937 he travelled to Switzerland, seeking relief from tuberculosis, returning via Pisa, Florence and Siena. After university he wrote novels, of which the best-known are *L'Étranger* (*The Stranger*) and *La Peste* (*The Plague*). He edited the journal of the French Resistance during the German occupation of France in the Second World War and in 1957 was awarded the Nobel Prize for Literature at the exceptionally young age of 44, but was killed in a car accident three years later.

Bruce Chatwin (1940–89)

English novelist and travel writer, best known for his travel-based books. He gave up his career as art consultant at Sotheby's to study archaeology and in 1976 began the journeys that resulted in his award-winning *In Patagonia*. Several of his books were filmed, including *On the Black Hill* and *The Viceroy of Ouidah*. He worked in a Tuscan writers' retreat in Donnini, and spent his last years in Seillans on the French Riviera, dying from AIDS-related illness in hospital in Nice.

Geoffrey Chaucer (1343–1400)

English author, generally considered England's greatest poet of the Middle Ages and the father of English literature. He married a member of the Queen's household, and in addition to achieving fame as an author, philosopher and diplomat, held a number of court positions under King Edward III, in which capacity he visited Genoa and Florence in 1372 and 1373 respectively. His works include *Legend of Good Women*, and *Troilus and Criseyde*, but he is best known for *The Canterbury Tales*. He was the first poet to be buried in Westminster Abbey.

Arthur Hugh Clough (1819–61)

English poet best known now for his short poems 'Say Not the Struggle Naught Availeth', and 'The Last Decalogue', a satirical take on the Ten Commandments. The couplet on murder in particular 'Thou shalt not kill; but need'st not strive officiously to keep alive' was no doubt intended to be ironic, but is now often quoted by doctors in debates on medical ethics. He first visited Florence in 1843, where he wrote several poems supporting Italian independence, and died there in the year of the unification of Italy. He is buried in the English Cemetery in Florence.

James Fenimore Cooper (1789–1851)

American author who wrote prolifically, both in fiction – in which his best-known work was *The Last of the Mohicans* – and non-fiction, which included *History of the Navy of the United States of America*. He came to Florence in 1828, where he wrote his novel *The Wept of Wish-Ton-Wish*. He became a friend of Grand Duke Leopold II, and his presentation copy of the novel to the Grand Duke is preserved in the National Library in Florence.

Noël Coward (1899–1973)

English playwright, actor and composer, known for highly polished comedies of manners. His successes included *Private Lives*, *Cavalcade*, *Present Laughter* and *Blithe Spirit*. He rewrote his *Still Life* to become the film *Brief Encounter*. He stayed in Florence in 1950 as the guest of the American art historian Bernard Berenson. He was knighted in 1970 and spent his last years mainly in the Caribbean.

Dante Alighieri (1265–1321)

The Italian poet and dramatist born in Florence, best known for his epic poem *The Divine Comedy*, which he wrote in Italian rather than in Latin to encourage the use of Tuscan Italian as a literary language, resulting eventually in its being adopted as the national language. He was exiled from Florence in 1302 because of the political struggles of the time and travelled extensively in Provence and Italy, dying in Ravenna in 1321, where he is buried.

Hunter Davies (1936–)

Scottish-born journalist and author with strong ties to Cumbria. He worked as a journalist after leaving university and wrote his first novel, *Here We Go Round the Mulberry Bush* in 1965, since which time he has tended to concentrate on children's books and non-fiction works, including ghost-written biographies of famous people and chronicles of his adopted county, while continuing his journalistic career. He visited Italy while researching his 1986 travel book, *Grand Tour*, which included interviews with Tuscany residents Sir Harold Acton and Muriel Spark.

Charles Dickens (1812–70)

Probably the most famous English novelist of the Victorian era, who began his career contributing to popular magazines. His prodigious output included *The Pickwick Papers*, *Oliver Twist*, *A Tale of Two Cities*, *Great Expectations* and *Nicholas Nickleby*. In July 1844 he travelled with his family by steamer along the coast from Marseilles to Genoa, then overland to Florence. He remained in Italy until June 1845, visiting Pisa, Rome, Livorno, Florence and Naples. Towards the end of his life he made many tours in Britain and abroad, giving readings from his works.

Fyodor Mikhailovich Dostoevsky (1821–81)

Russian prose writer who was born in Moscow and moved to St Petersburg as a teenager. He is best known for his novels *Crime and Punishment, The Idiot* and *The Brothers Karamazov*. He was arrested in 1849 for being part of the Petrashevsky Circle and sentenced to death. After a bizarre mock execution, in which he and other members of the group stood outside in icy weather waiting to be shot by a firing squad, his sentence was commuted to hard labour in Siberia. Later he spent four years in the army, followed in 1862 by visits to England, France and Italy, where he visited Florence. Dostoevsky was devastated by his wife's death in 1864, but afterwards met Anna Grigorevna Snitkina, whom he married in 1867, and he returned with her to Florence the following year, where he finished writing *The Idiot*. He died in St Petersburg of a lung haemorrhage following an epileptic seizure.

Alexandre Dumas, Père (1802–70)

French author best remembered for his historical novels such as *The Count of Monte Cristo* and *The Three Musketeers*. He worked in the household of the future King Louis-Philippe, but took up writing and wrote successful plays such as *Napoléon Bonaparte* and *Antony*. He lived in the Villa Palmieri – formerly the home of Boccaccio – in Fiesole, where he wrote *Une Année à Florence*, and while there was the occasional guest of Jérôme Bonaparte, Napoleon's youngest brother.

George Eliot, Mary Ann – later Marian – Evans (1819–80)

English novelist and poet, born in Warwickshire. better known by her pen name George Eliot, was also a translator and journalist, and one of the leading writers of the Victorian era. She wrote seven novels, including *Adam Bede, The Mill on the Floss* and *Silas Marner*, most of them set in provincial England and appreciated for their psychological insight. She visited Florence in 1860 with her partner G. H. Lewes and decided to write the novel *Romola*, based on the life of Savonarola, returning in later years for further research, and published the novel *Middlemarch* in instalments in 1871–2.

Ralph Waldo Emerson (1803–82)

American philospher, essayist, lecturer and poet, born in Boston, Massachusetts, who helped to establish the neo-religious movement of Transcendentalism in the mid-nineteenth century. Emerson left for Europe in 1832, arriving first at Malta, and later spent several months in Italy – mainly in Naples, Rome (where he met John Stuart Mill), Florence and Venice – and England, where he met Coleridge, Wordsworth and Carlyle. He later wrote of his travels in *English Traits*.

John Evelyn (1620–1706)

English author of books on fine arts, forestry and religious topics, who in 1644 became one of the first English writers to visit Tuscany, travelling to Livorno, Pisa, Florence and Lucca. His diaries – published 100 years after his death – are an important source of information on the social, cultural, religious and political life of seventeenth-century England.

Edward Morgan Forster, (1879–1970)

English novelist, short story writer and essayist, best known for his novels highlighting social and racial differences in twentieth-century British society. He was brought up in Stevenage and Tonbridge and went to King's College, Cambridge. In 1901 he visited Italy and Greece with his mother and in 1912/13, and 1921/2 spent several months in India, leading to his novel *A Passage to India*. His stays in Tuscany provided backgrounds for his first two novels: *Where Angels Fear to Tread* and *A Room with a View*. The strong visual aspect of his novels led to their being successfully adapted for film and television.

André Gide (1869–1951)

French novelist and critic. Much of his work reflects his conflict with conventional and religious morality. His novels include *Les Caves du Vatican* (*The Vatican Cellars*) and *Les Faux-Monnayeurs* (*The Counterfeiters*). His *Journal*, which he kept from 1885 until his death, is a major work of literary autobiography. A former Stalinist, he was disillusioned by a visit to Russia in 1936 and wrote *Retouches à mon Retour* (*Afterthoughts*), and won the Nobel Prize for Literature in 1947. He spent the winter of 1895/6 in Florence.

Johann Wolfgang von Goethe (1749–1832)

German author and lyric poet born in Frankfurt-am-Main whose most famous works included the dramatic poem *Faust* and *The Sorrows of Young Werther*, an epistolary novel. He travelled extensively in Europe, visiting England, Switzerland and, in 1786, Italy, particularly Rome and Florence resulting in his *Italienische Reise* (*Italian Journey*) and *Römanische Elegien* (*Roman Elegies*).

Thomas Gray (1716–71)

English poet, born in London, the only one of 12 children to survive infancy. His most famous work was 'Elegy Written in a Country Churchyard', which he began writing in the graveyard of the church in Stoke Poges, Buckinghamshire in 1742 and published eight years later. At Eton College he became a close friend of Horace Walpole, and in 1738 the couple visited Florence, where they stayed for 15 months with the Crown Representative to the Tuscan court, Horace Mann. Gray spent much of his later life in Cambridge, where he died on 30 July 1771. He was buried beside his mother in the churchyard at Stoke Poges.

Thomas Hardy (1840–1928)

English poet and novelist who saw himself as a poet but earned his living from novels, for which he was better known, with works such as *Tess of the d'Urbervilles* and *Far from the Madding Crowd*. Most of his novels are set in 'Wessex', which was strongly reminiscent of his native Dorset. He visited Florence in 1887, admiring the Piazza della Signoria, and was especially interested in the Etruscan and Roman relics in Fiesole.

Nathaniel Hawthorne (1804–64)

American short story writer and novelist of Quaker descent from Salem, Massachusetts. Most of his works were set in New England and explored themes of Puritan morality. He achieved his first success with the novel *The Scarlet Letter*, and went on to write other Romantic novels including *The House of Seven Gables* and *The Blithedale Romance*. From 1853 to 1857 he was the American consul in Liverpool, after which he moved with his family to Florence, where they lived in the southern heights of Bellosguardo. The house, and in particular its tower, became the setting for his next novel, *The Marble Faun* (published in England as *Transformations*). His wife, Sophia, an artist whom he had married in Boston in 1842, travelled with him, and moved to England after his death in 1864, where she wrote *Notes in England and Italy*, her personal memoir of their travels.

Ernest Hemingway (1899–1961)

American novelist and short-story writer, awarded the Nobel Prize for Literature in 1954. He worked as a journalist in Paris, associating with a number of contemporary American writers. His first successful novel was *The Sun also Rises*, followed by his novel set in the Spanish Civil War, *For Whom the Bell Tolls*. His other works include *The Old Man and the Sea* (for which he received the Pulitzer Prize) and *To Have and Have Not*. He was an ambulance driver in Italy in the First World War (fictionalised in *A Farewell to Arms*) and returned to Tuscany in 1923 with Ezra Pound. After he left Cuba in 1960 he settled in Ketchum, Idaho, where, after severe bouts of illness and depression, he shot himself.

Leigh Hunt (1784–1859)
English poet, essayist and journalist, born in Middlesex, whose interest in political reform brought him into contact with similarly minded contemporaries such as Shelley, Byron and Hazlitt. It also brought him into conflict with the establishment and he was finally sentenced to two years in prison for criticism of the Prince Regent. In 1821, Hunt was invited by Byron and Shelley to join them in Tuscany with a view to producing a literary magazine. After a long sea journey with his large family, they came to live with Byron in Pisa. The magazine project was short-lived, and, his attempts to start his own magazine being unsuccessful, he returned to England in 1824.

Aldous Huxley (1894–1963)
English novelist and critic. He developed keratitis at Eton and became partially blind. His first two published novels, *Crome Yellow*, which caricatured the country house lifestyle, and *Antic Hay*, established him as a major author, and were followed by *Those Barren Leaves* and *Point Counter Point*. His best-known work, *Brave New World*, portrayed a prophetic and concerned vision of the future. In the late 1920s he and his wife lived in Forte dei Marmi in coastal Tuscany, then moved to Sanary in southern France.

Henry James (1843–1916)
American novelist, short-story writer and critic. After education in London, Paris and Geneva, he studied law at Harvard and moved to Europe in 1875, becoming a British citizen in 1915. He received the Order of Merit in 1916. The central theme of many of his novels is of Americans confronting European culture, and his major works include *Daisy Miller, Portrait of a Lady, Washington Square, The Bostonians* and *The Ambassadors*. Starting in 1869, he travelled extensively in Tuscany, staying in Bellosguardo, Florence, Lucca and Siena, making his last visit in 1907.

Walter Savage Landor (1775–1864)

English poet and essayist who claimed to be a poet for pleasure but a prose writer by profession: a view confirmed by the fact that his best-known works were his *Imaginary Conversations*, a collection of 150 'discussions' between famous people from a wide range of eras, nationalities and professions. He was known for his intractable temper, being expelled from both Rugby School and Oxford University for indiscipline, and was frequently in court as a result of his irrational outbursts. In 1815, after inheriting a fortune and losing it, he moved to Florence, where, with the exception of a 22-year absence following a domestic dispute, he remained for the rest of his life, and is buried in the English Cemetery

D. H. Lawrence (1885–1930)

English novelist, poet and short-story writer, best known for his controversial novel *Lady Chatterley's Lover*. He began his career teaching, but his talent was recognised by the *English Review*, which led to the publication of his first novel, *The White Peacock*, in 1911. His other novels include *Sons and Lovers*, *The Rainbow* and *Women in Love*. In 1914 he eloped with and married Frieda Weekley (née von Richthofen) and they travelled for the next decade, settling for a time in Taos, New Mexico. They moved to Tuscany in 1919 and lived in the Gulf of La Spezia and Florence, where he published *Lady Chatterley's Lover* privately in 1927 before moving to southern France, where he died from tuberculosis.

Sinclair Lewis (1885–1951)

American novelist born in Minnesota who wrote satirically of everyday life in small mid-western towns such as 'Gopher Prairie'. His first great success was *Main Street* in 1920, and he continued the genre with *Babbitt*, *Arrowsmith*, *Elmer Gantry* and *Dodsworth*. He received the Nobel Prize for Literature in 1930 – the first American to do so. In 1950 he moved to Florence, where he lived in the southern hills near Arcetri and wrote *World so Wide*, a novel about expatriate life in Florence. He died in a Rome hospital from alcoholic poisoning in 1951; *World so Wide* was published posthumously the same year.

Eric Linklater (1899–1974)

Welsh-born, Orkney-based novelist and scenarist whose first success was his novel, *Juan in America*, in 1930, based on his experiences as a student in the United States. Three years later he moved to Lerici, in the Gulf of La Spezia, where he worked on his biography *Robert the Bruce* and wrote the novel *Private Angelo*, based on Italian campaigns in the First World War. In the Second World War he was in Tuscany in 1945 as a communications officer with the Allied forces, and was there in the invasion of Italy, during which time he wrote war memoirs under the title *Fanfare for a Tin Hat*.

Henry Wadsworth Longfellow (1807–82)

American poet born in Maine, a schoolmate of Nathaniel Hawthorne. In 1836 he began his teaching career at Harvard and started to write, first in prose and later poetry. He met Dickens in America in 1843 and came to England the following year, and achieved fame with his hexameter narrative poems, in particular *The Song of Hiawatha*. He came to Florence in 1928, staying in the Piazza Santa Maria Novella, as part of a plan to learn Italian with a view to translating Dante's *Divine Comedy*, which was finally published in 1867.

W. Somerset Maugham (1874–1965)

English novelist, playwright and short-story writer. He qualified as a doctor in 1897, but abandoned medicine on the success of his first novel, *Liza of Lambeth*. In 1894, on holiday from the hospital, he visited Pisa and Florence, 'Ruskin in hand'. His plays were outstandingly successful in Edwardian London, but he is best known now for his novels: in particular *Of Human Bondage*, *The Moon and Sixpence*, *Cakes and Ale* and *The Razor's Edge*. In 1926 he settled on the French Riviera, where he remained until his death 39 years later He revisited Florence on his way back from India in 1938.

Herman Melville (1819–91)

American poet and novelist born in New York City, who went to sea in 1839. In 1841 he signed on to another ship, which he left in the South Seas and joined the US Navy. Largely self-taught, he later returned to New England and started to write. His first completed work was set in the South Sea Islands and was his most successful novel in his lifetime: *Typee or a Peep at Polynesian Life*. He continued to write sea adventures, but his most famous work, *Moby Dick*, based on life aboard a New England whaler, was not published until 1851 and was not acclaimed at the time. In the mid-1850s he set off on a tour of Europe and the Holy Land, during which he spent several months of 1857 in Florence, where, like fellow New Englander Emerson, he lived in the Hôtel du Nord on the Via Tuornobuoni.

John Milton (1608–74)

English poet who supported the Puritan revolution and wrote defending civil liberties. After the Restoration he became blind but wrote his best-known works, including his master work *Paradise Lost*, its sequel *Paradise Regained* and *Samson Agonistes*. An early visitor to Tuscany, he travelled to Livorno and Lucca in 1638–9, meeting the blind and ageing Galileo in Florence.

Michel Eyquem de Montaigne (1533–92)

French author, philosopher and statesman who popularised the essay as a literary medium. On his thirty-eighth birthday he retired from public life to the library in the tower of his château for a 10-year period, during which he dedicated himself to writing. The resulting *Essays* have influenced the work of writers of many nationalities and eras, from his contemporaries to the present day. In his late forties, Montaigne began to travel throughout Europe in search of a cure for his inherited problem of kidney stones, eventually reaching Lucca in 1581, where he heard that he had been elected mayor of Bordeaux and returned home. His record of this quest was published as *Travel Journal*.

Iris Origo (1902–88)

Anglo-Irish historian and biographer. Following the death of her father, William Cutting, in 1910, she and her mother settled in Italy, buying the Villa Medici in Fiesole. In 1924, Iris Cutting married Antonio Origo, becoming Marchesa of Val d'Orcia, and the couple bought a neglected estate, La Foce, in the Val d'Orcia. She took up writing in 1925, her first published work being a biography, *Giacomo Leopardi*. During the Second World War, the Origos remained at La Foce and housed refugee children and escaped Allied prisoners of war. In recognition of this work she was appointed Dame Commander of the Order of the British Empire in 1976. Her moving account of this time, *War in the Val D'Orcia*, established her career as a historical author.

Francesco Petrarca, Petrarch (1304–74)

Italian poet and humanist, born in Arezzo and considered the greatest scholar of his time. With his parents, he fled from political conflict in Florence and settled in Avignon, returning to Tuscany in 1353. His best-known surviving poems are about the death of his mother and his *Canzoniere*, proclaiming his chaste love for 'Laura', whose identity he never revealed.

Ezra Pound (1885–1972)

American poet and critic recognised as a leader of the modernist movement. He moved to London in 1908, where he met his wife, English artist Dorothy Shakespear. They moved to Paris in 1920 and four years later to Italy, settling in Rapallo, where he was host and patron to W. B. Yeats, James Joyce and Ernest Hemingway. His pro-Fascist broadcasts from Rome during the Second World War led to his arrest in 1945 by American troops and his confinement, first in an army camp near Pisa, where he began his widely acclaimed *Pisan Cantos*, and then 12 years in an asylum for the criminally insane in Washington DC. On his release, he returned to Rapallo, then lived in Venice for the rest of his life.

John Ruskin (1819–1900)

English art critic, author, historian and essayist of the Victorian era with a broad range of interests. He grew up in Surrey and London and was educated at home and at Oxford University. He was especially influential in the latter part of the nineteenth century, and his *Modern Painters* in 1843 was effective in promoting the careers of a number of contemporary artists, in particular Turner. He sketched and painted in watercolour, and was the author of over two hundred works, including *Giotto and his Works in Padua* and *The Stones of Venice*, a detailed architectural study of the city. On his thirteenth birthday he was given a copy of Samuel Rogers's poem, *Italy* (1830), which initiated a lasting affection for the country, and at the age of 14 he paid his first visit to Tuscany with his parents, becoming a regular visitor, especially to Florence, over the next 40 years, in the course of which he published his *Mornings in Florence*, a guide to the religious art of the city.

Vita Sackville-West (1892–1962)

English novelist and poet, daughter of the Third Baron Sackville and married to the diplomat and author Harold Nicolson. Her best-known works include the novels *The Edwardians* and *All Passion Spent*, and her poem about the English countryside, 'The Land'. She gained notoriety in part through her friendship with Virginia Woolf – who based the main character in *Orlando* on her – and her open lesbian relationship with Violet Trefusis, who, like her mother, a former mistress of Edward VII, spent her last years, including the years of the Second World War, at Bellosguardo in Florence.

José de Sousa Saramago (1922–2010)

Portuguese novelist, poet and playwright whose works first became popular in Britain with the translation of his *Memorial do Convento* (with the English title *Baltasar and Blimunda*), set in pre-Second World War Portugal. His works tended to use allegory to illustrate the savagery of war. He was awarded the Nobel Prize for Literature in 1998 but left Portugal in protest against religious censorship and, while considering where to live, came to Tuscany, where he was enthusiastic about settling in Siena, but eventually moved to Spain, where he died in 2010.

Mary Shelley (1797–1851)

English novelist, short story writer and essayist, best known for her novel *Frankenstein*. She was the daughter of early feminist philosopher Mary Wollstonecraft and the political writer and novelist William Godwin. In 1816 she married the Romantic poet Percy Bysshe Shelley following the suicide of his first wife. After the death of Shelley by drowning off Viareggio in 1822, she returned to England with her son, Percy, and died in Bournemouth from a brain tumour at the age of 53.

Percy Bysshe Shelley (1792–1822)

English poet born in Sussex and educated at Eton and Oxford. He was one of the most important of the Romantic poets and is considered one of the finest lyric poets in the English language. Shelley is famous for such classic poems as *Ozymandias*, 'Ode to the West Wind' and 'To a Skylark', among many others. His unconventional lifestyle and strident atheism made him unpopular among contemporaries, as did his abandonment of his first wife and subsequent elopement to Italy with the 16-year-old Mary Godwin (later known as the novelist Mary Shelley, the author of *Frankenstein*), and many of his works were suppressed on publication and did not reach the public in his lifetime. Percy and Mary Shelley came first to Bagni di Lucca, but also lived in Livorno, Venice, Rome, Pisa and finally Lerici. In July 1822 Shelley drowned in a sudden storm while sailing from Livorno to Lerici, just days before his thirtieth birthday.

Osbert Sitwell (1892–1969)

English poet, novelist, short-story writer and critic, the younger brother of Dame Edith Louisa Sitwell and older brother of Sacheverell Sitwell. Like them, he was dedicated to the arts, especially literature, and led an unconventional lifestyle. The three were a cultural clique known collectively as the Sitwells, a dynasty fathered by the equally eccentric Sir George Sitwell, and were involved in various joint literary and artistic ventures. Osbert began his literary career as a poet, the result of 'some instinct, and a combination of feelings not hitherto experienced'. His first novel was *Before the Bombardment*, published in 1924 and set in a slightly war-torn Scarborough. He succeeded to the baronetcy on the death of his father in 1943, and took over Castello Montegufoni, a castle in the Tuscan countryside near Florence, where he completed a five-volume autobiography, *Left Hand, Right Hand*, between 1945 and 1962 and died of Parkinson's disease.

Tobias George Smollett (1721–71)

Scottish surgeon, novelist and historian, whose writing influenced many authors, in particular Charles Dickens. He was best known for his novels, the most famous of which was *The Expedition of Humphry Clinker*. His works included translations of Voltaire and Cervantes and, in 1757–8, his successful *Complete History of England*. As editor of the *Critical Review*, he libelled Admiral Sir Charles Knowles and was sentenced to three months' imprisonment. In 1763, he went to Nice for his health, where he stayed for two years and wrote his still-read book *Travels through France and Italy*. In 1768 he returned to Italy, living first in Pisa, then Livorno, where he died at the age of 50.

Muriel Spark (1918–2006)

Scottish novelist, born in Edinburgh. She left her husband and son after the Second World War and began writing seriously under her married name, first with poetry and biography, turning to fiction after winning a national short-story competition. She became a Roman Catholic in 1954, which she claimed was fundamental to her literary success. Graham Greene, another convert, helped to support her in her early career. Her first successful novel, *The Prime of Miss Jean Brodie*, published in 1961, was set in Edinburgh and demonstrated her originality of style. She came to live in the village of Civitella della Chiana, near Arezzo, in 1979, with the sculptor Penelope Jardine, and remained there for the rest of her life.

John Steinbeck (1902–68)

American writer best known for his novels, of which he wrote 16, the most famous being the Pulitzer Prize-winning *The Grapes of Wrath*, the novella *Of Mice and Men* and *East of Eden*. He also published non-fiction and collections of short stories. He first came to Italy during the Second World

War as a war correspondent based in the Naples area, and visited Florence after the war. He received the Nobel Prize for Literature in 1962.

Stendhal, Marie-Henri Beyle (1783–1842)

French novelist and critic, whose major works were the novels *The Red and the Black* and *The Charterhouse of Parma*. He also wrote books on travel, music and painting. After the fall of the French First Empire in 1814 he travelled in Italy, where he spent more than a year and wrote *Rome, Naples et Florence* and his essay *La Villa Palmieri*, about his home in Florence.

Harriet Beecher Stowe (1811–96)

American religious author and journalist born in Connecticut, who wrote more than twenty works. An ardent critic of slavery, she and her husband supported the 'Underground Railroad', a network to help fugitive slaves to escape. Her most important work, *Uncle Tom's Cabin*, told of the suffering of Africans under slavery, and had a strong influence on political thought in the United States and Europe. She was received by Queen Victoria on her visit to England in 1853, and between 1856 and 1859 lived in Florence and visited other parts of Tuscany, becoming a close friend of Elizabeth Barrett Browning and the Trollope family.

Algernon Swinburne (1837–1909)

English poet and critic. He left Oxford without a degree, but was able, with an allowance from his father, to follow a literary career. His successful works include the verse drama *Atalanta in Calydon* and *Poems and Ballads*, but many readers were troubled by their anarchistic content. His penchant for excessive drinking and self-abuse seriously damaged his health. He came to Florence in 1864 and visited his literary idol, Walter Savage Landor, who died soon afterwards. Swinburne wrote the poetic epitaph for Landor's grave in Florence.

Anton Pavlovich Chekhov (1860–1904)

Russian dramatist and short-story writer. He wrote hundreds of stories while studying medicine at the University of Moscow, but is best remembered for his plays, which he wrote after he developed tuberculosis. His most famous works include *Uncle Vanya*, *The Three Sisters* and *The Cherry Orchard*, which he wrote for the Moscow Art Theatre, where he met and married the actress Olga Knipper. He stayed in Florence on a tour of Italy in the spring of 1891, when he was writing *The Three Sisters*, and returned 10 years later, when he also visited Pisa.

Alfred, Lord Tennyson (1809–92)

English poet who was one of 12 children, brought up in a Lincolnshire rectory. At Trinity College, Cambridge he began a lifelong friendship with Arthur Hallam, and in 1830 they went to Spain to help in the unsuccessful revolution against Ferdinand VII. He became poet laureate in 1850 and published *In Memoriam*, mourning the death of Hallam. His best-known work was *Idylls of the King*. A favourite of Queen Victoria, he received a peerage in 1884. A regular visitor to the oriental Pyrenees, he passed through La Turbie on his way to Florence, where he lived with his brother, the musician Frederick Tennyson in Bellosguardo.

William Makepeace Thackeray (1811–63)

English novelist and journalist born in Calcutta. He came to England after his father's death and went to Charterhouse School, and spent a year at Cambridge University, but had to leave early without a degree for financial reasons. He studied painting in Paris and turned to journalism as subeditor of *Galignano's Messenger*, France's first English-language magazine. Thackeray returned to England and began to make his name contributing articles to a wide variety of journals. His first important novel was *Vanity Fair*, initially published in monthly instalments from 1847, followed by *The History of Henry Esmond*, *The Newcomes*, and a number of children's stories which he illustrated himself, while continuing to write for satirical magazines. He visited Tuscany and Rome with his daughters and lived in Florence with the Irish novelist Charles Lever in Bellosguardo.

Dylan Marlais Thomas (1914–53)

Welsh poet and writer born in Swansea and educated at Swansea Grammar School, where his father taught English. Thomas wrote exclusively in English, at first poetry but later film and radio scripts, many of which he presented. His strong voice and accent made him a popular public speaker and he made successful tours of the United States giving readings of his works. His prose and poetry collection *Portrait of the Artist as a Young Dog* attracted critical attention, but his best-known poem was one of his last: the celebrated villanelle for his dying father, 'Do Not Go Gentle into that Good Night'. His most famous work was his 'play for voices', *Under Milk Wood*, in which he played the role of narrator in New York shortly before his death there from alcoholic poisoning. He came to Tuscany only once, on a travelling scholarship in 1947: it was his only trip abroad, and he stayed first in Scandicci, in the southern suburbs of Florence, then on the island of Elba.

Violet Trefusis (1894–1972)

English socialite and novelist, daughter of Alice Keppel, the last mistress of King Edward VII, and sister of Sonia Keppel, the grandmother of Camilla Parker-Bowles. Violet was notorious for her long and public affair with the poet and novelist Vita Sackville-West. She married at the end of the First World War in an attempt to allay gossip, and on her mother's death inherited her large villa, Villa dell'Ombrellino, in Bellosguardo, overlooking Florence, where she published a number of novels in English and French and entertained the cream of European society, including senior politicians and minor royalty. She was awarded the Legion d'Honneur for her broadcasts during the Second World War.

Frances 'Fanny' Milton Trollope (1779–1863)

English novelist and writer born in Hampshire. On the failure of her husband's business she tried unsuccessfully to establish herself and family in the USA. On returning to England she published her caustic, but successful, *Domestic Manners of the Americans*, which set her on a career as a writer. She published more than forty books, an output that both made her rich and brought her some literary recognition, and she became hostess and friend of many contemporary writers, including Charles Dickens, the Brownings and Landor. She established a home in central Florence with her oldest son, the author Thomas Adolphus Trollope, and his wife. The Villino Trollope became a rendezvous for Anglo-Florentine writers. Her third son, the more successful author, Anthony Trollope, visited occasionally but lived in England.

Mark Twain (1835–1910)

The pen name of Samuel Langhorne Clemens, American humourist, writer and lecturer born in Hannibal, Missouri, best known for his stories *The Adventures of Tom Sawyer* and *The Adventures of Huckleberry Finn*. He lived close to the Mississippi River and worked as a steamboat pilot. After his first visit to Rome, Pisa and Florence in 1867 he published a satirical account of his travels, *The Innocents Abroad*. He returned to Florence several times and was negotiating to buy a villa there when his wife died. Following a petition by British writers, including Graham Greene and Somerset Maugham, a commemorative stone was placed in Westminster Abbey after his death.

Horace Walpole (1717–97)

English historian, playwright and novelist, third son of Sir Robert Walpole, Britain's longest-serving Prime Minister. He left Cambridge in 1738 without finishing his degree, and began the Grand Tour with his fellow Etonian, the poet Thomas Gray. After spending time in Paris and Rheims, they spent 15 months in Florence as guests of the Crown Representative in Tuscany, Horace Mann. Walpole wrote the Gothic novel *The Castle of Otranto*, which was published in 1764. Walpole and Gray quarrelled on leaving Florence and did not re-establish their friendship for another three years.

Edith Wharton (1862–1937)

American author best known for her stories and novels set in the upper-class society into which she was born. Her major literary model was Henry James, and she acknowledged her debt to him in her manual, *The Writing of Fiction*. She published more than fifty books, including fiction, short stories and travel and historical works. Her best-known work was *Ethan Frome*, but others include *The House of Mirth* and *The Age of Innocence*, which won her a Pulitzer Prize. During the First World War, Wharton dedicated herself to the war effort and was honoured by the French government for her work with refugees. A compulsive and involved traveller throughout her life, she wrote three books on Italy and travelled over much of Tuscany in the early twentieth century, and was particularly knowledgeable about Italian religious art.

Oscar Wilde (1854–1900)

Irish poet, wit and dramatist. He was born in Dublin, but became a leading figure in London society. He became as famous for the trial arising from his homosexual relationship with Lord Alfred Douglas and subsequent two-year prison sentence, as he was for his works, which include his social comedies such as *Lady Windermere's Fan*, *An Ideal Husband* and *The Importance of Being Earnest*, a novel, *The Picture of Dorian Gray*, and poetry. He visited Tuscany in 1877, and in 1895, the year of his trial, stayed with his friend Lord Alfred Douglas in his apartment in the Palazzo Spini-Feroni. After his release from prison he produced his best-known poem, *The Ballad of Reading Gaol*, and in 1898 went to the south of France, but returned the same year to Paris, where he died two years later.

Virginia Woolf (1882–1941)

English novelist who was a central figure in the Bloomsbury group. Her best-known works include *Mrs Dalloway*, *To the Lighthouse* and her historical fantasy *Orlando*. With her husband Leonard Woolf she founded the Hogarth Press and published her own works and those of modernist writers such as James Joyce and D. H. Lawrence. She visited Siena with her sister, Vanessa, in 1908, and returned in the 1930s with her husband Leonard Woolf. They visited Rome, Siena and Florence and Lerici before returning home by way of Vence to visit Lawrence's grave. A sufferer from depression, she drowned herself during the Second World War.

William Zinsser (1922–)

American journalist, essayist and academic, author of 17 books, mostly non-fiction works on the art of writing. His most successful work was the best-selling *On Writing Well*. He served in the US Army in North Africa in the Second World War before being transferred to a base near Livorno in 1945 after the end of hostilities in Italy, and took the opportunity to visit Volterra and Siena, returning to New York in 1946 as a journalist with the *New York Herald Tribune*. He returned to Siena with his wife to celebrate his seventieth birthday.

CHRONOLOGY OF EVENTS

	Literary and Cultural Events	Political Events
59 BC		Roman military settlement Florentia is founded on the Arno River.
552–68		Byzantine occupation of Florence.
1155		Resumption of struggles between Roman Empire and Papacy.
1265	Dante Alighieri born, Florence.	
1294		The commune of Florence decides to build a new cathedral.
c.1294		Construction begins on Church of Santa Croce.
1302	Dante exiled.	
1304	Petrarch born, Arezzo.	
1313	Boccaccio born, Florence.	
1321	Dante Alighieri dies, Ravenna.	
1337	Giotto dies; buried in the new cathedral in Florence.	
1343?	Chaucer born, London.	
1348		Outbreak of the plague.
1353	Boccaccio's *Decameron* published.	
1359		Giotto campanile in Florence completed.
1364		Sir John Hawkwood fights for the Pisans.
1373	Geoffrey Chaucer visits Florence.	

	Literary and Cultural Events	Political Events
1374	Petrarch dies, Arquà.	
1375	Boccaccio dies, Certaldo.	
1394		Sir John Hawkwood dies, Florence.
1400	Chaucer dies; buried in Westminster Abbey.	
1434		Cosimo de' Medici returns to Florence from a year in exile to take control.
1436		Brunelleschi's dome in Florence completed.
1440?	Monument to Sir John Hawkwood painted by Uccello.	
1446		Filippo Brunelleschi dies.
1452	Leonardo da Vinci born.	
1478		The Pazzi Conspiracy.
1482–7	Girolamo Savonarola preaches at the convent of San Marco in Florence.	
1492		Death of Lorenzo the Magnificent.
1498		Savonarola executed in Florence.
1511	Giorgio Vasari born, Arezzo.	
1512	Machiavelli begins *The Prince*.	
1527	Machiavelli dies, Florence.	
1564	Galileo born, Florence; Michelangelo dies.	
1580–1	Montaigne visits Florence and Lucca.	
1635		A proposed plan for new façade of Florence Duomo presented.
1638	John Milton visits Florence for two months; meets Galileo.	
1642	Galileo dies.	
1644	John Evelyn arrives in Livorno.	

	Literary and Cultural Events	Political Events
1737–86	Sir Horace Mann in Florence.	
1739–41	Thomas Gray and Horace Walpole in Florence.	
1755	Oliver Goldsmith in Florence.	
1760	Maria Hadfield Cosway born, Florence.	
1764	Edward Gibbon in Florence.	
1764–71	Tobias Smollett visits Tuscany.	
1765	James Boswell in Pisa, Florence, Siena.	
1768	Tobias Smollett moves to Livorno; dies there 1771.	
1774		Charles Edward Stuart, 'Young Pretender', moves to Florence.
1786 & 1788	Goethe visits Florence and Siena.	
1796		Napoleon invades Italy.
1800	Stendhal's first visit to Italy; writes *Rome, Naples et Florence.*	
1814		Napoleon confined on Elba.
1815		Napoleon escapes; is defeated at Waterloo.
1818	P. B. Shelley marries Mary Godwin; they leave for Italy.	
1818–19	Arthur Schopenhauer in Florence.	
1819	Stendhal in Volterra.	
1820	Florence Nightingale born, Via Colombaia, Florence.	
1821	Byron moves to Villa Lanfranchi in Pisa; moves to Livorno.	
1821–64	Walter Savage Landor in Pisa and Florence.	
1822	P. B. Shelley drowned at Viareggio.	
1823–5	Leigh Hunt in Florence and Pisa.	
1824	William Hazlitt in Florence. Byron dies, Missolonghi.	

	Literary and Cultural Events	Political Events
1828	Henry Wadsworth Longfellow in Florence; returns 1868–9.	
1828–9	James Fenimore Cooper in Florence.	
1833	Hans Christian Andersen in Florence; returns 1834 and 1840.	
1835	Alexandre Dumas in Livorno, Pisa, Florence and Arezzo; returns 1840. Writes *Une Année à Florence.*	
	Ralph Waldo Emerson first in Florence.	
1837	William Wordsworth in Florence.	
1838	Robert Browning visits Florence, Pisa and Livorno.	
1840	John Ruskin first visits Florence: returns over next 40 years, writes *Mornings in Florence.*	
1843	Frances Trollope visits Florence. Builds Villino Trollope in 1850 and dies there in 1863.	
1843–61	Arthur Hugh Clough in Florence.	
1845	Charles Dickens in Florence; visits Smollett's grave in Livorno.	
	Ruskin visits Pisa and Lucca.	
1847	Robert and Elizabeth Barrett Browning arrive in Florence; live in Casa Guidi.	
1850–7	Alfred, Lord Tennyson in Florence.	
1850–75	Anthony Trollope visits Florence.	
1854–5	William Thackeray in Florence.	
1855	Frances Trollope moves to Florence.	
	James Russell Lowell arrives in Florence.	
1857	Herman Melville in Florence.	

	Literary and Cultural Events	*Political Events*
1857–65	Harriett Beecher Stowe in Florence.	
1858	Nathaniel Hawthorne in Florence and Siena.	
1858–68	Charles Lever in La Spezia, Lucca and Florence.	
1860	Matthew Arnold first in Florence.	
1861	Death of Elizabeth B. Browning, Florence. Death of Arthur Hugh Clough, Florence.	Unification: Vittorio Emanuele becomes first King of Italy.
1861–2	George Eliot first in Florence.	
1863	Death of Frances Trollope, Florence.	Façade of Santa Croce completed.
1864	Algernon Swinburne in Florence.	
1862–3	Dostoevsky first visits Florence.	
1864 & 1879	Algernon Swinburne in Florence.	
1865		Florence declared capital of kingdom of Italy.
1867	Mark Twain visits Florence and Siena; returns three times until 1904.	
1868–9	Dostoevsky in Florence; finishes *The Idiot*.	
1869	Henry James arrives Florence; returns to Tuscany many times until 1907.	
1871		Rome becomes capital of united Italy.
1877	Oscar Wilde in Florence.	
1887	Thomas Hardy in Florence and Livorno.	Inauguration of the façade of the Duomo in Florence.
1889		Queen Victoria visits Florence; returns 1893.
1891	Anton Chekhov in Florence.	
1895–6	André Gide in Florence. Oscar Wilde in Florence.	

	Literary and Cultural Events	*Political Events*
1898	Rainer Maria Rilke in Florence and Lucca.	
1900	Sir Henry Rider Haggard in Florence.	
1901	Hilaire Belloc walks to Rome via Tuscany; writes *The Path to Rome*.	
	E. M. Forster in Florence and San Gimignano.	
1903	Edith Wharton in Florence and San Gimignano.	
1904–33	Virginia Woolf visits Siena and Lerici.	
1908	Rupert Brooke in Florence and Siena; returns in 1912.	
1909	George Sitwell acquires Montegufoni for his son, Osbert.	
1910	Iris Origo comes to Florence as a child.	
1912	Arnold Bennett in Florence.	
1914	D. H. Lawrence in Florence.	
1914–18		First World War.
1919	D. H. Lawrence returns to Florence; prints *Lady Chatterley's Lover* in Florence.	
1922		Mussolini becomes dictator.
1922–5	Aldous Huxley intermittently at Florence and Forte dei Marmi; returns in 1927–8.	
1923	Ernest Hemingway and Ezra Pound visit Siena.	
	Aldous Huxley moves to Florence.	
1930	D. H. Lawrence dies in Vence.	
1933	Eric Linklater arrives in Lerici.	
1937	Albert Camus visits Pisa and Florence.	

	Literary and Cultural Events	Political Events
1939		Outbreak of Second World War.
1943	Sir George Sitwell dies.	Italy surrenders.
1945	William Zinsser in Siena and Florence.	Allies reconquer Italy; Mussolini shot.
	Eric Linklater at Montegufoni.	End of Second World War.
1946	Eric Newby marries in Santa Croce; moves to Fosdinovo.	
1947	Dylan Thomas in Florence and Elba.	
	Violet Trefusis inherits Villa dell'Ombrellino.	
1948–9	Laurie Lee in Florence, Siena and San Gimignano.	
1950	Sinclair Lewis in Florence.	
1951	Sinclair Lewis dies in Rome; *World so Wide* published.	
1956	Mary McCarthy's first visit to Florence.	
1966		Flooding of the river Arno damages Florence Duomo, Baptistery, Museum, and the Uffizi.
1987	Bruce Chatwin in Donnini, Florence; writes *Tower in Tuscany*.	
1991–2	Saul Bellow in Florence and Montecatini.	
1995	William Zinsser in Siena.	

SELECT BIBLIOGRAPHY

Acton, H., *Memoirs of an Aesthete*, London, Methuen, 1948.
—— *More Memoirs of an Aesthete*, London, Methuen, 1970.
—— *The Villas of Tuscany*, London, Thames & Hudson, 1984.
Aldington, R., *Portrait of a Genius, but . .* , London, Heinemann, 1950.
Bartlett, V., *Tuscan Retreat*, London, Chatto & Windus, 1964.
Bedford, S., *Aldous Huxley: A Biography, Volume. 1*, London, Chatto & Windus, 1973.
Beevor, K., *A Tuscan Childhood*, London, Viking, 1993.
Belloc, Hilaire, *The Path to Rome*, Edinburgh, Thomas Nelson, 1916.
Bellow, S., *It All Adds Up*, London, Secker & Warburg, 1994.
Blanch, L, *The Wider Shores of Love*, London, John Murray, 1954.
Boccaccio, G., *The Decameron*, trans. J. M. Rigg, London, Angus & Robertson, 1954.
—— *The Nymph of Fiesole*, trans. D. J. Donno, New York, Columbia University Press, 1960.
Borm, J. (ed.), *Anatomy of Restlessness*, New York, Viking Penguin USA, 1966.
Borsook, E., *The Companion Guide to Florence*, London, Collins, 1979.
Bostridge, M., *Florence Nightingale*, London, Viking, 2008.
Boswell, J., *Journal of a Tour of Corsica*, Cambridge, Cambridge University Press, 1923.
Boulton, J. T., (Ed.) *The Letters of D. H. Lawrence*, Cambridge, Cambridge University Press, 2002
Brady, F. (ed.), *Boswell on the Grand Tour*, London, Heinemann, 1955.
Brucker, G. A., *Renaissance Florence*, Berkeley, University of California Press, 1983.
Caferro, W., *John Hawkwood*, Baltimore, Johns Hopkins University Press, 2006.
Carmichael, M, *In Tuscany*, London, Burns & Oates, 1913.
Chaucer, G., *The Canterbury Tales*, trans. D. Wright, Oxford, Oxford University Press, 1985.
Cooper, J. F., *Excursions in Italy*, London, Richard Bentley, 1838.
—— *The Last of the Mohicans*, London, John Miller, 1826.
Dante Alighieri, *The Divine Comedy*, trans. R. Kirkpatrick, London, Penguin, 2007.

Davies, H., *The Grand Tour*, London, Hamish Hamilton, 1986.

Dentler, C. L., *Famous Foreigners in Florence*, Florence, Bemporad Marzocco, 1964.

Dickens, C., *Pictures from Italy*, London, Penguin, 1998.

Dostoevsky, F. M., *The Idiot*, Toronto, Dent, 1914.

—— *Complete Letters*, Ann Arbour, MI, Ardis, 1991.

Dumas, A., *Une Année à Florence*, Paris, Calmann-Levy, 1894.

—— *La Villa Palmieri*, Paris, Calmann-Levy, 1894.

Fitzgibbon, C., *The Life of Dylan Thomas*, London, Dent & Sons, 1965.

de Filippis, S. (ed.), *Sketches of Etruscan Places*, Cambridge, Cambridge University Press, 1992.

Forster, E. M., *Where Angels Fear to Tread*, Penguin, London, 1946.

—— *A Room with a View*, London, Edward Arnold, 1977.

Frank, J., *Dostoevsky: The Miraculous Years: 1865–71*, London, Robson Books, 1995.

Fraser, H., *Victorians and Renaissance Italy*, Oxford, Blackwell, 1992.

Gibbon, E., *History of the Decline and Fall of the Roman Empire*, London, Chatto & Windus, 1960.

Goethe, J. W. von, *Italian Journey*, London, Collins, 1962.

Guiccioli, T., *Lord Byron's Life in Italy*, Newark, DE, University of Delaware Press, 2005.

Haggard, H. R., *Winter Pilgrimage*, London, Longmans, Greene, 1901.

Hall, E. F., *Florence Nightingale*, New York, Nightingale Society, 1920.

Hamilton, O., *Paradise of Exiles: Tuscany and the British*, London, André Deutsch, 1974.

—— *The Divine Country: The British in Tuscany, 1372–1980*, London, André Deutsch, 1982.

Hare, A. C., *Italian Cities, Vol.II*, London, George Allen, 1891.

Hawthorne, S., *Notes in England and Italy*, London, Sampson Low, 1872.

Hersholt, J. (ed.), *The Complete Andersen*, Berkeley, University of California Press, 1949.

Hobday, C., *A Golden Ring: English Poets in Florence from 1373 to the Present Day*, London, Peter Owen, 1997.

Holmes, R., *Footsteps*, London, Hodder & Stoughton, 1985.

—— *Sidetracks*, London, HarperCollins, 2000.

Holroyd, M., *Works on Paper*, London, Little, Brown, 2002.

Hotchner, A., *Papa Hemingway*, London, Weidenfeld & Nicolson, 1966.

Jacks, P. (ed.), *Vasari's Florence: Artists and Literati at the Medicean Court*, Cambridge, Cambridge University Press, 1998.

James, H., *Italian Hours*, London, Heinemann, 1909.

Johnson, P., *The Renaissance*, London, Phoenix, 2001.

Jones, J., *Lost Battles*, London, Simon & Schuster, 2010.

Jones, T., *The French Riviera Literary Guide*, London, I.B.Tauris, 2007.

Kelly, L. (ed.), *Tobias Smollett: Critical Heritage*, London, Routledge & Paul, 1987.

King, F., *Florence*, London, John Murray, 1991.

King, R., *Brunelleschi's Dome*, London, Penguin Books, 2000.

—— *Machiavelli*, London, Atlas Books, 2007.

Knapp, L. M. (ed.), *The Letters of Tobias Smollett*, Oxford, Clarendon Press, 1949.

Labande, E.-R., *Florence*, London, Nicholas Kate, 1962.

Landor, W. S., *Imaginary Conversations*, London, Walter Scott, 1886.

Lawrence, D. H., *Aaron's Rod*, New York, Martin Secker, 1922.

—— *Etruscan Places*, New York, Viking Penguin, 1932.

—— *Lady Chatterley's Lover*, London, Heinemann, 1960.

Leavitt, D., *Florence: A Delicate Case*, London, Bloomsbury, 2002.

Lee, H., *Virginia Woolf*, London, Chatto & Windus, 2005.

—— *Edith Wharton*, London, Chatto & Windus, 2007.

Lewis, J, *Tobias Smollett*, London, Pimlico, 2003.

Lewis, S., *World so Wide*, London, Heinemann, 1951.

Lewis, S. W., (ed.), *Selected Letters of Horace Walpole*, New Haven, CT, Yale University Press, 1973,

Lingeman, R. R., *Rebel from Main Street*, New York, Random House, 1992.

Linklater, E., *Fanfare for a Tin Hat*, London, Macmillan, 1970.

Lottman, H. R., *Albert Camus*, London, Weidenfeld & Nicolson, 1979.

Luzzi, J., *Romantic Europe and the Ghost of Italy*, London, Yale University Press, 2008.

Lyall, A., *The Companion Guide to Tuscany*, London, Collins, 1973.

Macadam, A, *Americans in Florence*, Florence, Giunti, 2003.

McCarthy, M., *Stones of Florence*, London, Heinemann, 1959.

Maddox, B., *D. H. Lawrence*, London, Simon & Schuster, 1994.

Mayes, F., *Under the Tuscan Sun*, San Francisco, Chronicle Books, 1996.

Mayle, P., *A Year in Provence*, London, Hamish Hamilton, 1989.

Miller, E. H., *Salem is my Resting Place*, London, Duckworth, 1991.

Morton, H. V., *A Traveller in Italy*, London, Methuen, 1964.

Najemy, J. M., *History of Florence, 1200–1575*, Oxford, Blackwell, 2006.

Nelson, M. E., *Queen Victoria and the Discovery of the French Riviera*, London, I.B.Tauris, 2001.

Newby, E., *A Merry Dance Around the World*, London, HarperCollins, 1995.

Norwich, J. J., *The Italian World*, London, Thomas Hudson, 1983.

Novick, S. M., *Henry James*, London, Random House, 2007.

O'Reilly, J., and T. Weaver (eds), *Travelers' Tales, Tuscany*, San Francisco, Travelers' Tales, 2002.

Origo, I., *Images and Shadows*, London, John Murray, 1970.

—— *War in the Val D'Orcia*, London, John Murray, 1984.

Parnell, M., *Eric Linklater: Critical Biography*, London, John Murray, 1984.

Pemble, J., *The Mediterranean Passion*, Oxford, Clarendon Press, 1987.

Platt, D. F., *Through Italy with Car and Camera*, London, Putnam's Sons, 1908.

Pound, E. L., *Pisan Cantos*, New York, New Directions, 2003.

Purdy, R., and M. Millgate (eds), *Collected Letters of Thomas Hardy*, Oxford, Clarendon Press, 1988.

Quennell, P., *Byron in Italy*, London, Collins, 1941.

Roeck, B., *Florence 1900: The Quest for Arcadia*, New Haven, CT, Yale University Press, 2009.

Rushdie, S., *The Enchantress of Florence*, London, Cape, 2008.

Ruskin, J., *Mornings in Florence*, London, George Allen, 1901.

Saine, T. P. (ed.), *Goethe: Italian Journey*, Princeton, NJ, Princeton University Press, 1994.

Shapiro, H. I. (ed.), *Ruskin in Italy: Letters to his Parents, 1845*, Clarendon Press, 1972.

Shelden, M., *Graham Greene: The Man Within*, London, Heinemann, 1994.

Raiman, D. H., and N. Fraistat (eds), *Complete Poetry of P. B. Shelley*, Baltimore, MD, Johns Hopkins University Press, 2004.

Sitwell, O., *Left Hand, Right Hand!*, Macmillan, London, 1948.

Smith, H. E. (ed.), *Autobiography of Mark Twain*, Berkeley, University of California Press, 2010.

Smollett, T. G., *Travels through France and Italy*, London, Tauris Parke, 2010.

Stannard, M., *Muriel Spark: The Biography*, London, Weidenfeld & Nicolson, 2009.

Stendhal, H., *Rome, Naples et Florence*, Paris, Calmann-Levy, 1927.

—— *Une Dépêche sur la Toscane*, Paris, Calmann-Levy, 1927.

Sterne, L., *A Sentimental Journey through France and Italy*, London, Oxford University Press, 1968.

Taine, H., *Voyage en Italie: Florence et Venise*, trans. J. Durand, New York, Leypold & Holt, 1869.

Todd, O., *Albert Camus: A Life*, New York, Alfred A. Knopf, 1997.

Trelawny, E., *Last Days of Shelley and Byron*, London, Robinson, 2000.

Treves, G., *The Golden Ring: Anglo-Florentines 1847–1862*, London, Longmans Greene, 1956.

Trollope, F., *A Visit to Italy*, London, Bentley, 1842.

Twain, M., *The Innocents Abroad*, Bloomington, MN, American Publishing Co., 1875.

Tytell, J., *Ezra Pound: The Solitary Volcano*, London, Bloomsbury, 1987.

Vasari, G., *Lives of the Painters, Sculptors and Architects*, London, David Campbell, 1996.

West, R., *Chaucer: 1340–1400*, London, Constable, 2000.

Wharton, E., *Italian Backgrounds*, London, Macmillan, 1905.

Williams, W. C., *Voyage to Pagany*, New York, Macaulay, 1928.

Worthen, J., *D. H. Lawrence*, London, Allen Lane, 2005.

INDEX